Artistic Video
with Master
Bob Klein
VOL 1

FAMILY
VHS

CHRISTY

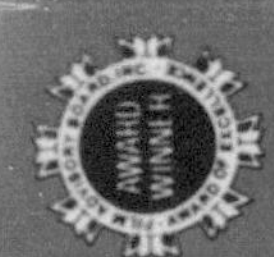

90271 00013 6

"Toilet Training the Feline"

Smart Cat Productions

AWARD WINNER

MAGIC STAR TRAVELER Vol. 3

80052009 .50

VHS CMK202

VHS

Deluxe Edition

Painting Wizard's Workshop 1

Face Aerobics

with Judith Olivia

"Jingle Bell Rockin' Christmas"

With Bobby Helms

Performing his #1 original Christmas classic *Jingle Bell Rock*

Chart
Breaker
Video

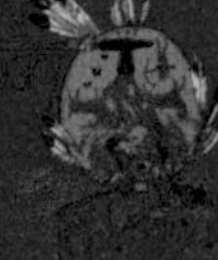

LEGENDS OF OLD MOSSY
DEATH BY THE ELEMENTS

VHS

T-120

THE REAL SHOTGUN RED®

VIDEOCASSETTE STEREO

The ultimate body contouring and sculpting workout!
PRISM
ENTERTAINMENT

VHS

ABSURD, ODD, AND RIDICULOUS RELICS FROM THE VIDEOTAPE ERA

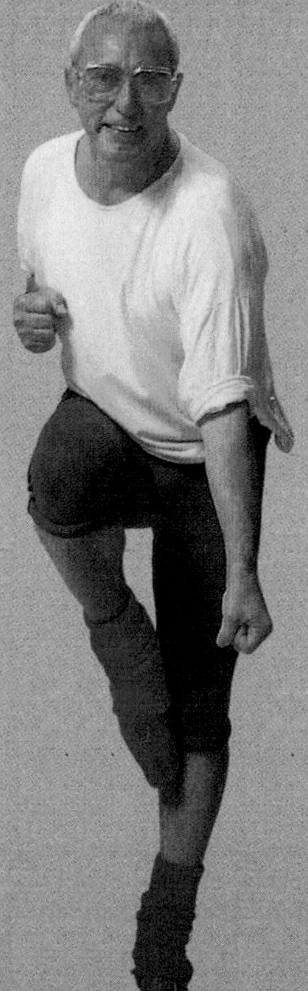

JOE PICKETT AND NICK PRUEHER

RUNNING PRESS
PHILADELPHIA · LONDON

Published by Running Press,
A Member of the Perseus Books Group

Printed in China

ISBN 978-0-7624-4259-1
Library of Congress Control Number: 2011929081

E-book ISBN 978-0-7624-4480-9

9 8 7 6 5 4 3 2 1
Digit on the right indicates the number of this printing

Cover design and interior design by Joshua McDonnell
Edited by Jennifer Kasius
Typography: Impact and St Ryde

Running Press Book Publishers
2300 Chestnut Street
Philadelphia, PA 19103-4371

Visit us on the web!
www.runningpress.com

CONTENTS DATE

Kmart

FOREWORD BY DAVY ROTHBART,

FOUND Magazine & This American Life

Soon after my ninth birthday, when melting plastic army guys with a magnifying glass had lost its luster, I started spending afternoons at our corner video store—a place called Video Watch, which sat between a kebab joint and a Domino's Pizza, but had the distinct odor of an old sneaker found in the woods. I hadn't the cash to rent any movies, nor an account with which to rent one, but still I'd haunt the aisles, gazing up at the VHS tape covers crammed along the shelves, utterly mesmerized by movies my folks would never agree to rent, from *Can't Buy Me Love* to *Faces of Death*. The cover art on each box peddled glimpses of thrilling, forbidden worlds still beyond my grasp. Every day, neck aching as I stared up at the shelves, my simple, earnest longing performed a strange bit of alchemy, turning even the crummiest and most forgettable flicks into gold.

Now, twenty-five years later, I can't leave a garage sale or thrift store without a stack of VHS tapes under my arm. It's as though I'm making up for all those years of paucity. I love the reliable heft of each cassette tape, and have become an expert at spotting jewels in the rough—a favorite documentary or cult classic or 80s gem in a *Titanic*- and *Jerry Maguire*-filled sea. Friends in my town know that I operate a unique sort of traveling VHS infirmary—whenever they get sick, I deliver to their door five hand-picked movies, plus a VCR, remote, and RCA cables to boot. Nothing cures the flu like *Trading Places*, *Pelle The Conqueror*, *The Third Man*, *Hands On A Hard Body*, and *American Movie*.

While I've spent the 2000s harvesting classics from Goodwills and St. Vincent de Pauls, Joe Pickett and Nick Prueher of the Found Footage Festival have been panning for a different sort of gold. Any average film aficionado can pull *The Thin Blue Line* out of a haystack, but it takes a particular brand of genius to pay attention to the VHS tapes that no one else might think to give a second glance: instructional videos, motivational seminars, exercise tapes, work-safety demonstrations, perversely low-budget horror and sci-fi flicks, public access TV shows, home videos, and even blank, mystery tapes which reveal themselves only once the VCR heads start spinning. By sharing juicy morsels from these tapes in their Found Footage show, Joe and Nick have opened a trenchant window on the moving, rousing, bizarre, and utterly ridiculous nature of human endeavor.

Here, in this book, the Found Footage guys have brought out the most sacred and sacrilegious prizes of their VHS treasure chest. It's a gripping, mind-bending collection. Many of the tapes recall a brighter, not-so-distant past, when people weren't working three jobs and had a desire to better themselves in their spare time by mastering the yo-yo or doing aerobics with newborn babies in tow. Others stand as evidence to some of the awfullest-looking movies ever filmed. I think it's important to keep in mind, though, that every one of these tapes, no matter how weird or terrible or fucking insane, was the result of someone's real passion, an attempt to fulfill a dream. Knowing that someone poured their heart and soul into producing these videotapes may complicate the enjoyment we feel at their existence, but it shouldn't dampen our appreciation, it should only deepen it. Because as wildly funny as these VHS tapes may be to us, they're no joke. Almost unbelievably, they're all one-thousand-percent genuine. Someone devoted their lives to making these tapes, and others consumed them. That, to me, is the real magic here, and what makes this incredible book so rich. Enjoy!

INTRODUCTION

1988 was a good year. NWA's "Straight Outta Compton" was blasting from suburban boom boxes, Nintendo owners everywhere learned the cheat code to Contra, and all those unanswered questions from *Crocodile Dundee* were finally answered in *Crocodile Dundee II*. But most importantly, there was a VCR in every home in America.

The VHS format was so ubiquitous, so affordable, and so easy-to-produce, that anybody with a pulse, a camcorder, and a few bucks could make his own video. And luckily for us, a lot of them did.

Need an exercise video for your baby? Try *Baby-N-Momerobics*. Need to learn how to flash-fry a turkey in under eight minutes? Pick up *Garbage Can Turkey*. Attracted to male country singers wearing Stetsons? Check out *Hunks With Hats*. Always wanted to teach your cat how to crap like a human? Find a copy of *Toilet Training the Feline*. Truly, it was the Golden Age of VHS.

Alas, the honeymoon didn't last long. By the late 90s, a sexy young newcomer known as the Digital Versatile Disc was becoming the format of choice. It was better looking, easier to use, and didn't require any fancy automatic rewinders shaped like red Corvettes. As DVD players entered more and more homes, people started to get rid of their once cherished VHS tapes in droves. The videos ended up by the boxful at thrift stores, garage sales, and in garbage cans.

And that's where we come in.

In 1991, Nick was working at a McDonald's in his hometown of Stoughton, Wisconsin (and generally winning at life) when he stumbled across a video in the break room that would change his life forever. It was called *Inside & Outside Custodial Duties*, and it featured a dopey trainee named Chris, an overly perky crew trainer named Jennifer, the palpable sexual tension between them, and a convoluted plot. It was as if McDonald's thought a cute storyline would somehow make cleaning up barf go down easier. It didn't.

Remember that scene in *Raiders of the Lost Ark* where they open the Ark of the Covenant and it melts the faces of the Nazis who look at it? That comes close to describing how Nick felt while first viewing this training video, except instead of melting off his face, it compelled him to take it home and show it to fellow pop culture masochist, Joe, who instantly fell in love with the tape.

In a town where we had to make our fun by tying fishing line to a stuffed animal beaver and yanking it across the road to scare motorists (we called it Beaverin' and it was a lot more fun than it sounds), the prospect of a new source of entertainment excited us. We invited friends over to watch *Inside & Outside Custodial Duties* again and again while developing a running commentary of smartass remarks to keep ourselves amused.

And that got us to thinking, "If there are videos this dumb right under our noses, imagine what else is out there." Thus began the quest to look in out-of-the-way places like break rooms, Salvation Armys, and Dumpsters to rescue more VHS gems from obscurity.

Over the years, our collection grew exponentially. We turned up wonderfully bad exercise videos, instructional videos, public access shows, and home movies that other people had discarded. Other times, we had to get more creative to procure VHS oddities.

In 1999, Joe heard a rumor that Suncoast Video, that overpriced mall repository for mainstream VHS titles, was showing employees a training video where two hosts impersonated Wayne and Garth from *Wayne's World*. It sounded like a tape we needed for the collection, so Joe applied for a job at a Suncoast, got hired, worked a four-hour shift, and hid their entire training video collection in his backpack at the end of the night. Having dubbed the videos overnight, Joe returned to the store the next day, returned the videos, and said, "I can no longer work here." Unfortunately, the *Wayne's World*-inspired training video was nowhere to be found. But there was a customer service video hosted by Siskel and Ebert impersonators, so the mission wasn't a complete loss.

Through our tenacity and utter lack of scruples, we had amassed a pretty impressive collection of over 3,000 tapes that spilled out over both of our apartments and two storage lockers in the glamorous metropolis of Queens, New York. No longer content to show off our finds to a handful of friends in a living room, we launched the Found Footage Festival in 2004 to spread the gospel of VHS to audiences all over the country.

And not a moment too soon. In December of 2008, the last supplier of new VHS tapes unceremoniously shipped the last of its supply, officially marking the death of the format. But fear not. VHS is alive and well at the Found Footage Festival. We have made it our mission to resurrect these clunky, analog relics for the ages.

Herein, for the first time, we collect and comment on our favorite VHS covers from more than 20 years of video scavenging. All the neon colors, shiny leotards, and regrettable graphic design from the 1980s and 90s come vividly back to life in this ode to the disposable video culture of yesteryear. So sit back, adjust the tracking on your VCR, and enjoy.

LEOTARDS & SWEAT

By far the most common type of video we find at thrift stores across the country is the exercise tape. Fitness videos meant you could work out at home without suffering any of the humiliation of exercising in front of strangers at a gym. You had your own personal trainer right there in your living room, cheerily barking orders at you any time you pressed *play*. And best of all, you could always hit *pause* when *Card Sharks* came on. But no matter how attractive the idea of exercising at home seemed, people inevitably grew tired of watching the same video every day and power-stepped© these videos to their nearest Goodwill.

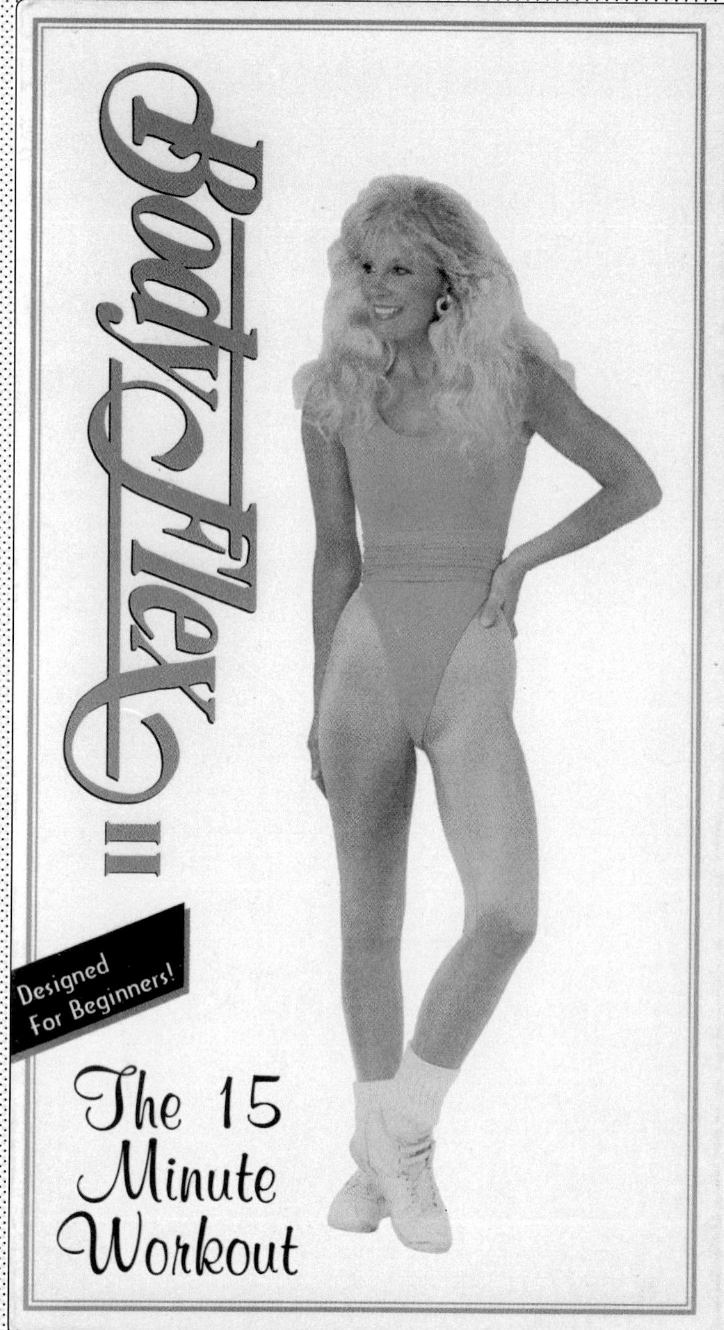
Body Flex
II
Designed For Beginners!
The 15 Minute Workout

We'd prefer it if that leotard left about 75% more to the imagination.

BODY BREAK

THE TOTAL BODY PROGRAM

GET FIT
&
HAVE FUN

HAL JOHNSON & JOANNE McLEOD
HOSTS OF TV'S BODY BREAK

After posing this unnaturally, you'll need a body break, too.

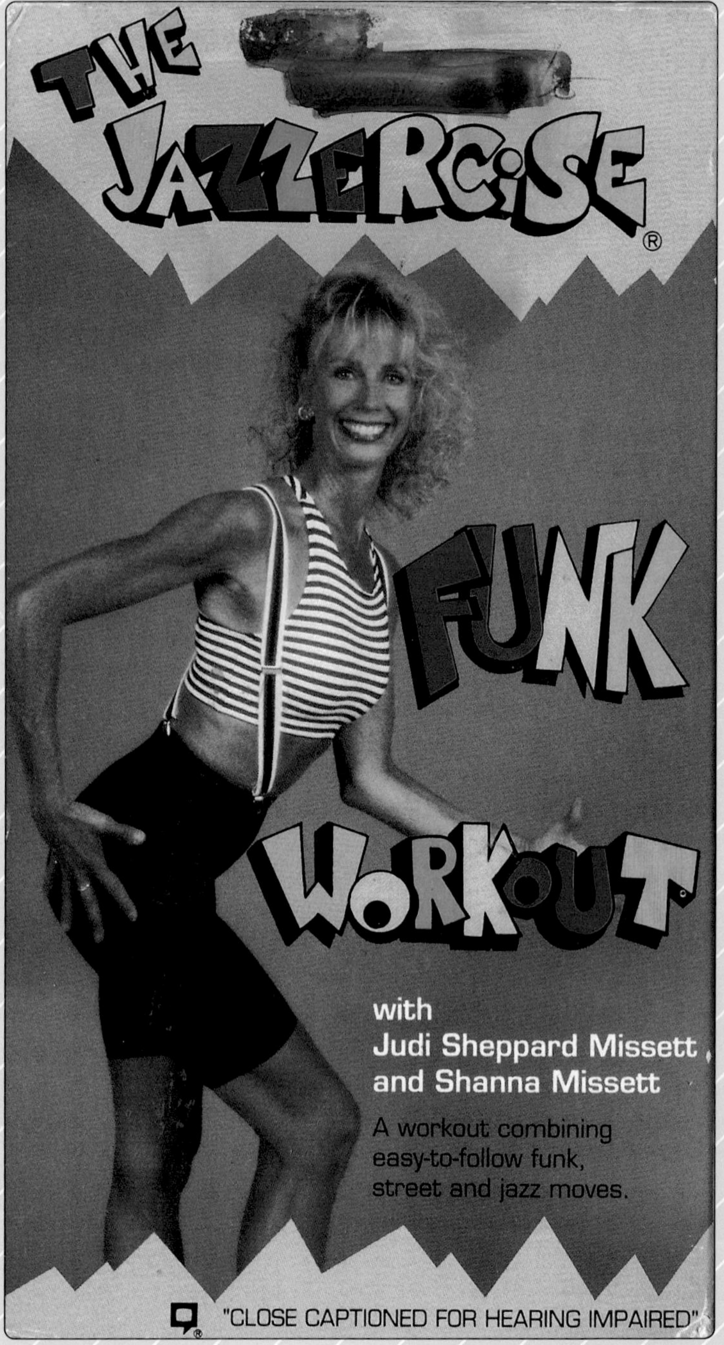
THE
JAZZERCISE®
FUNK
WORKOUT
with
Judi Sheppard Missett
and Shanna Missett
A workout combining
easy-to-follow funk,
street and jazz moves.
"CLOSE CAPTIONED FOR HEARING IMPAIRED"

This woman is everybody in the world's aunt.

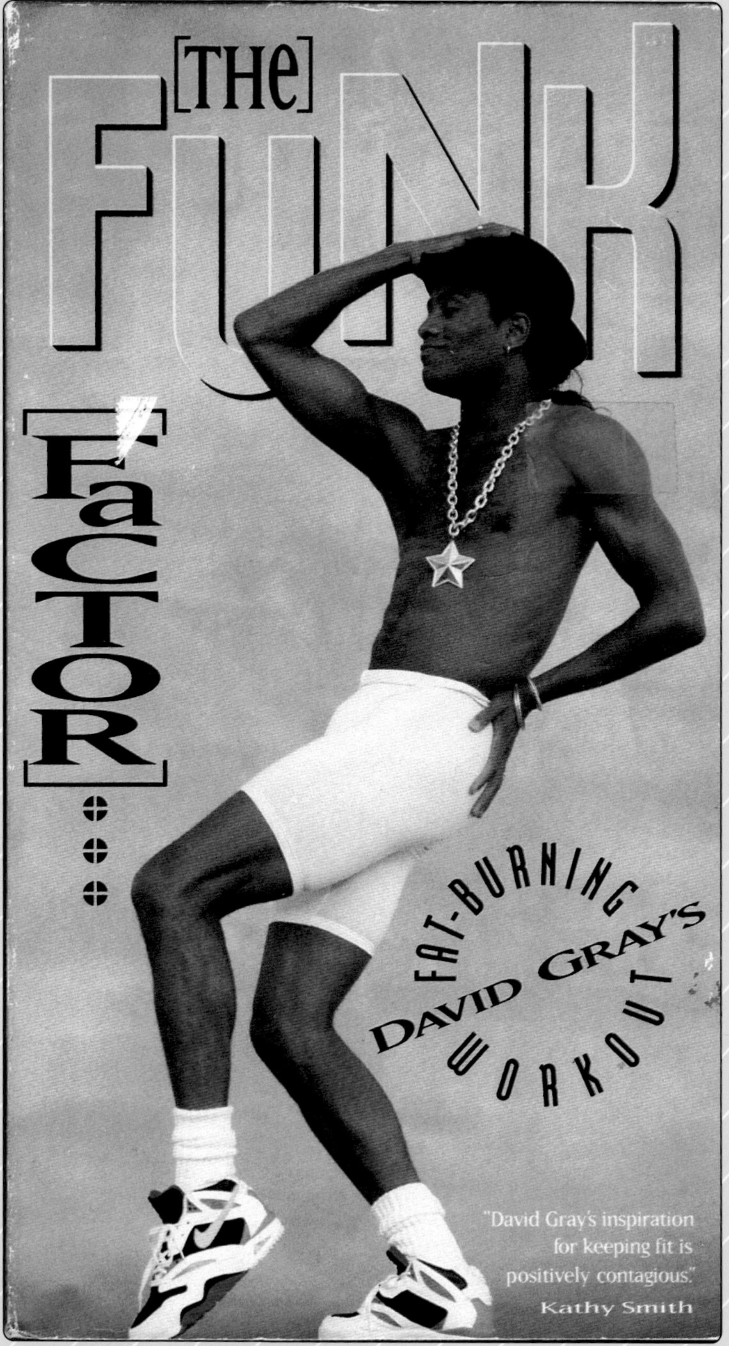
[THE] FUNK
[FaCTOR]
DAVID GRAY'S
FAT-BURNING WORKOUT
"David Gray's inspiration for keeping fit is positively contagious."
Kathy Smith

The photographer asked him to put on his "funk face."

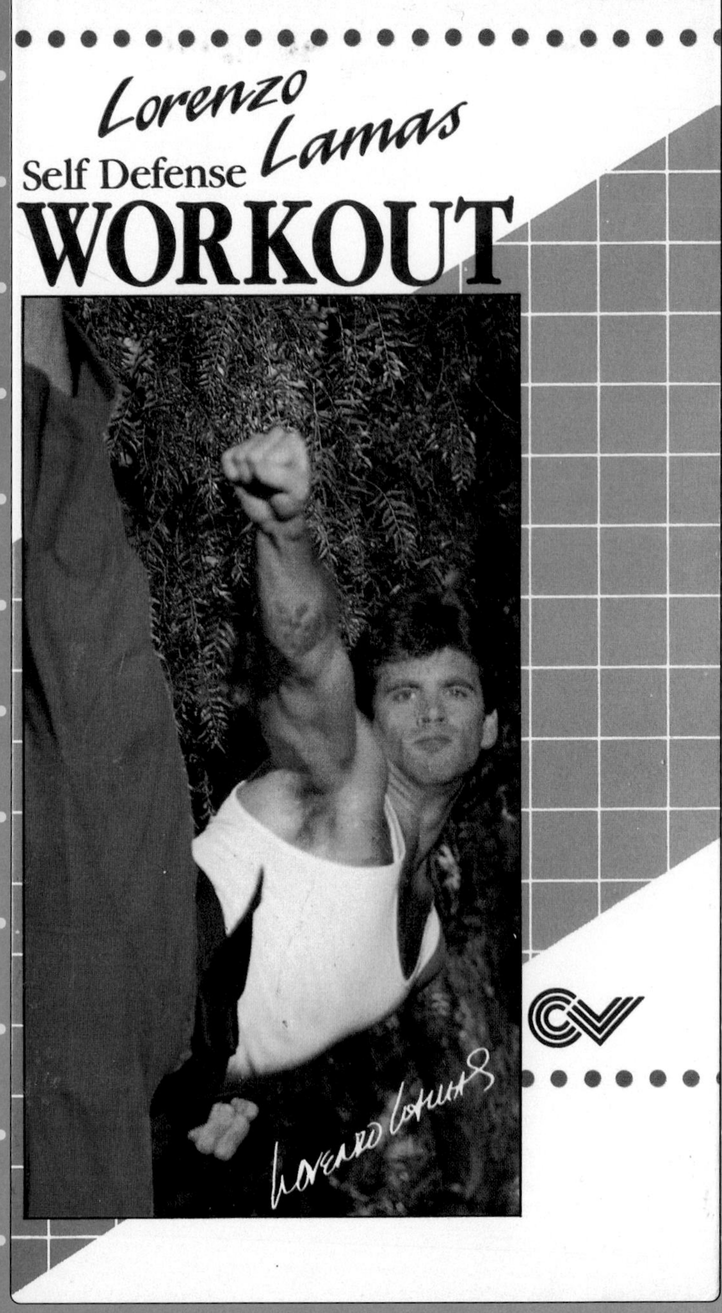
Lorenzo Lamas
Self Defense
WORKOUT
Lorenzo Lamas

Really comes in handy when surrounded by B-movie bad guys.

FTM SPORTS PRESENTS
SILVER FOXES™ II
SHAPE UP
AMERICA
FITNESS FOR
SILVER
CITIZENS
FEATURING
LAURIE WILLIAMS
HARRY HOFFMAN
JACKIE STALLONE
SAL PACINO
JCI VIDEO
SPONSORED BY Great Earth

Get that "celebrity parent" physique.

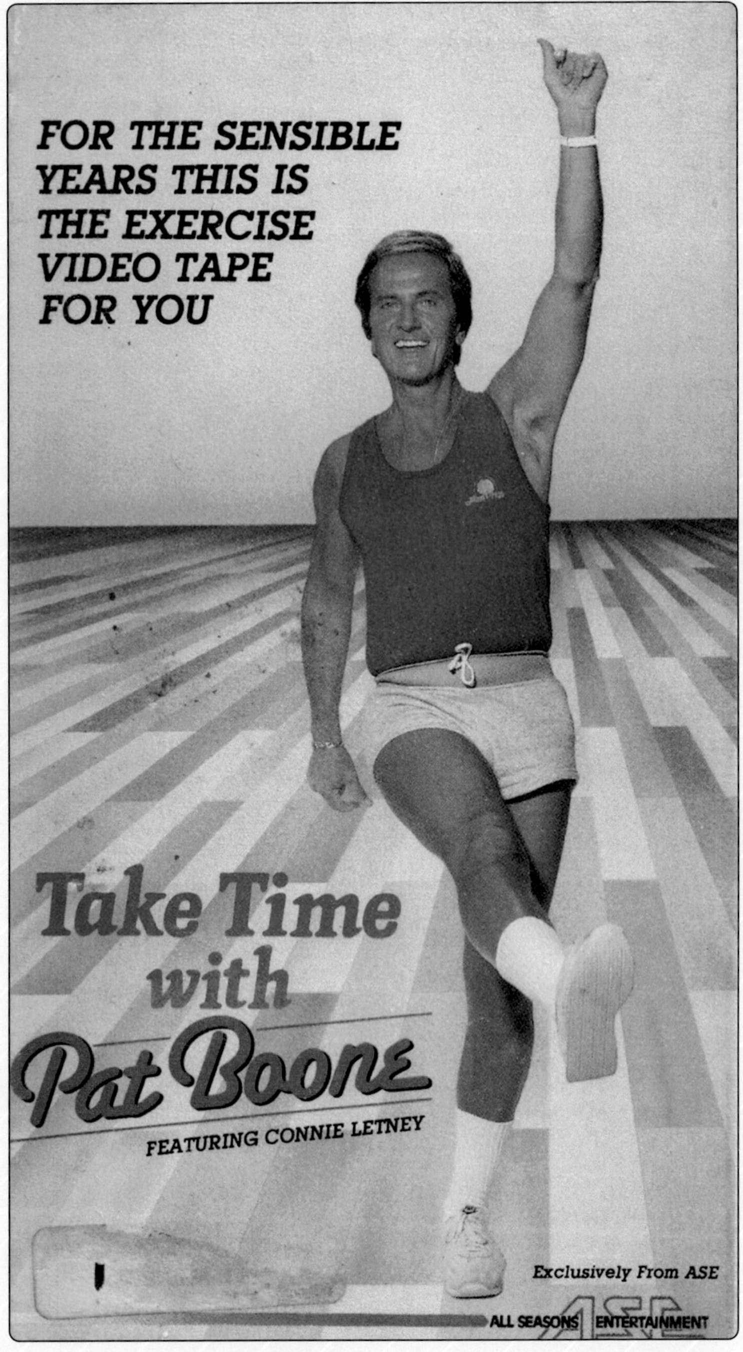
FOR THE SENSIBLE
YEARS THIS IS
THE EXERCISE
VIDEO TAPE
FOR YOU
Take Time
with
Pat Boone
FEATURING CONNIE LETNEY
Exclusively From ASE
ALL SEASONS ENTERTAINMENT

This photo was taken moments after Pat Boone's game-winning field goal.

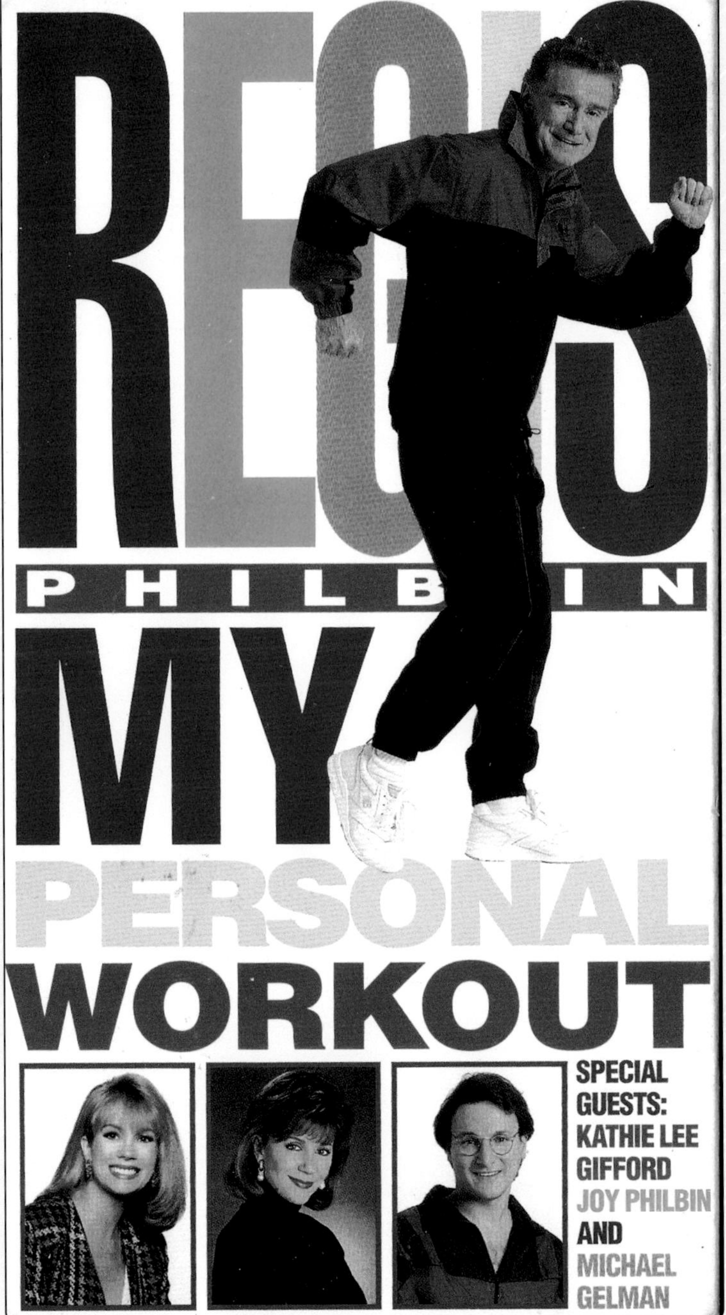
REGIS
PHILBIN
MY
PERSONAL
WORKOUT
SPECIAL GUESTS:
KATHIE LEE GIFFORD
JOY PHILBIN
AND
MICHAEL GELMAN

We bet he still has that jumpsuit.

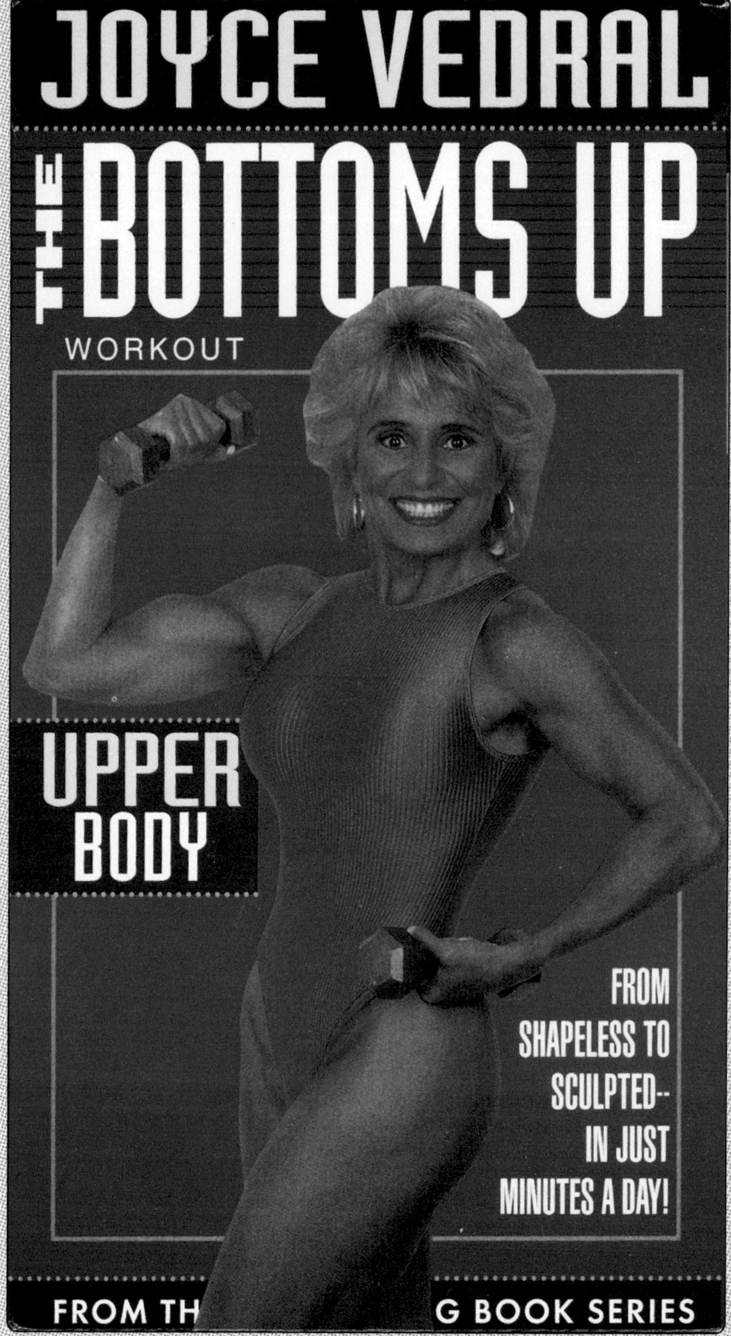
JOYCE VEDRAL
THE BOTTOMS UP
WORKOUT
UPPER BODY
FROM SHAPELESS TO SCULPTED-- IN JUST MINUTES A DAY!
FROM TH
G BOOK SERIES

Her smile is so aggressive, it actually looks like she's mad at you.

TIGHT ASSETS
BODY SLI
INSTRUCTION BY FITNESS EXPERTS
PAT WADE & ANDRE HOULE

Heil fitness!

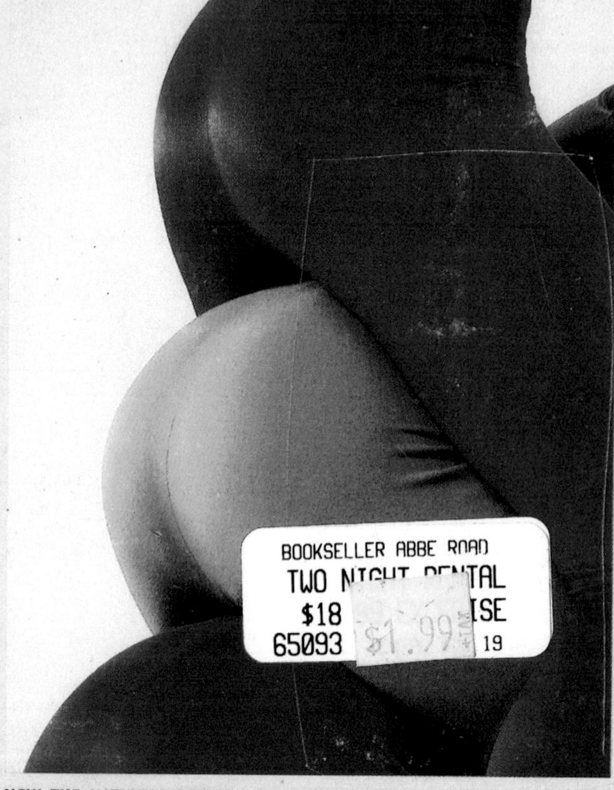
20 MINUTES TO THE
PERFECT BUTTOCKS
VID-28
Cal•del•Pozo's
Bunnetics
THE BUTTOCKS WORKOUT
BOOKSELLER ABBE
$18
65093
$1.99
NOW THE NATIONAL BESTSELLING BOOK, BUNNETICS, COMES TO LIFE ON VIDEO WITH A SIMPLE AND EFFECTIVE WORKOUT THAT WILL IMPROVE YOUR BACKSIDE IN JUST TWENTY MINUTES!

A stack of colorful asses for $1.99? Sounds fair.

Cal Pozo's
Bunnetics
"Exercise your way to a perfect posterior."
— New York Daily News

When you find two different but equally eye-catching Bunnetics covers in the same year, you make a wish.

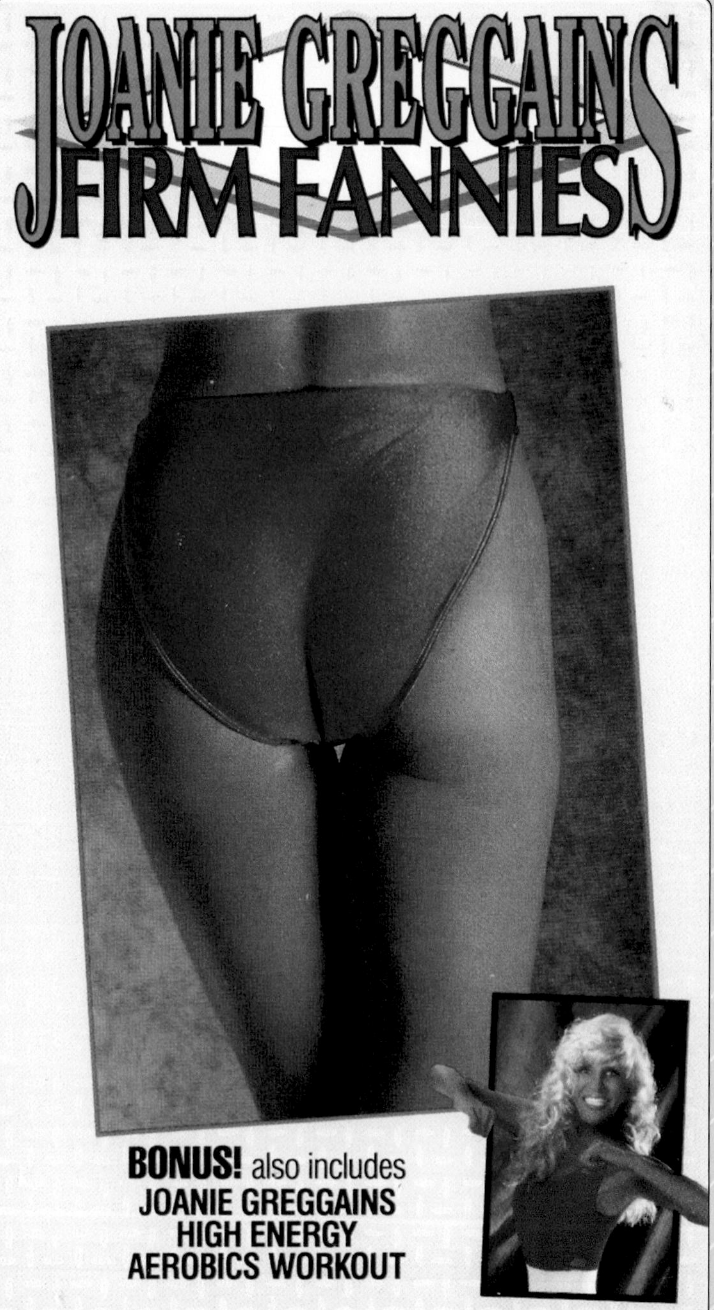
JOANIE GREGGAINS
FIRM FANNIES
BONUS! also includes
JOANIE GREGGAINS
HIGH ENERGY
AEROBICS WORKOUT

A cover like this is its own bonus.

FITNESS
PERSONAL
Action
FOR BETTER HEALTH

Here it is, the most generic VHS cover ever produced.

KIDZ & TEENZ*

Nothing speaks to the youth of America more clearly and efficiently than a video (just ask any substitute teacher) and during the VHS gold rush of the 80s and 90s, production companies eagerly sought to tap into this burgeoning market. Shaping young minds suddenly became very important to video peddlers, who employed everything from cartoons to puppets to Burt Reynolds to reach impressionable youngsters. Judging by these covers, the tapes didn't so much shape young minds as warp them irrevocably.

*Zs added for extra kid and teen appeal!

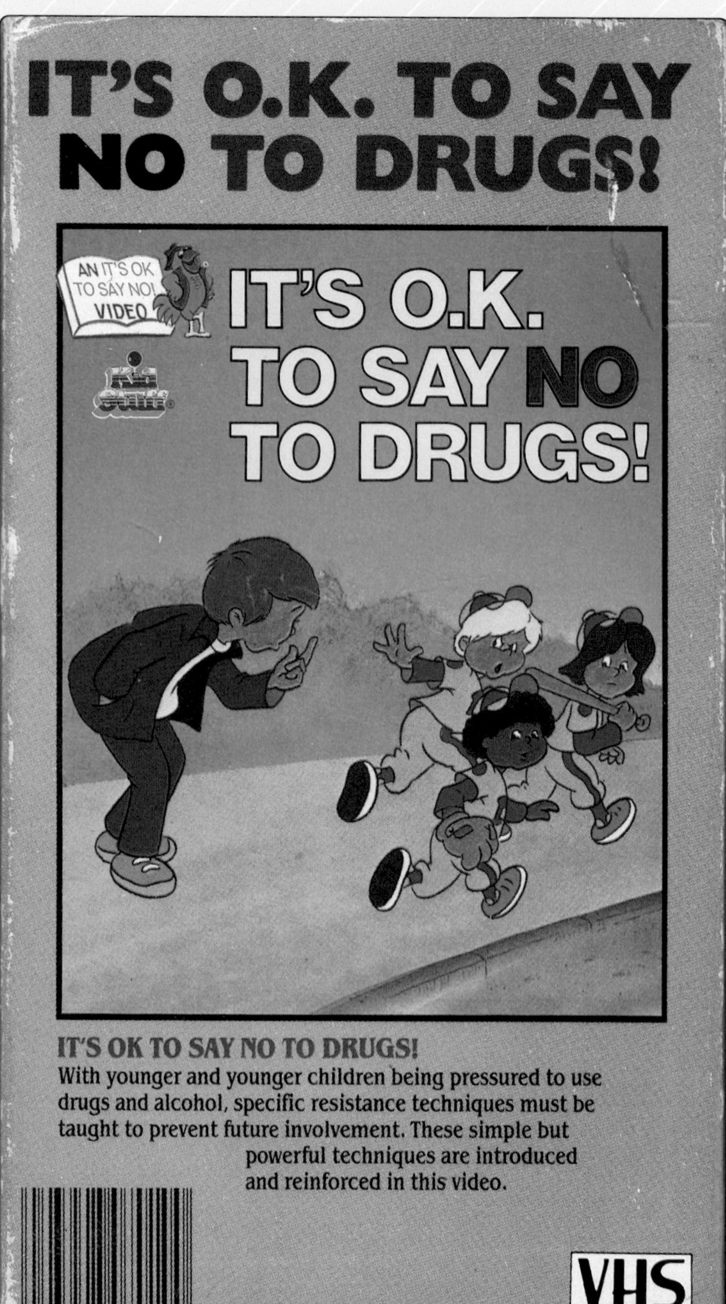
IT'S O.K. TO SAY NO TO DRUGS!
AN IT'S OK TO SAY NO! VIDEO
IT'S O.K. TO SAY NO TO DRUGS!
IT'S OK TO SAY NO TO DRUGS!
With younger and younger children being pressured to use drugs and alcohol, specific resistance techniques must be taught to prevent future involvement. These simple but powerful techniques are introduced and reinforced in this video.
43948 07010 0
I.S.B.N.0-87660-172-7
VHS
KOK 7010

If only there were some way to tell what the title of this video is.

THE REPPIES™
One Man Band
"You shall know the truth and
the truth shall set you FREE!"

Kids don't care about the truth. They want to see monsters rock out on guitars. So this video gets it half-right.

THE LEARNING TREEHOUSE SERIES
PHONICS
VOLUME ONE
MAKES LEARNING A FUN EXPERIENCE
FOR CHILDREN OF ALL AGES

They found this muppet in the Dumpster behind Jim Henson's Puppet Workshop.

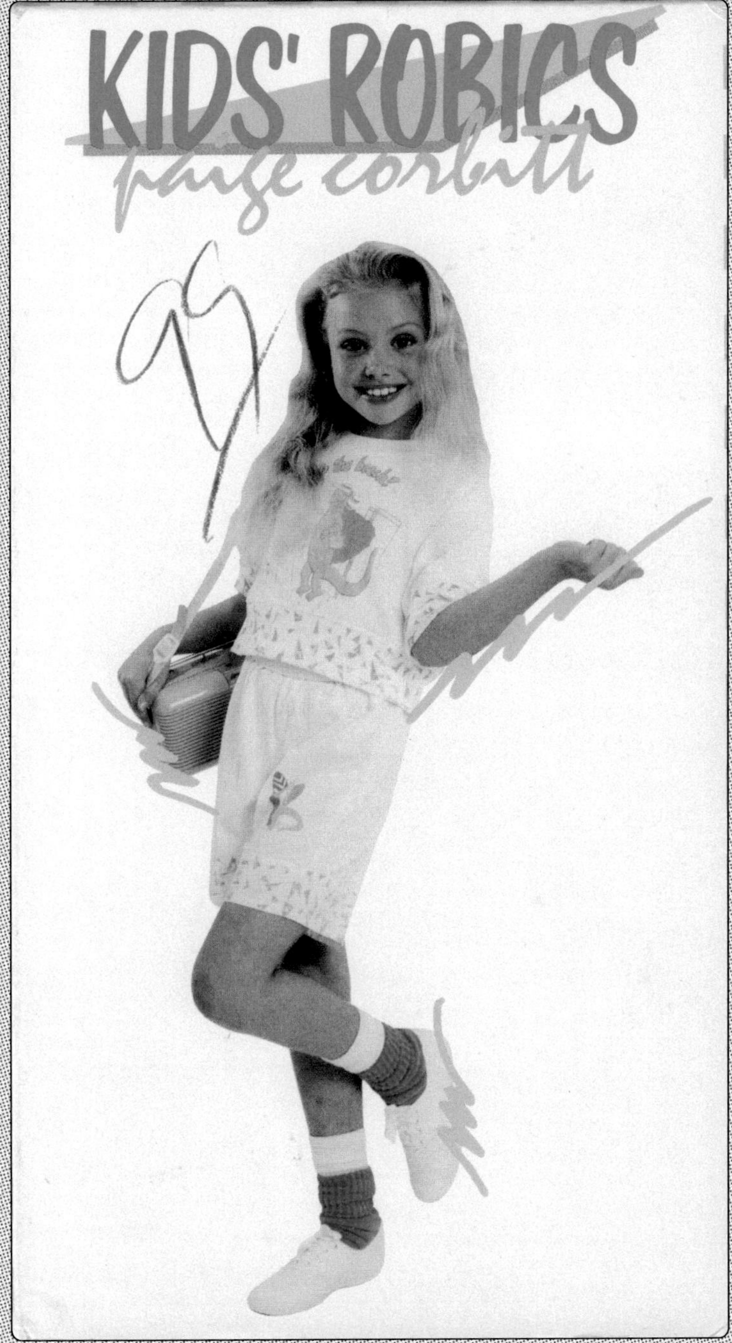
KIDS' ROBICS
paige corbitt

Helps your child get into pageant shape in no time!

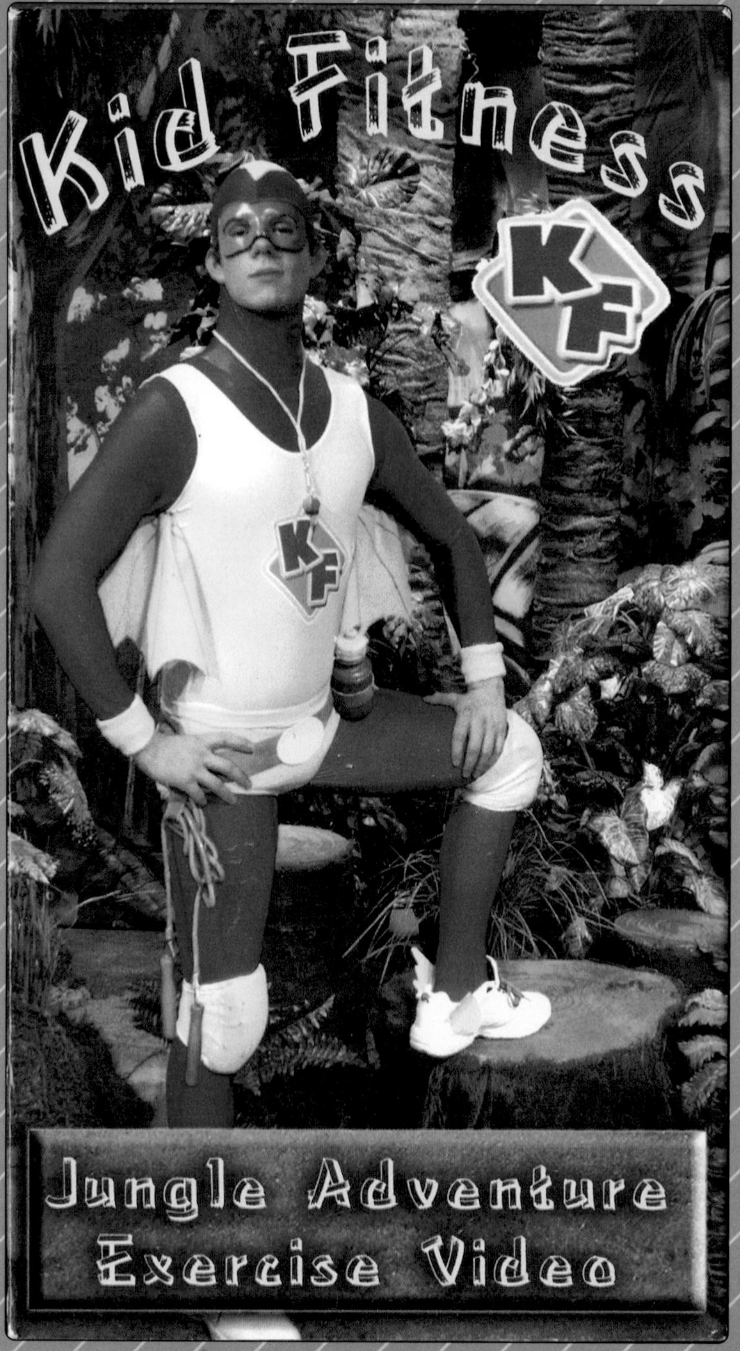
Kid Fitness
KF
KF
Jungle Adventure
Exercise Video

Looks like Kid Fitness is getting a little too cocky for his unitard.

SHATTERED
IF YOUR KID'S ON DRUGS
Special Appearances by BURT REYNOLDS & JUDD NELSON
MCA HOME VIDEO

Stay away from partying and drugs, kids.
Take it from Burt Reynolds and Judd Nelson.

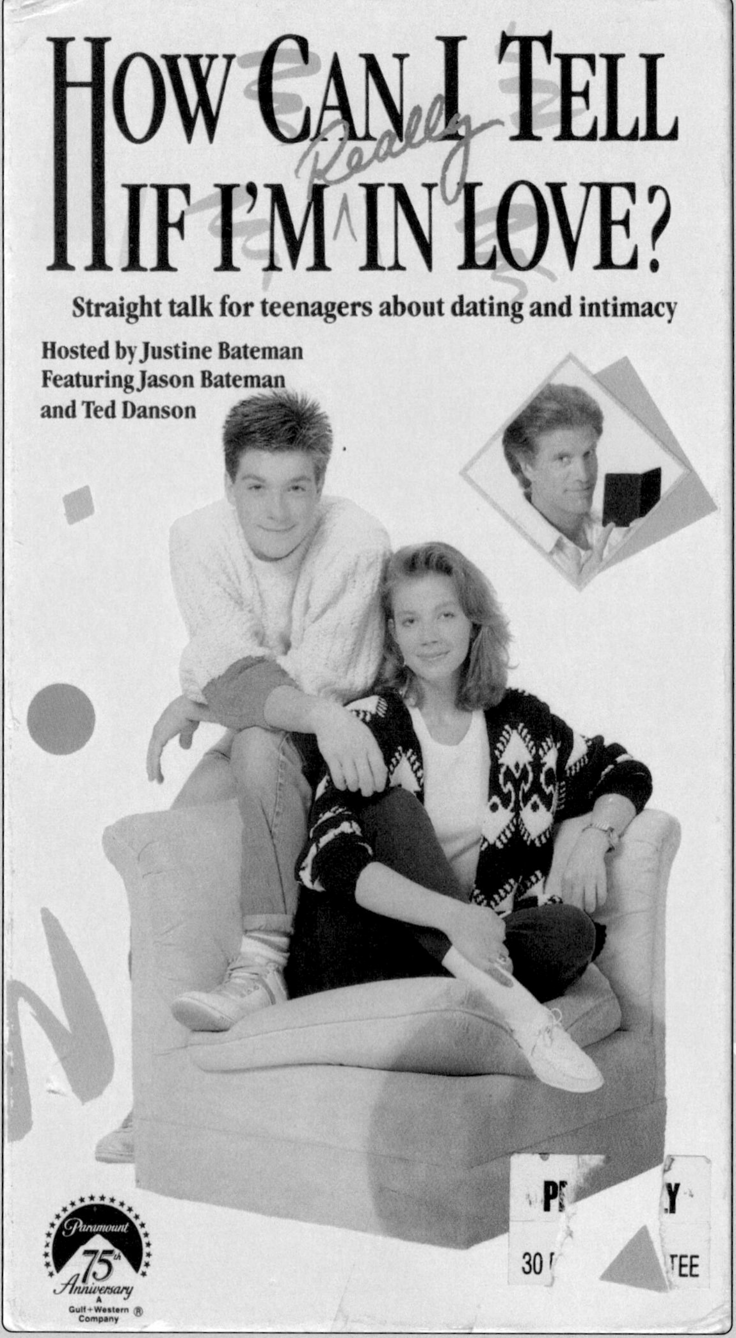
HOW CAN I TELL IF I'M IN LOVE?
Really
Straight talk for teenagers about dating and intimacy
Hosted by Justine Bateman
Featuring Jason Bateman
and Ted Danson
Paramount
75th
Anniversary
A
Gulf+Western
Company

Try as they might, the Batemans could never escape the watchful eye of Ted Danson.

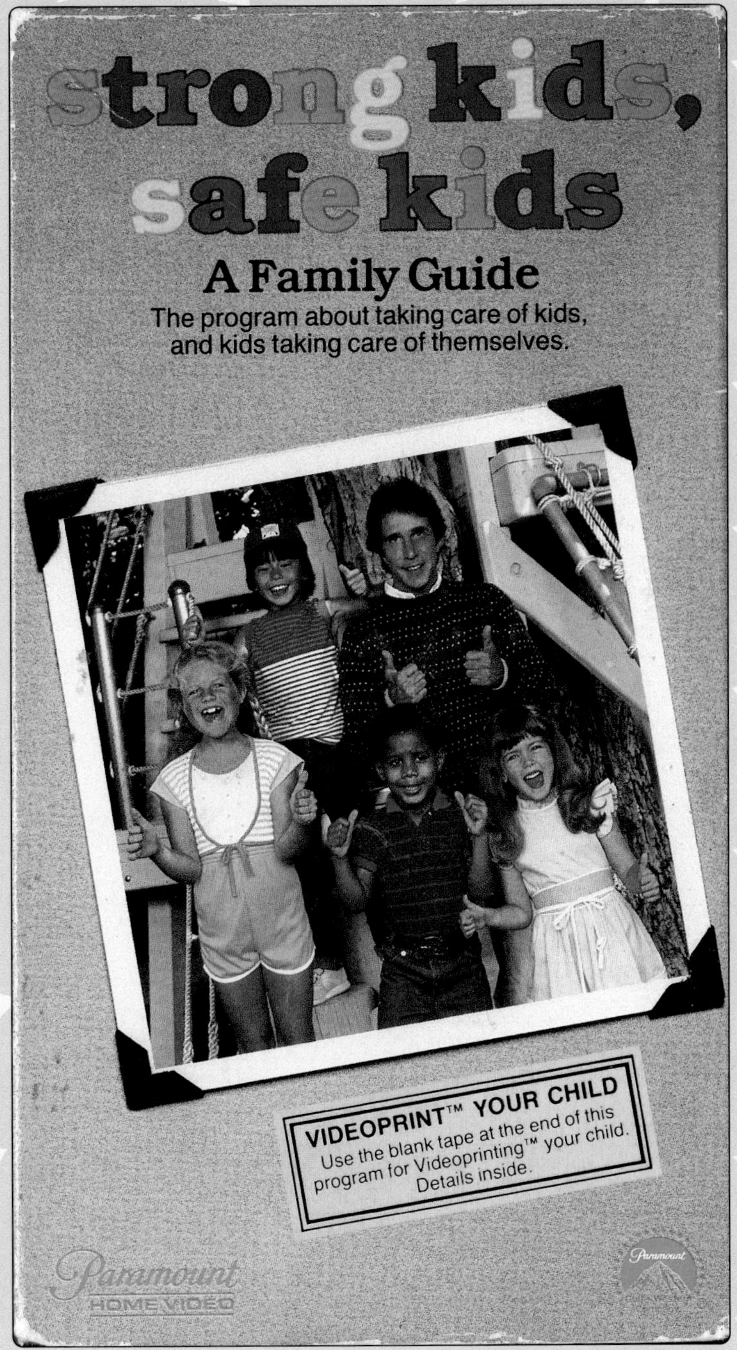
strong kids,
safe kids
A Family Guide
The program about taking care of kids,
and kids taking care of themselves.
VIDEOPRINT™ YOUR CHILD
Use the blank tape at the end of this
program for Videoprinting™ your child.
Details inside.
Paramount
HOME VIDEO
Paramount

You gotta think that Henry Winkler tried talking the director out of doing the Fonzie pose.

LET'S LEARN!

The desire to learn and the quest for greater knowledge are part of basic human nature, but let's face it, learning is boring. Our desire for laziness wins out every time. Hence, the educational video, which promises the tools to better ourselves while making the minimum amount of effort possible, and without all the pesky social interaction of school. But learning, no matter what form it comes in, will never be as entertaining as your copy of *Die Hard*, and thus, these videos quickly ended up at thrift stores.

LEARNING

ROCK 'N ROLL

PIANO

TAUGHT BY BOB HOBAN

HOMESPUN VIDEO

If this cover teaches us anything, it's don't get caught mid-whistle.

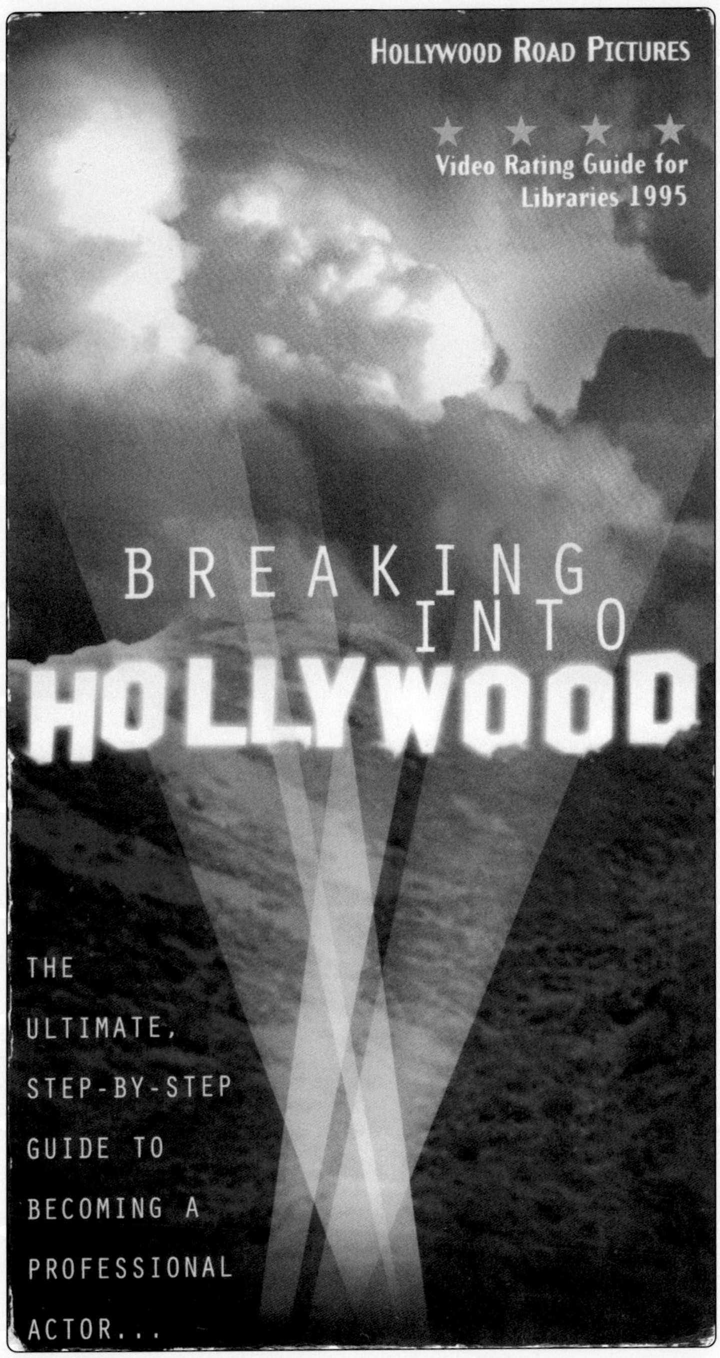
HOLLYWOOD ROAD PICTURES
★ ★ ★ ★
Video Rating Guide for Libraries 1995
BREAKING INTO HOLLYWOOD
THE ULTIMATE, STEP-BY-STEP GUIDE TO BECOMING A PROFESSIONAL ACTOR...

By setting it on fire?

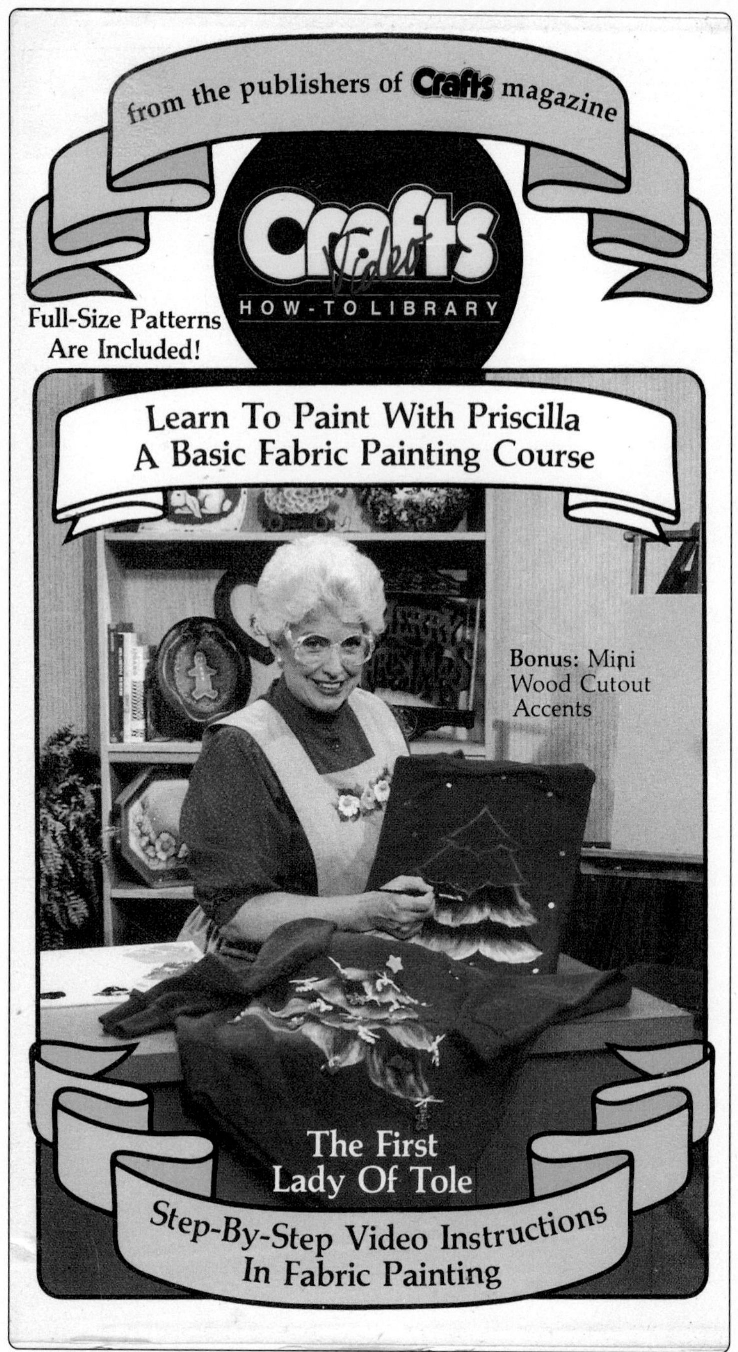
from the publishers of Crafts magazine
Crafts Video
HOW-TO LIBRARY
Full-Size Patterns
Are Included!
Learn To Paint With Priscilla
A Basic Fabric Painting Course
Bonus: Mini
Wood Cutout
Accents
The First
Lady Of Tole
Step-By-Step Video Instructions
In Fabric Painting

Learn how to make all the fashions you admired so much on your kindergarten teacher.

CRAFTS

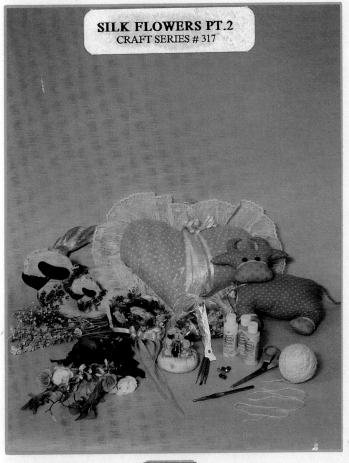

SILK FLOWERS PT.2
CRAFT SERIES # 317

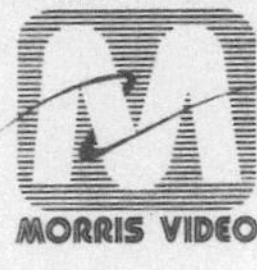
MORRIS VIDEO

That's certainly an impressive pile of crafts.

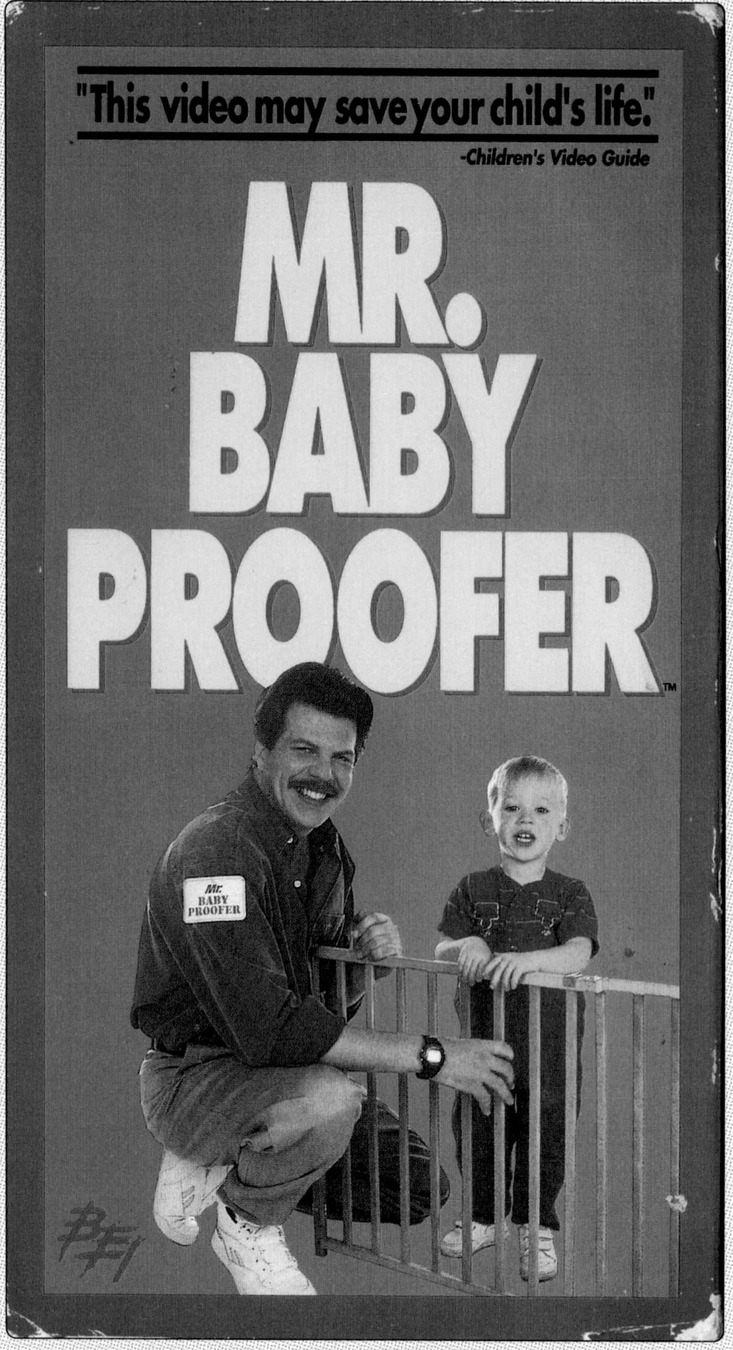
"This video may save your child's life."
-Children's Video Guide
MR. BABY PROOFER™
Mr. BABY PROOFER
BFI

"Please, call me Dennis.
My dad is Mr. Baby Proofer."

How To Retire
in
2 to 5 Years!
©2Xtreme Performance Intl.,L.L.C.
To reorder this video, call 1-800-616-1376

. . . To a transparent house with hundred dollar bills for grass and yellow blobs for trees.

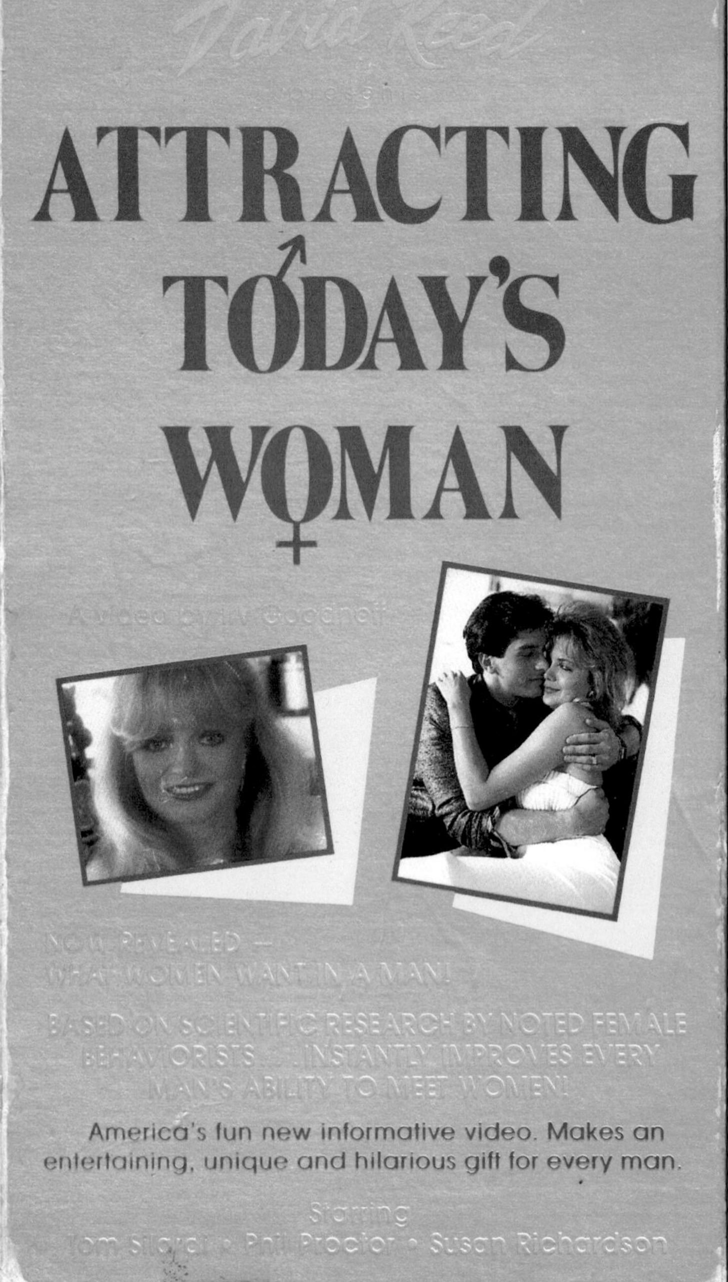
David Reed
presents
ATTRACTING TODAY'S WOMAN
NOW REVEALED —
WHAT WOMEN WANT IN A MAN!
BASED ON SCIENTIFIC RESEARCH BY NOTED FEMALE BEHAVIORISTS ... INSTANTLY IMPROVES EVERY MAN'S ABILITY TO MEET WOMEN!
America's fun new informative video. Makes an entertaining, unique and hilarious gift for every man.
Starring

Step 1: Hide this video where no woman will ever find it.

THE VIDEO GUIDE TO
SUCCESSFUL SEDUCTION
MAKE THE HONEYMOON LAST FOREVER

This video couldn't be any more 1987 if it tried.

How To Date God
HOLY
Featuring:
CHARLES BILLINGSLEY
Bonus Video:
THIS TRAIN "SHE'S A ROCKET"
ACQUIRE THE FIRE
VIDEO SERIES
WITH RON LUCE

There's no sugarcoating it: you're gonna have to put out.

A 75/R
Merry Heart
Doeth Good
Like
A
Medicine
VOLUME III
BY JESSE DUPLANTIS
$20

Mugging nonstop is apparently a side effect of having a merry heart.

CATCHY TITLES

In the overcrowded VHS market, it was absolutely necessary to make your tape stand out from the rest, otherwise your fishing lure video could get lost among the three to five other fishing lure videos out there. But how to do it? Flashy graphic design? A free enclosed poster? Perhaps. But the simplest, most basic technique was using the ancient art of scribe. A catchy title, a snappy turn-of-phrase, or some alliterative copy could lure consumers' brains into forking over their precious $19.95. It could also really confuse them.

BABE WINKELMAN PRESENTS
JIGS!
Expert Tactics for the
World's Most Versatile Lure
TEACHING AMERICA TO FISH®

If there was ever a word that deserved an exclamation point, it's "jigs."

C'mon Geese!

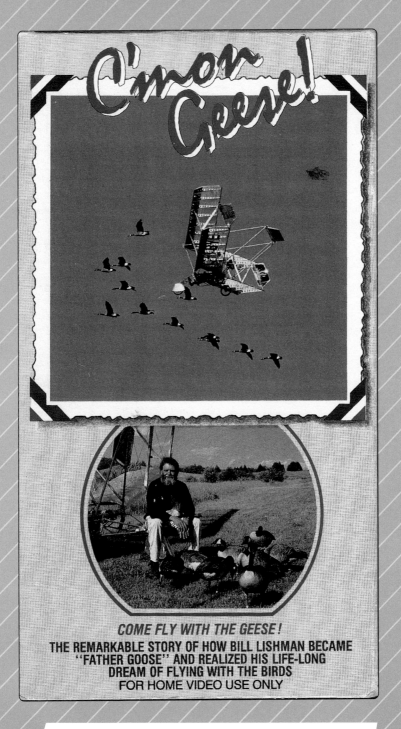

COME FLY WITH THE GEESE!

THE REMARKABLE STORY OF HOW BILL LISHMAN BECAME "FATHER GOOSE" AND REALIZED HIS LIFE-LONG DREAM OF FLYING WITH THE BIRDS

FOR HOME VIDEO USE ONLY

We think he might be expecting a little too much out of the geese.

HEY KIDS:
LET'S MAKE MILK!
FALL ON THE FARM VOL. 1
This 30-minute video takes you behind the scenes of a family farm during the fall season.

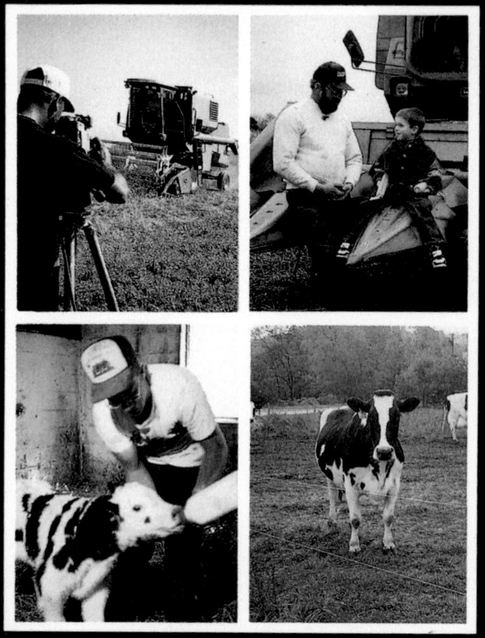

VHS

This title is way more excited than the kids are.

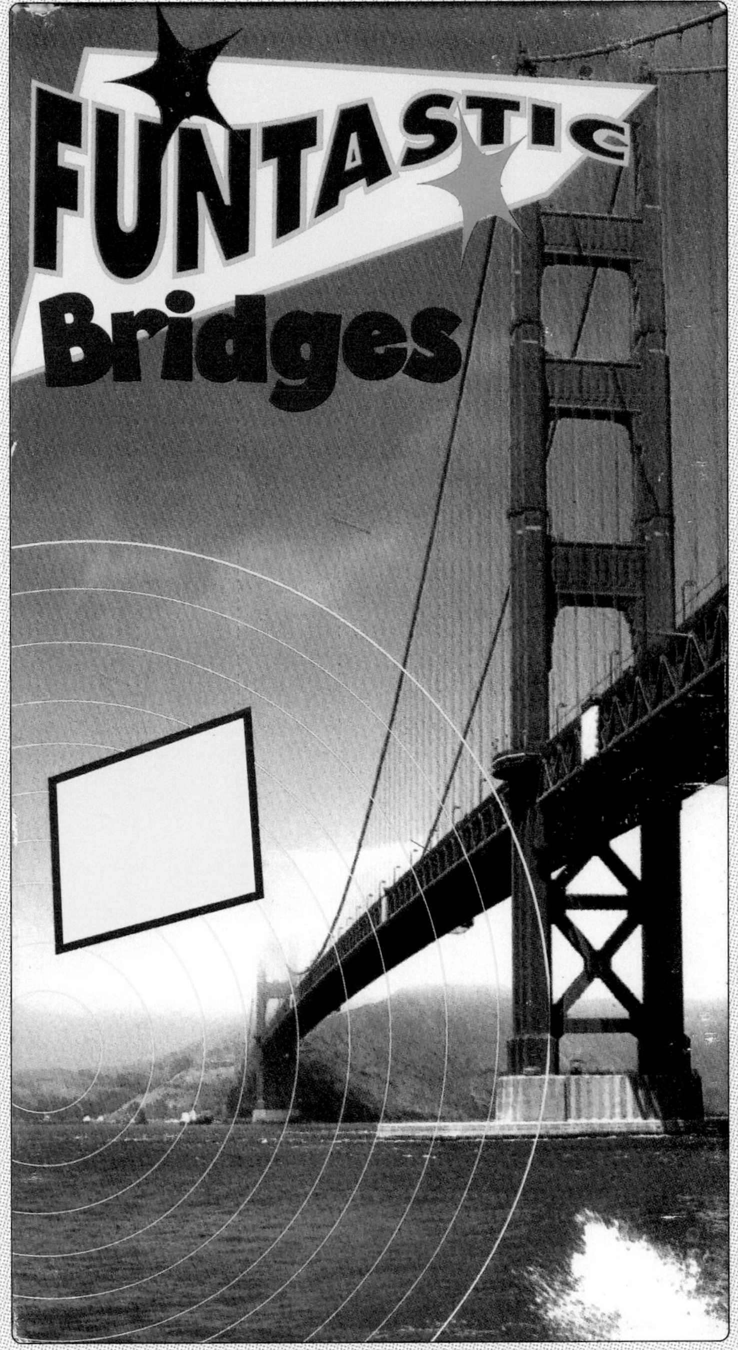
FUNTASTIC
Bridges

It's a nice bridge, to be sure, but we don't know if we'd go as far as "funtastic."

YES
WE'RE
walking
ANNE KASHIWA
TIM LEWIS
The complete fitness walking video from beginning technique to race walking.

This video answers the question: "Hey, are you guys walking?"

Am I Not Here
Who Am Your Mother?

The ongoing Miracle of
Our Lady of Guadalupe
hosted by
Bob and Penny Lord

Is this one of those trick questions where you'll end up in hell if you answer wrong?

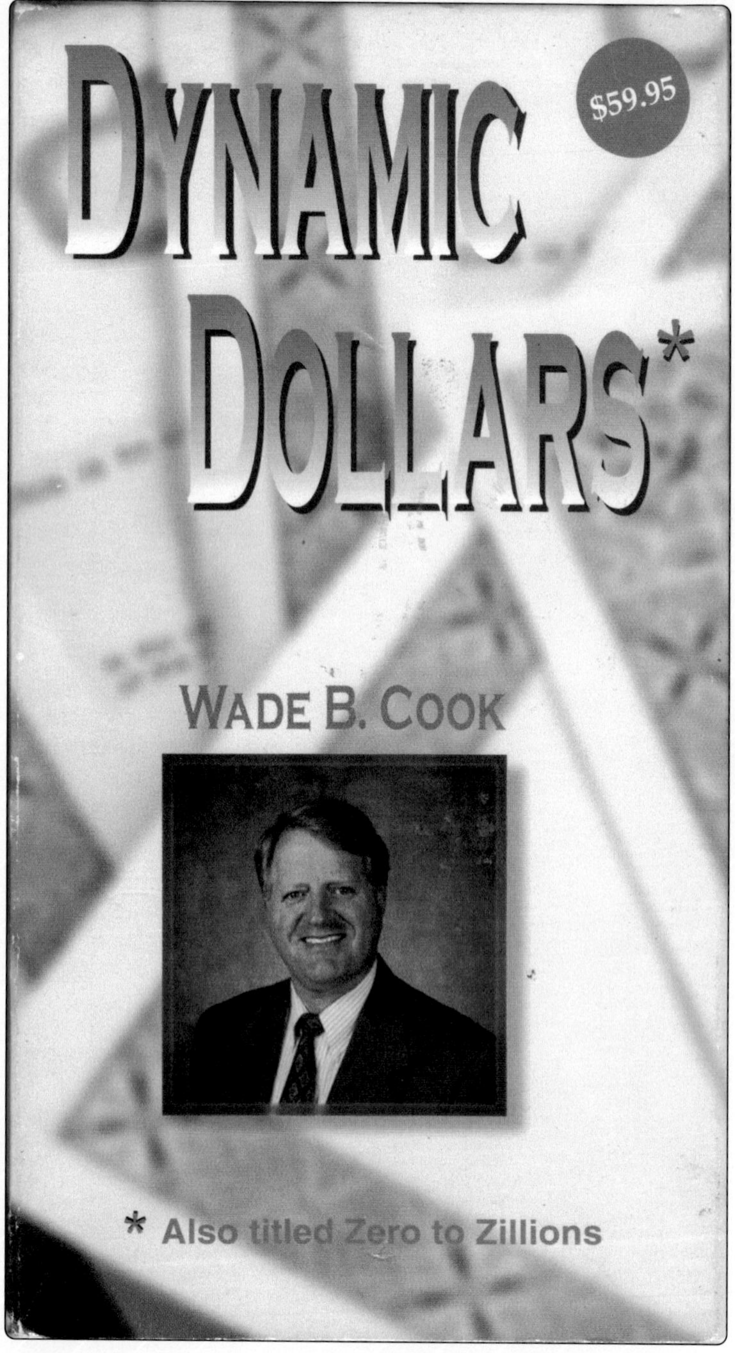
DYNAMIC
DOLLARS*
$59.95
WADE B. COOK
* Also titled Zero to Zillions

Wade B. Cook is a self-made zillionaire.

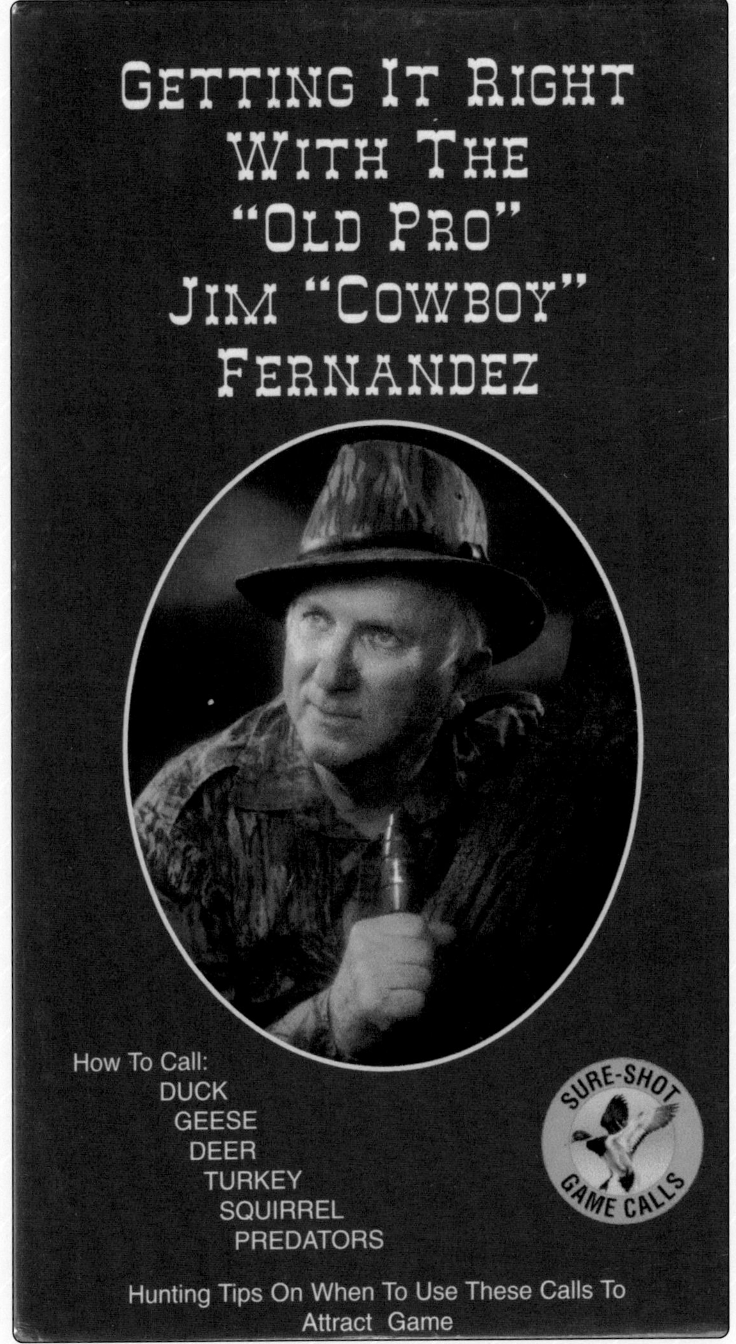
GETTING IT RIGHT
WITH THE
"OLD PRO"
JIM "COWBOY"
FERNANDEZ
How To Call:
DUCK
GEESE
DEER
TURKEY
SQUIRREL
PREDATORS
SURE-SHOT
GAME CALLS
Hunting Tips On When To Use These Calls To
Attract Game

They need a bigger cover to accommodate all of this guy's nicknames.

"ALL FISH-FINDERS ARE NOT CREATED EQUAL!"

LCG Buyer's Guide & Instructional Video

- 52 Minutes of Live-Action, Full Color Instruction.
- All The Facts You'll Need To Select The Recreational Sonar That's Right For You.
- How to get the most out of your LCG.

We hold these fish-finding truths to be self-evident.

THE
CHALLENGE
OF FLIGHT
Whispers of Death

Fun Fact: Adding the subtitle "Whispers of Death" to any video makes it 40% cooler.

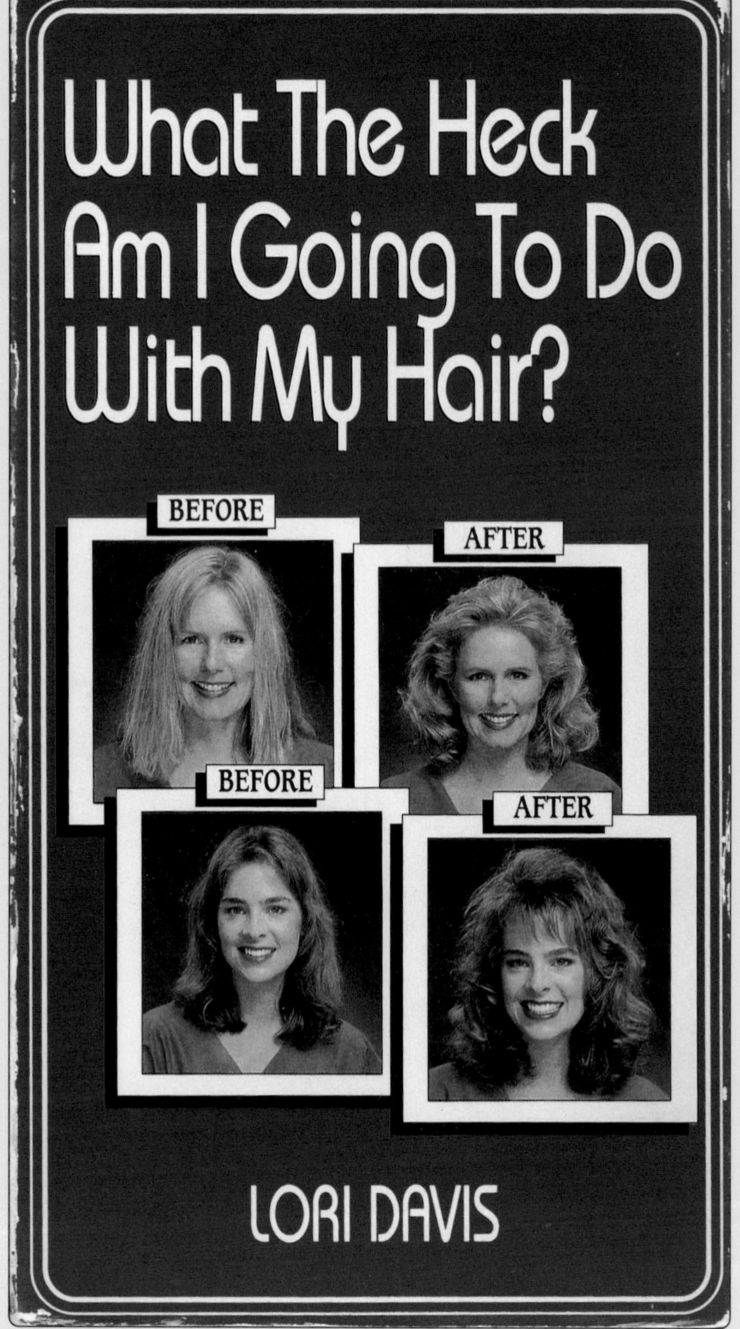
What The Heck
Am I Going To Do
With My Hair?
BEFORE
AFTER
BEFORE
AFTER
LORI DAVIS

Make it poofier?

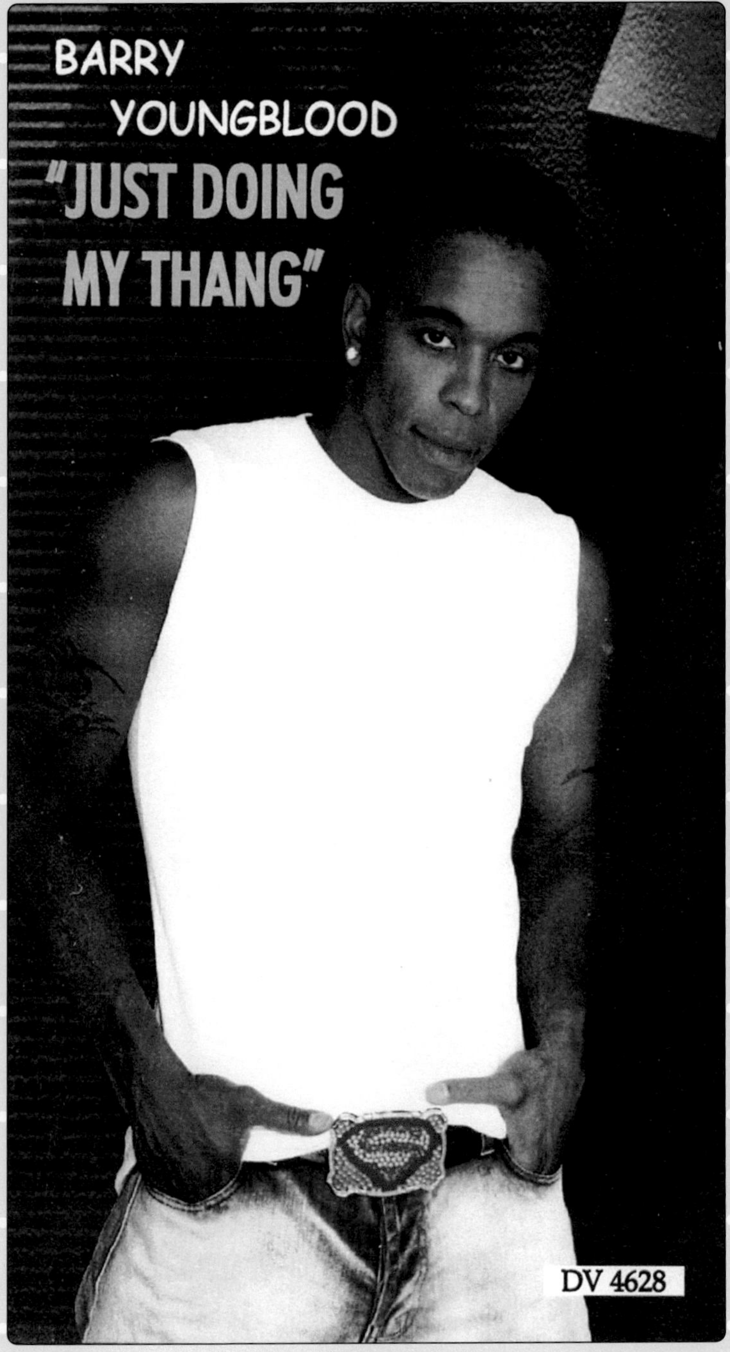
BARRY
YOUNGBLOOD
"JUST DOING
MY THANG"
DV 4628

Barry's "thang" looks kind of boring.

A good magician never reveals his secrets, but a good producer always puts the word "magic" in his video title. Ladies and gentlemen, prepare to be amazed by some magical videos that seem to contain a little bit of pixie dust. No, wait, that's actual dust.

Winner of NASA's prestigious Star Traveler of the Year Award

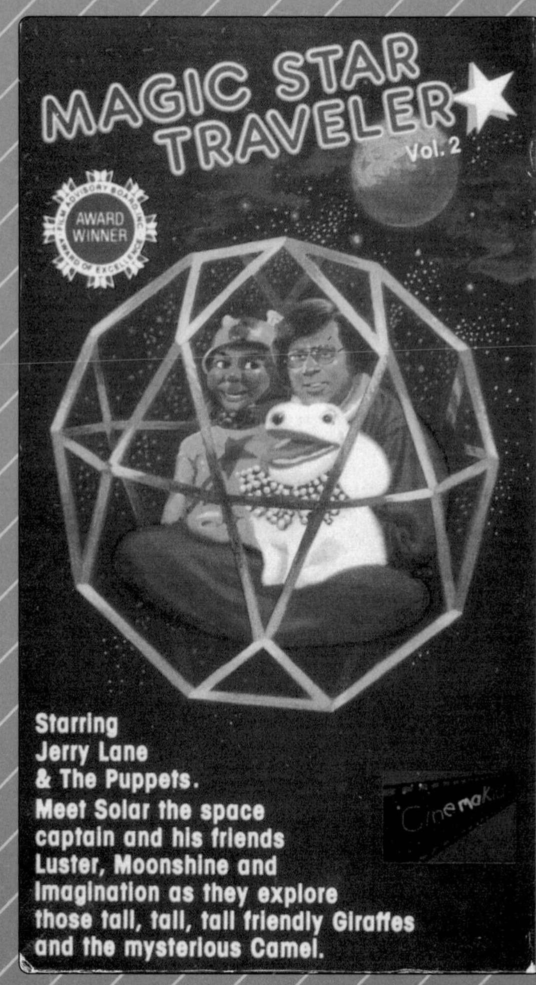
MAGIC STAR TRAVELER
Vol. 2
AWARD WINNER
Starring
Jerry Lane
& The Puppets.
Meet Solar the space
captain and his friends
Luster, Moonshine and
Imagination as they explore
those tall, tall, tall friendly Giraffes
and the mysterious Camel.

KNIGHT
GAME
INCORPORATED
& HALE
CALLS
Presents

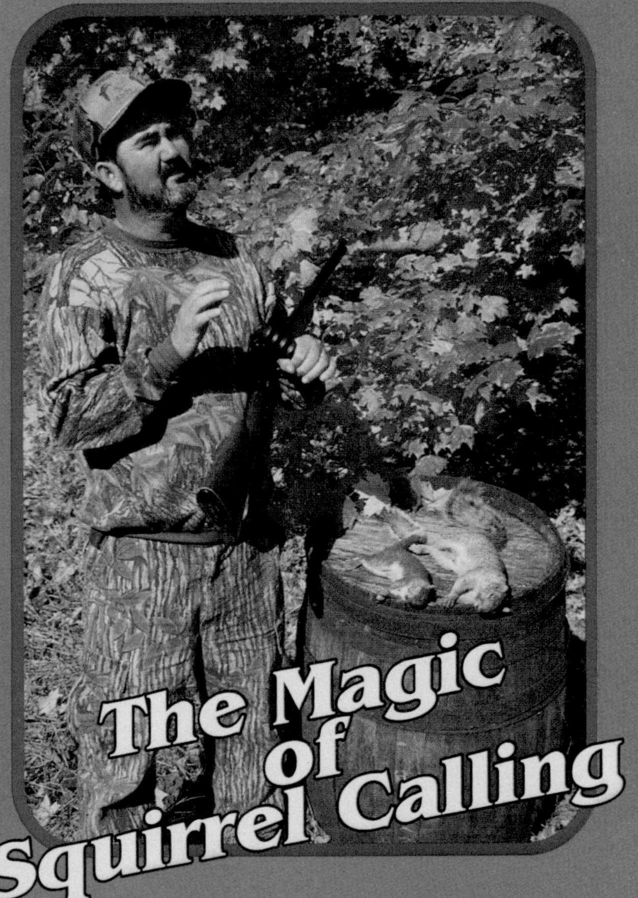
The Magic of Squirrel Calling

"He couldn't help but give away his location"

Two dead squirrels on a barrel.
Now that's what we call magic.

"C'mon! Let's go sponge some shit!"

Posh Impressions®
Magical Rainbow Sponge™
With Dee Gruenig
Learn To:
• Ink the Sponge
Mix & Blend Colors
Free Form Sponge
Rainbow Write
Dry Sponge
Wet Sponge
Create Tile
Effects
rox. Running
Time 35 min

DUNCAN THE MAGIC DRAGON©
Mighty Machines
Bulldozers • Trucks • Backhoes • Cranes • & More
See Them In Action!

We love Duncan's magically saggy ankles.

IT'S EASY
TO MEET PEOPLE,
ALL YOU NEED
IS A LITTLE
MAGIC!
Flirting With Magic

Calling all desperate men!

GET UP AND DANCE!

Dancing is embarrassing. Anybody who's ever been to a wedding reception knows this. But dancing can be fun if you feel like you know what you're doing. Video producers understood this and began releasing tapes where you could learn all the hottest dance moves in the privacy of your non-judgmental home. Dance crazes like country line dancing, hip-hop dancing, and dirty dancing further fueled the fire, leading to a whole host of videos designed to make you the king or queen of the dance floor. We're not sure if they worked or not, we just know the dad from *Footloose* would have tried to ban them. And you know what? He wouldn't be wrong.

Learn the art of
Dancing Dirty
"It's NOT dirty—It's just good clean fun—and a little bit sexy"
"Great for beginners and for experienced dancers as well."

It's rare to see a video contradict itself on its own cover.

Line Dancing For Seniors

with Dr. Grant Longley

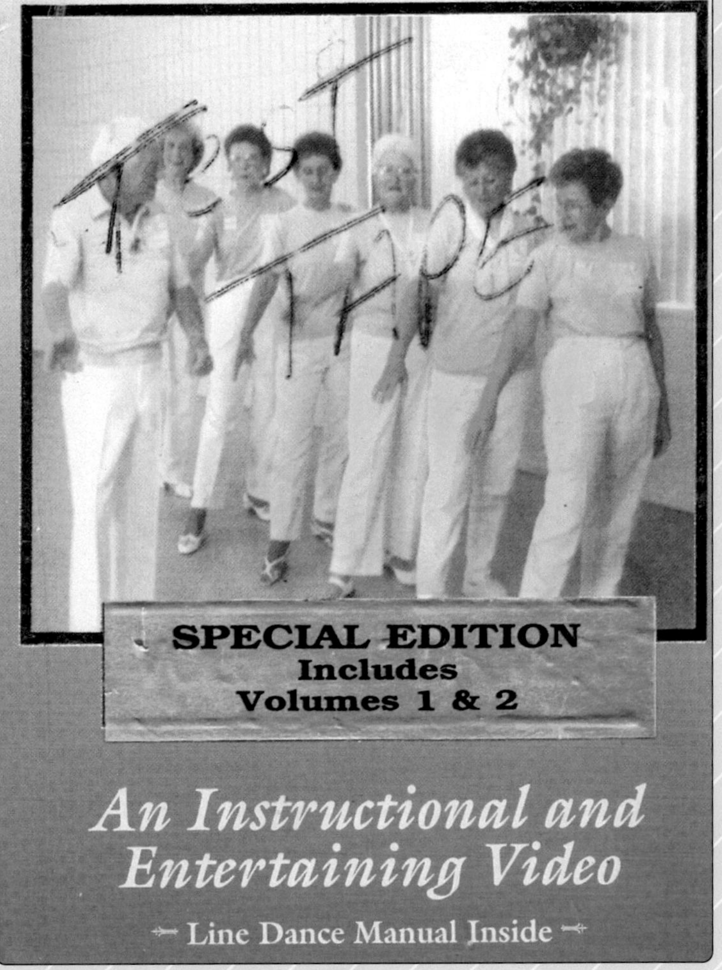
SPECIAL EDITION
Includes
Volumes 1 & 2
An Instructional and
Entertaining Video
Line Dance Manual Inside

This is a test tape only.
Not for actual use.

Dancin' Grannies®
Exercise Program
Beginners
Beverly Gemigniani,
IDEA Foundation certified,
is the founder of the Dancin' Grannies®

DANCIN' GRANNIES
NEW! Mature Fitness
TRIM & TONE

Special
Exercises
for
Arms &
Stomach!

DANCIN' GRANNIES™
Mature Fitness
Beginners

Helps work off all those Werther's Originals

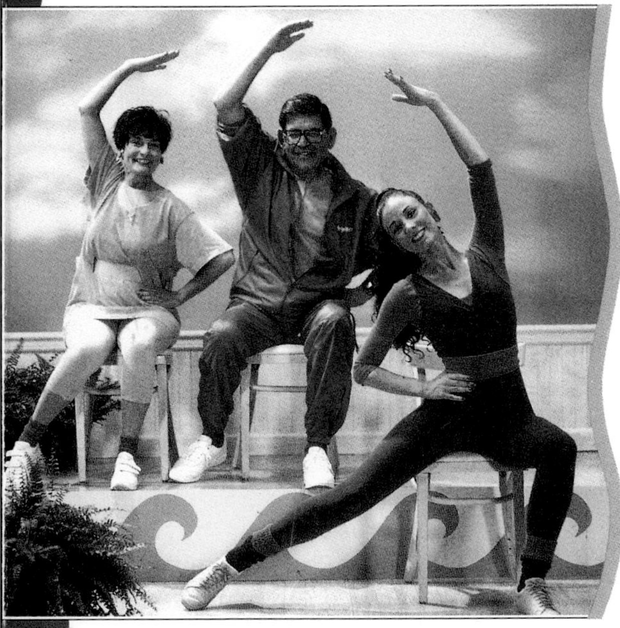
Jodi Stolove's
CHAIR DANCING®
A NEW CONCEPT IN AEROBICS FITNESS
Exercise to the Beat Without Leaving Your Seat!
Fun for Ages 5-95

It's only the cover photo and they're already way out of sync.

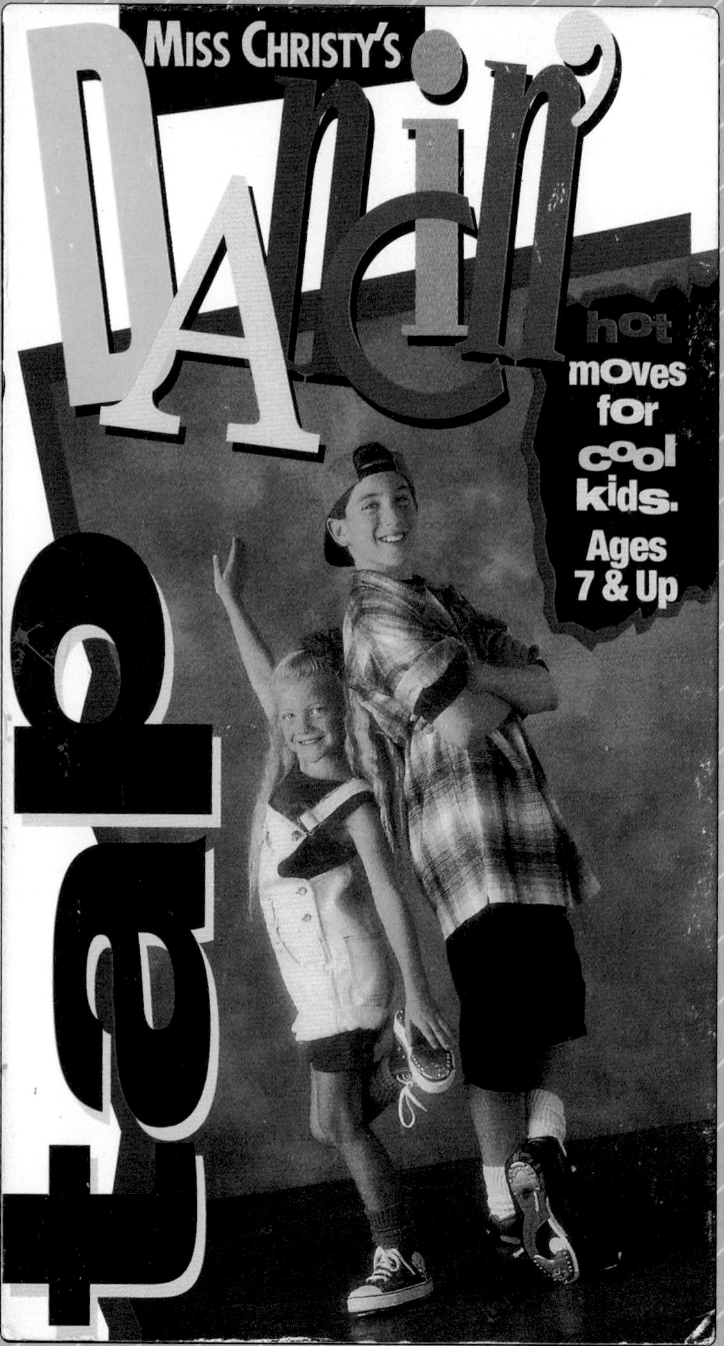
MISS CHRISTY'S
Dancin'
tap
hot moves for cool kids.
Ages 7 & Up

Bonus feature: How to tap your way out of a bully pounding.

Cal del Pozo's
VOL. 2
LEARN TO DANCE
THE SWING ERA

WITH JUST 4 EASY STEPS, YOU CAN DANCE
THE FOXTROT, LINDY & WALTZ

LEARN TO DANCE IN MINUTES

AM-710

Finally, a dance video
for white people.

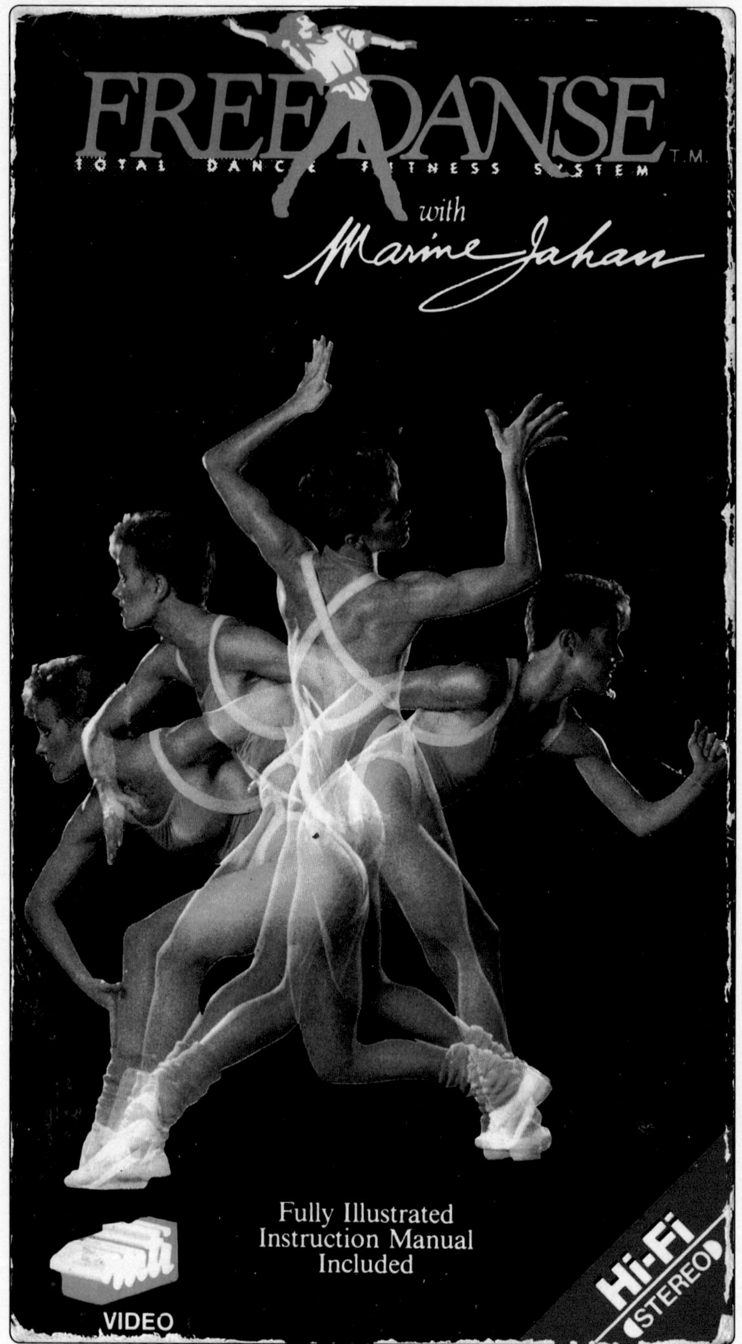
FREEDANSE
TOTAL DANCE FITNESS SYSTEM
T.M.
with
Marine Jahan
Fully Illustrated
Instruction Manual
Included
VIDEO
Hi-Fi
STEREO

The dance video that frees you of the trappings of just one body.

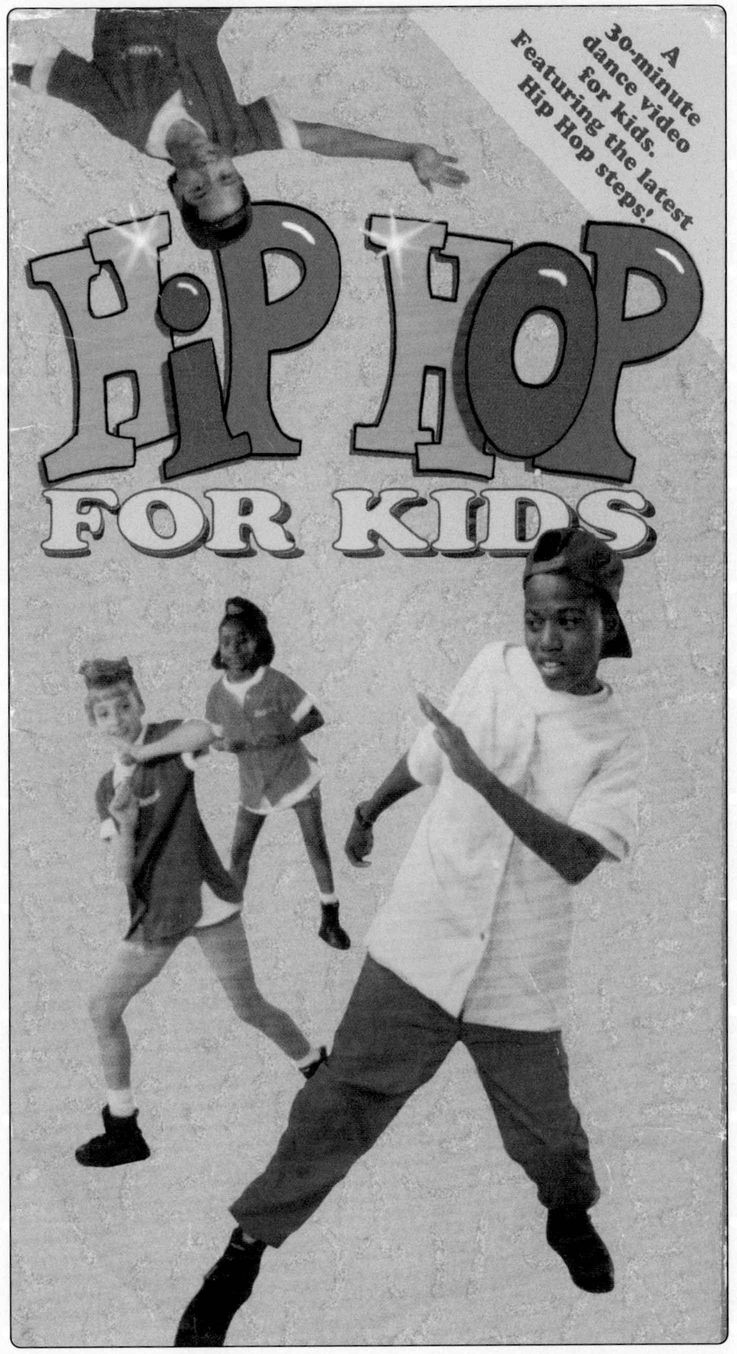
A
30-minute
dance video
for kids.
Featuring the latest
Hip Hop steps!
HiP HOP
FOR KIDS

Ah, the innocent days when hip-hop was little more than multiracial kids wearing backwards hats and pastel baseball jerseys.

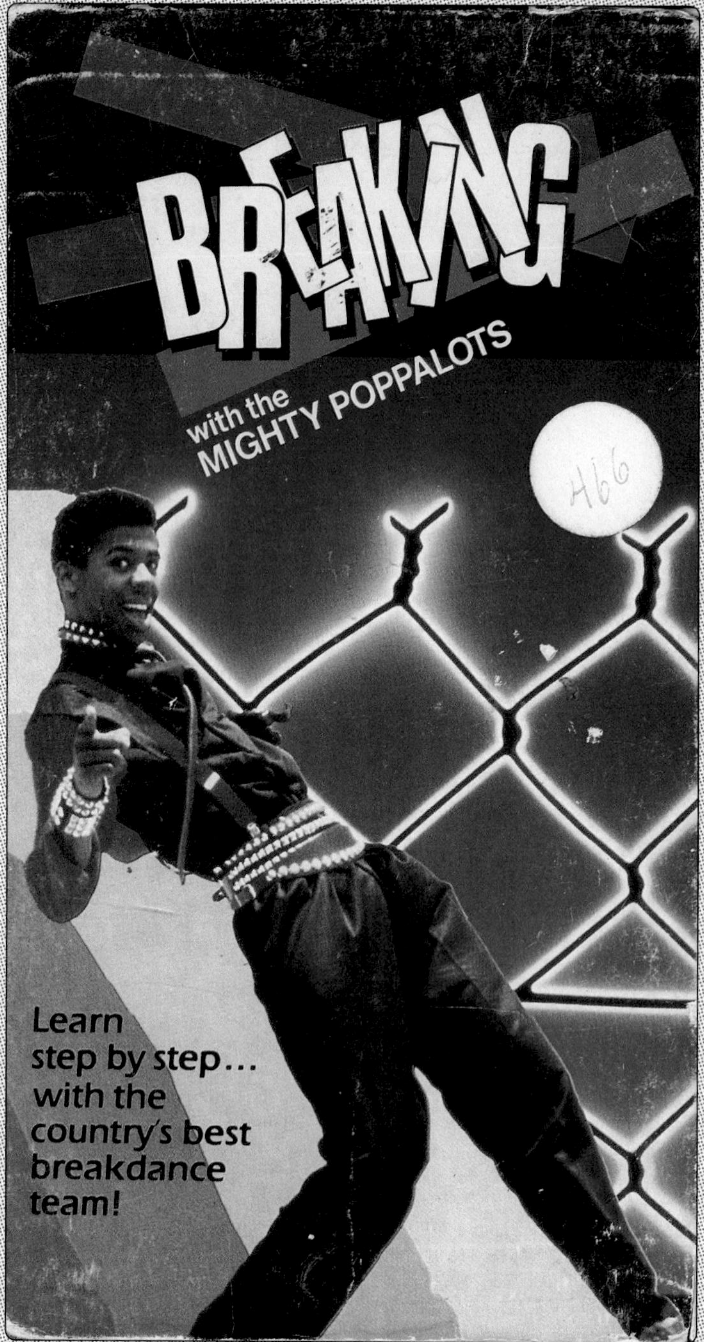
BREAKING
with the
MIGHTY POPPALOTS
A66
Learn
step by step...
with the
country's best
breakdance
team!

We used to poppalot. Now
we only poppoccasionally.

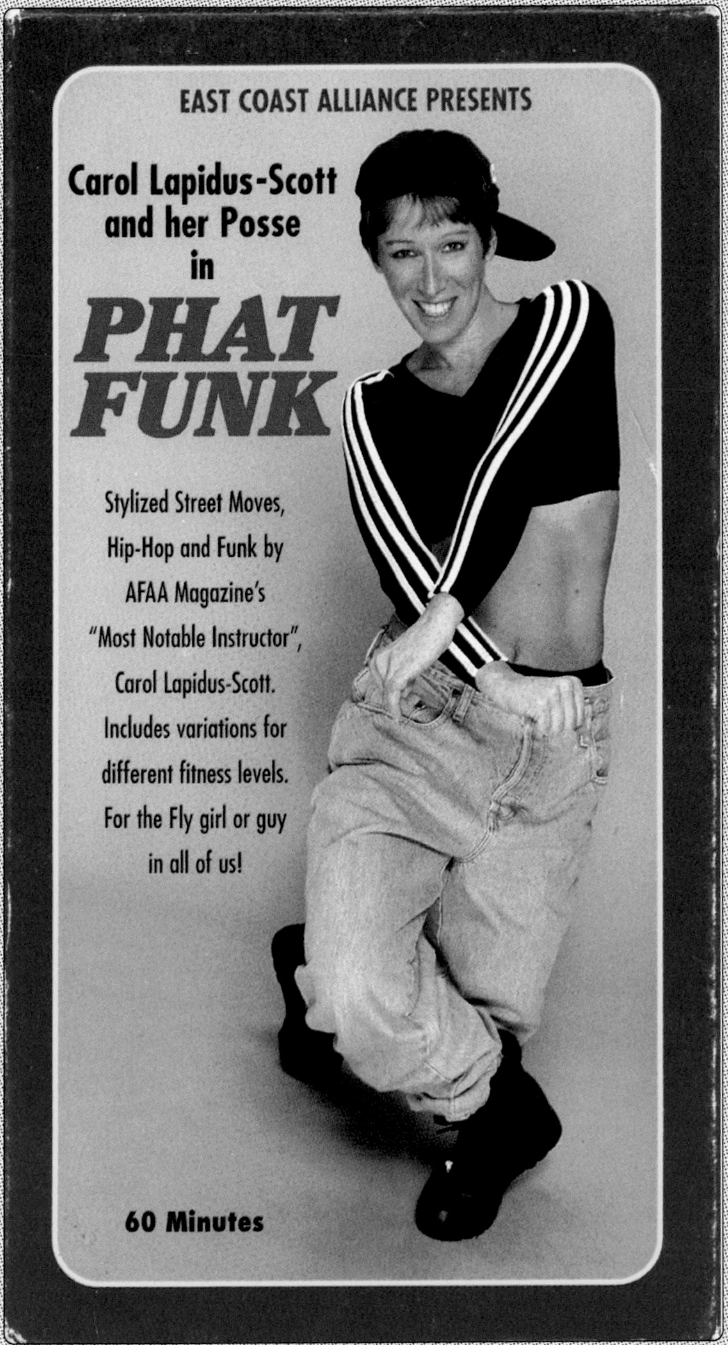
EAST COAST ALLIANCE PRESENTS
Carol Lapidus-Scott and her Posse in
PHAT FUNK
Stylized Street Moves, Hip-Hop and Funk by AFAA Magazine's "Most Notable Instructor", Carol Lapidus-Scott. Includes variations for different fitness levels. For the Fly girl or guy in all of us!
60 Minutes

Lose weight and dignity!

KICK-ASS COVERS

Time to tuck in your UFC Tapout shirt, swallow a couple of scoops of Creatine, and strap yourself in for a high-octane thrill ride through the world of kick-ass video covers. These tapes are swimming with so much testosterone that a few of them have already been arrested on domestic violence charges. Don't think you're man enough to handle it? No worries. We'll be your spotters. Now let's blast those VHS quads.

BARROOM
BRAWLING
The Art of Staying Alive in Beer Joints, Biker Bars, and Other Fun Places

with Peyton Quinn & Marc "Animal" MacYoung

When did staying alive become an art?

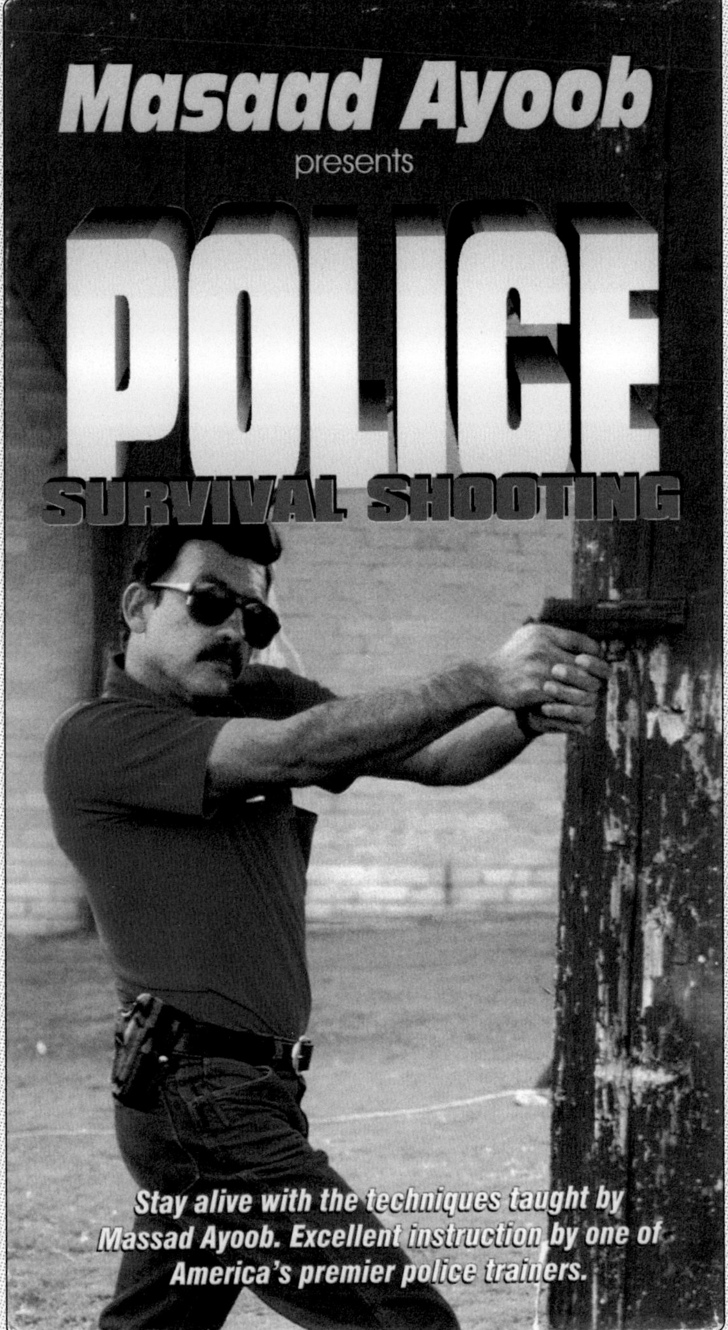
Masaad Ayoob
presents
POLICE
SURVIVAL SHOOTING
Stay alive with the techniques taught by Massad Ayoob. Excellent instruction by one of America's premier police trainers.

The most impressive part about Masaad Ayoob is that even while kicking ass, he manages to keep his polo tucked in.

THE ART OF
AIKIDO

featuring
DR. LEE, AH LOI, 7th DAN

There goes the 7th Dan.
Bring in the 8th Dan.

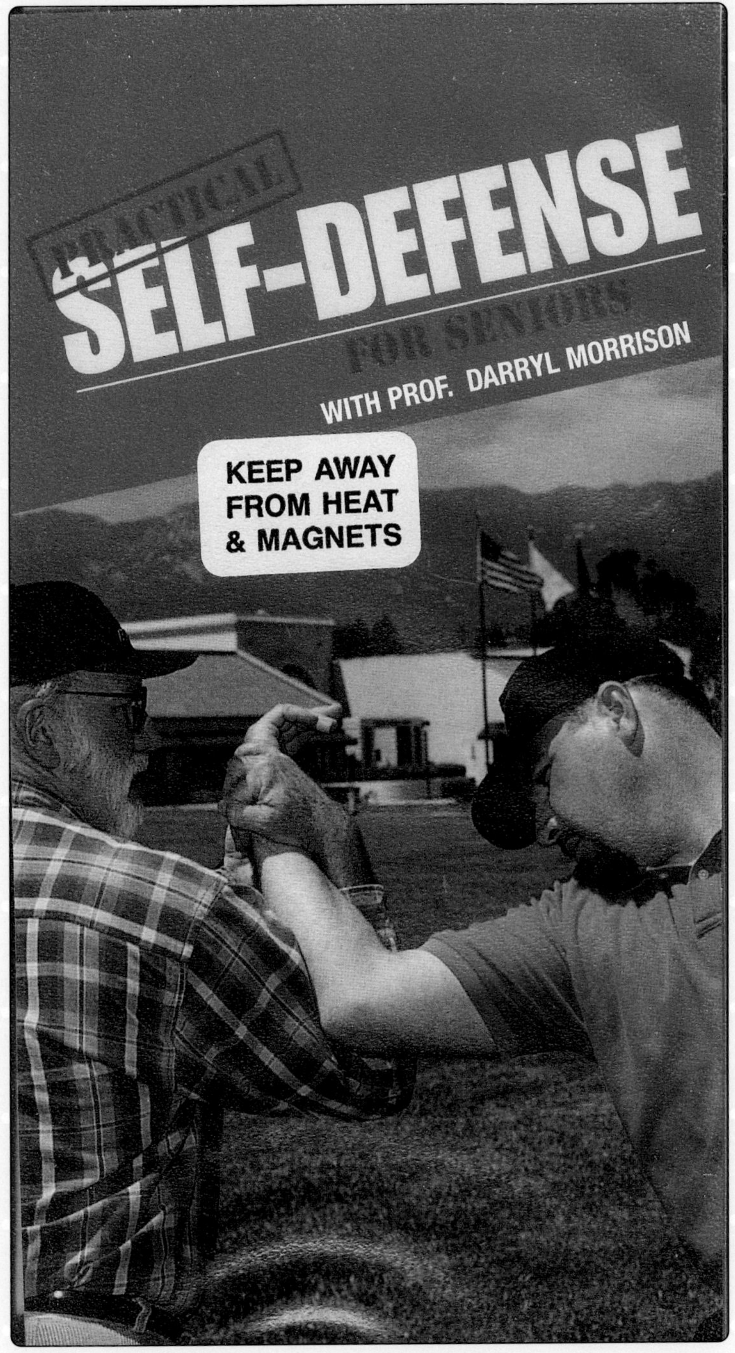
PRACTICAL
SELF-DEFENSE
FOR SENIORS
WITH PROF. DARRYL MORRISON
KEEP AWAY
FROM HEAT
& MAGNETS

Keep seniors away from heat and magnets. It's their kryptonite.

The Raising Canes Club Video

by: Ted Truscott

http://defendyourself101.ca

For when you need to defend yourself on the way to the gazebo.

AMERICAN
BOUNTY
HUNTER
With Bob Burton
INTERNATIONAL
BOUNTY
IBHA
HUNTER
A L.O.T.I. Group Film

It may be hard to capture criminals, but with this cover, Bob Burton has already captured our hearts.

9/01
HALF PRICE BOOKS
$ 3 98
Metal Method
Established 1981
DEMONSTRATION VIDEO
Created and Produced by Doug Marks

Taught by a very pretty lady named Doug.

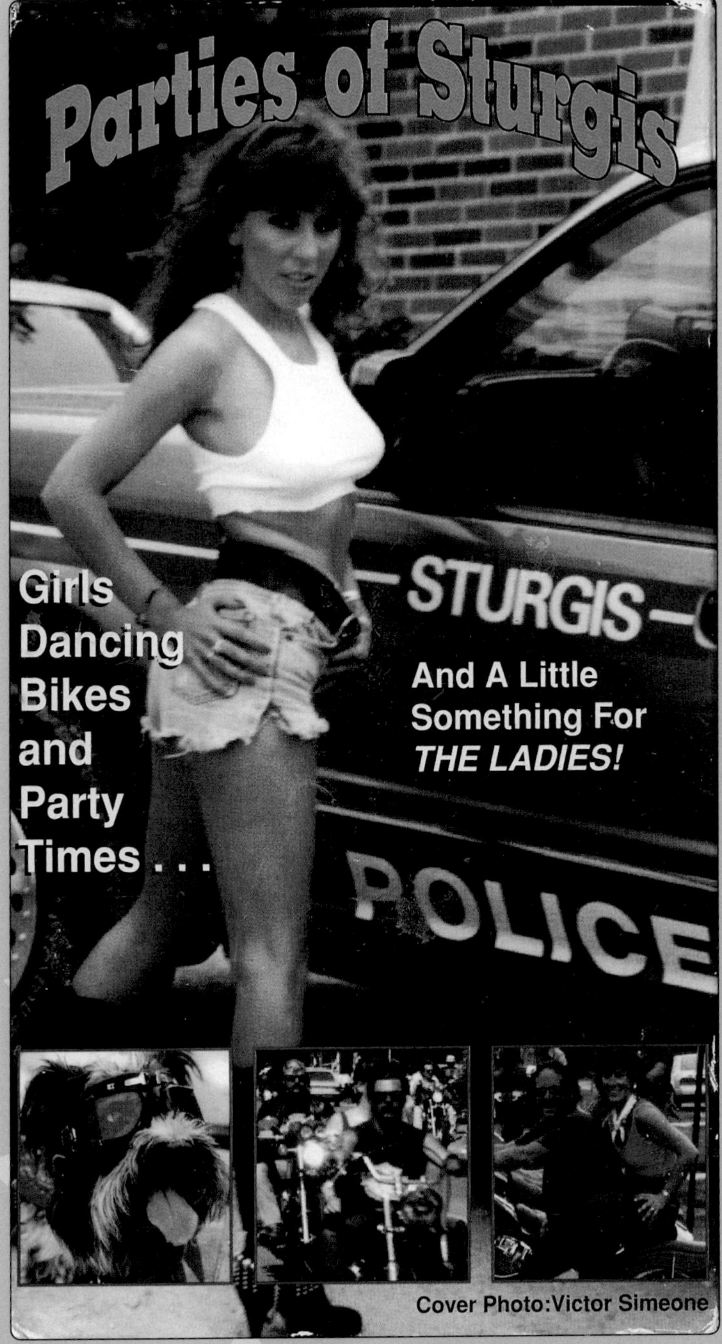
Parties of Sturgis
Girls
Dancing
Bikes
and
Party
Times . . .
STURGIS
And A Little
Something For
THE LADIES!
POLICE
Cover Photo:Victor Simeone

The dog wearing goggles is the "little something for the ladies."

Fast & Boats

Beautiful Women

An extraordinary view featuring two of Man's ultimate obsessions.

Together at last!

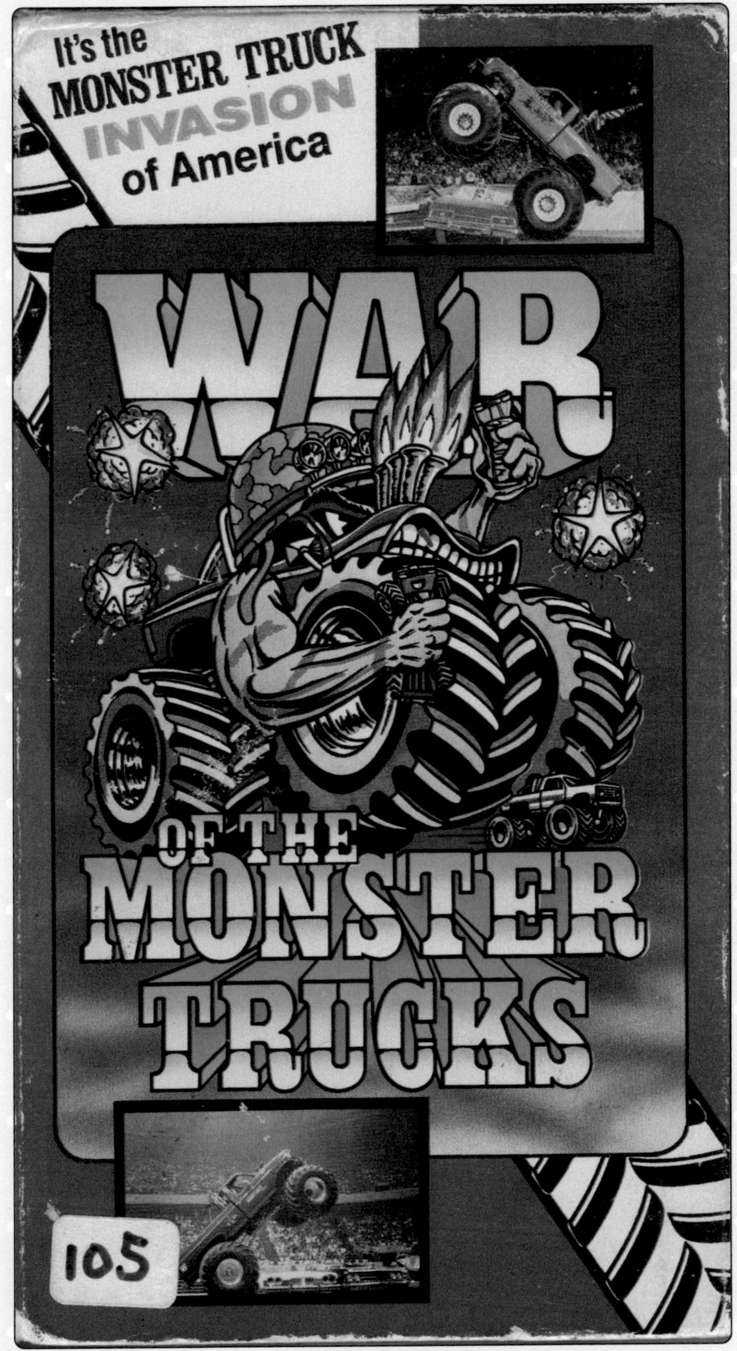
It's the
MONSTER TRUCK
INVASION
of America
WAR
OF THE
MONSTER
TRUCKS
105

This video sold way more copies than *Diplomacy of the Monster Trucks*.

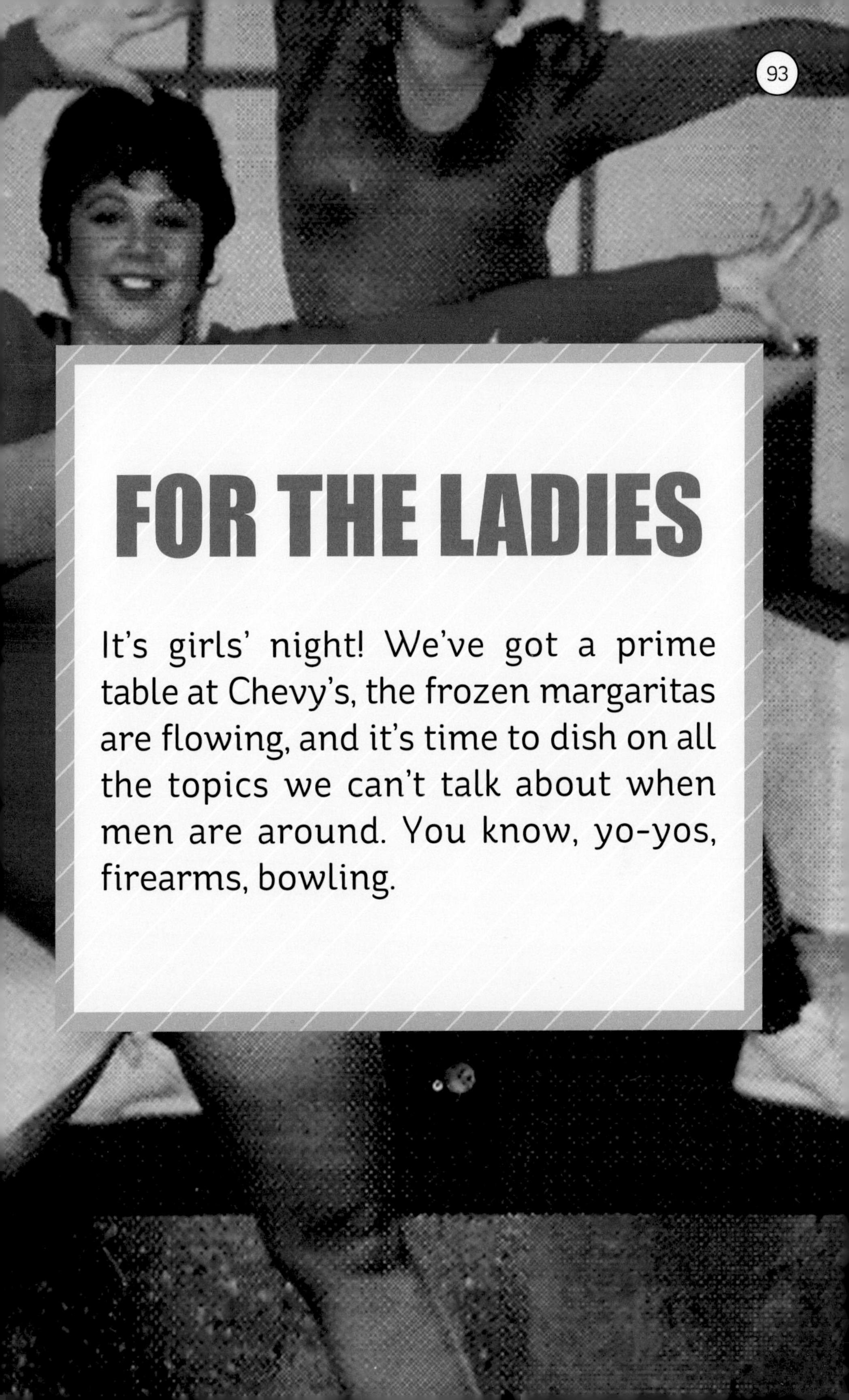

FOR THE LADIES

It's girls' night! We've got a prime table at Chevy's, the frozen margaritas are flowing, and it's time to dish on all the topics we can't talk about when men are around. You know, yo-yos, firearms, bowling.

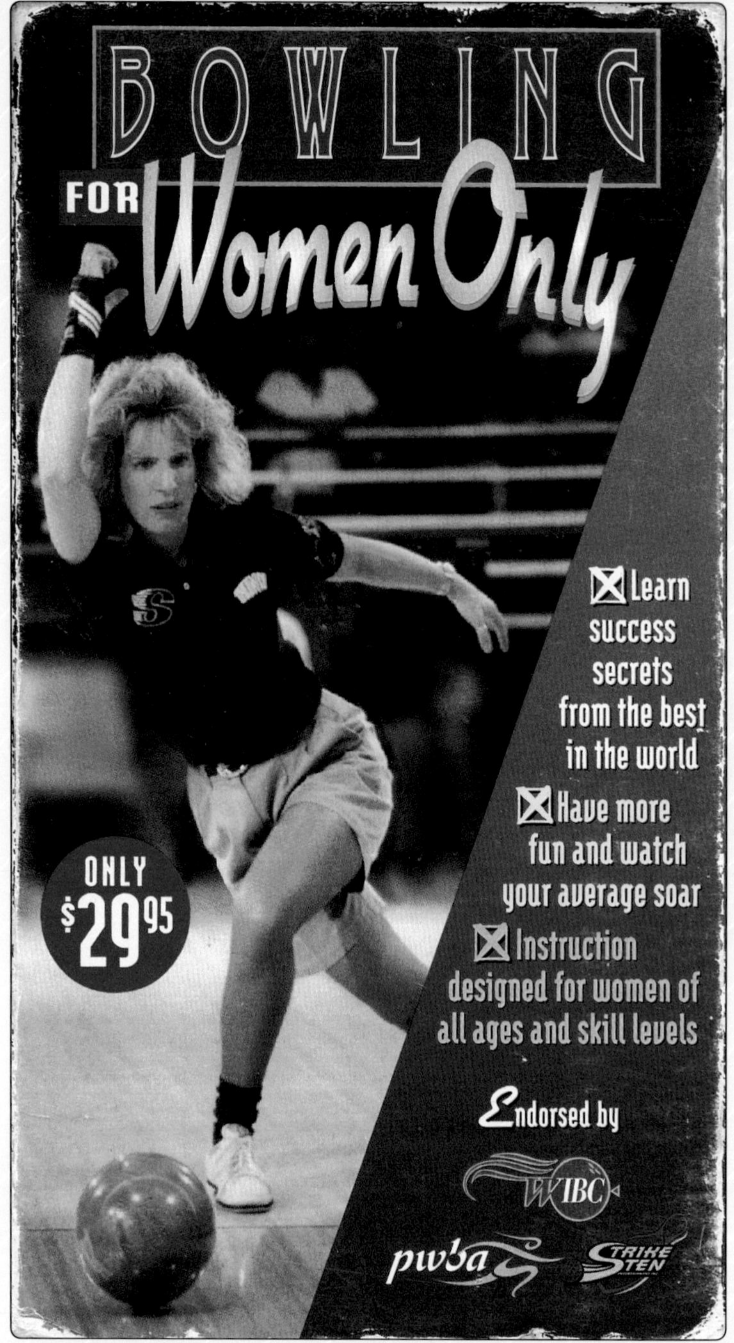
BOWLING
FOR Women Only
Learn success secrets from the best in the world
Have more fun and watch your average soar
Instruction designed for women of all ages and skill levels
ONLY $29.95
Endorsed by
WIBC
pwba
STRIKE TEN

"I'd love to sell you this video, sir, but the cover clearly states . . ."

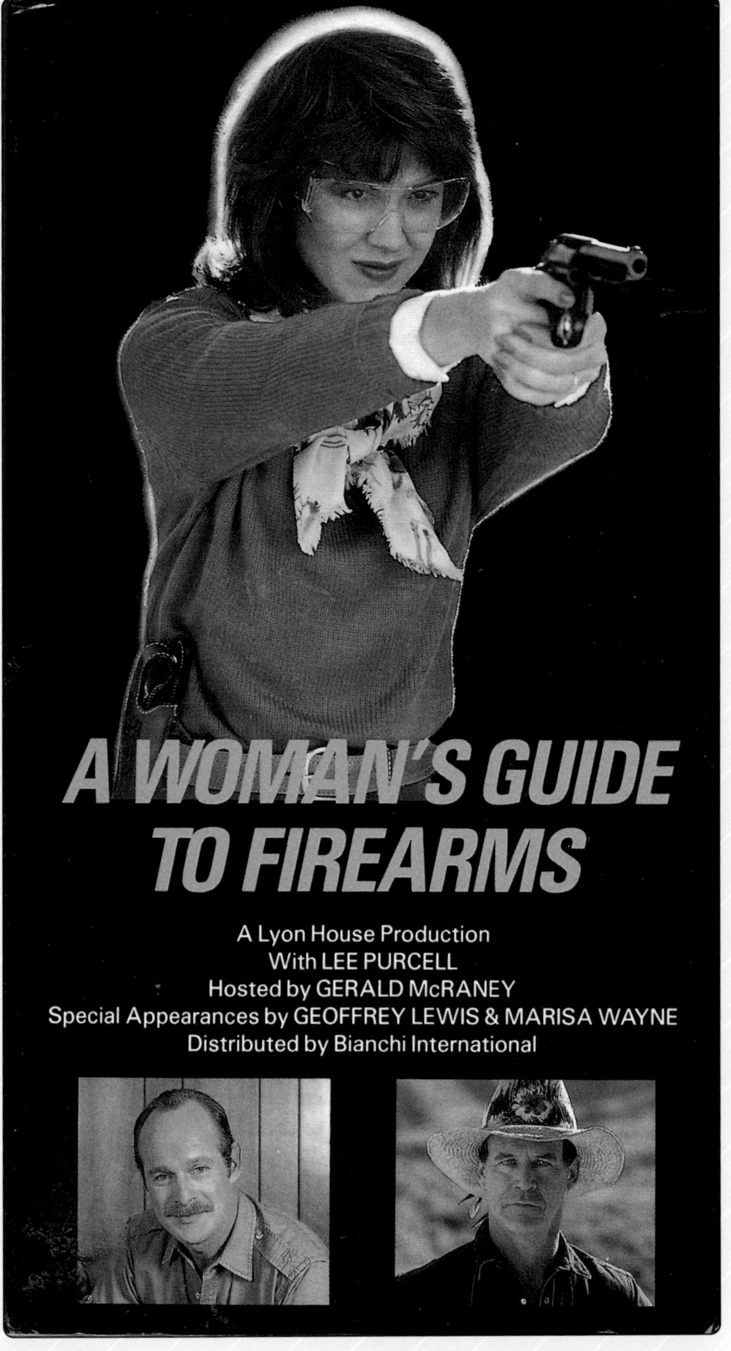
A WOMAN'S GUIDE
TO FIREARMS
A Lyon House Production
With LEE PURCELL
Hosted by GERALD McRANEY
Special Appearances by GEOFFREY LEWIS & MARISA WAYNE
Distributed by Bianchi International

Now if they only had a video called *A Man's Guide to Putting the Toilet Seat Down.* Am I right, ladies?

LISA SLIWA'S
COMMON SENSE
DEFENSE
SHE'S A HIGH-FASHION
MODEL BY DAY...
A GUARDIAN ANGEL
BY NIGHT.
GUARDIAN
SAFETY PATROL
ANGELS

She's a lot more intimidating as the high-fashion model.

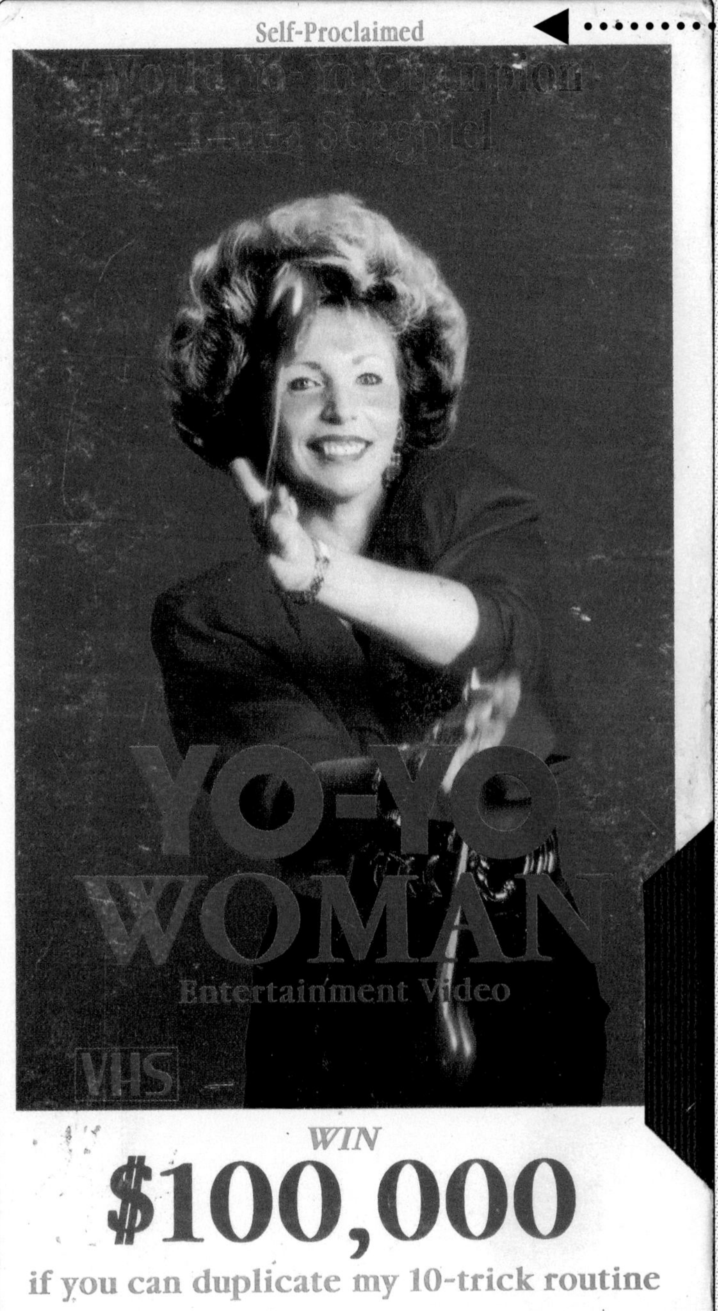
Self-Proclaimed
World Yo-Yo Champion
YO-YO
WOMAN
Entertainment Video
VHS
WIN
$100,000
if you can duplicate my 10-trick routine

The easiest way to become a world champion is to proclaim yourself one.

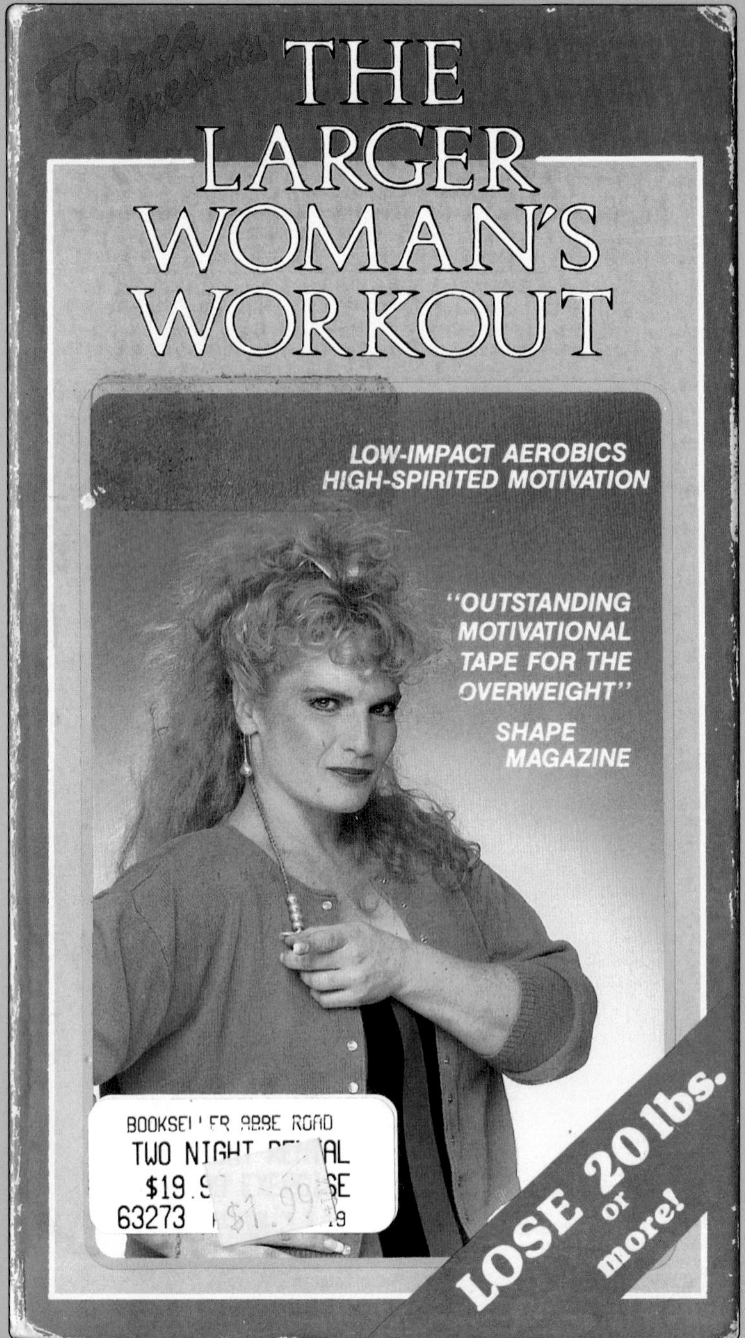
THE
LARGER
WOMAN'S
WORKOUT
LOW-IMPACT AEROBICS
HIGH-SPIRITED MOTIVATION
"OUTSTANDING MOTIVATIONAL TAPE FOR THE OVERWEIGHT"
SHAPE MAGAZINE
TWO NIGHT
$1.99
63273
LOSE 20 lbs. or more!

Larger than what?

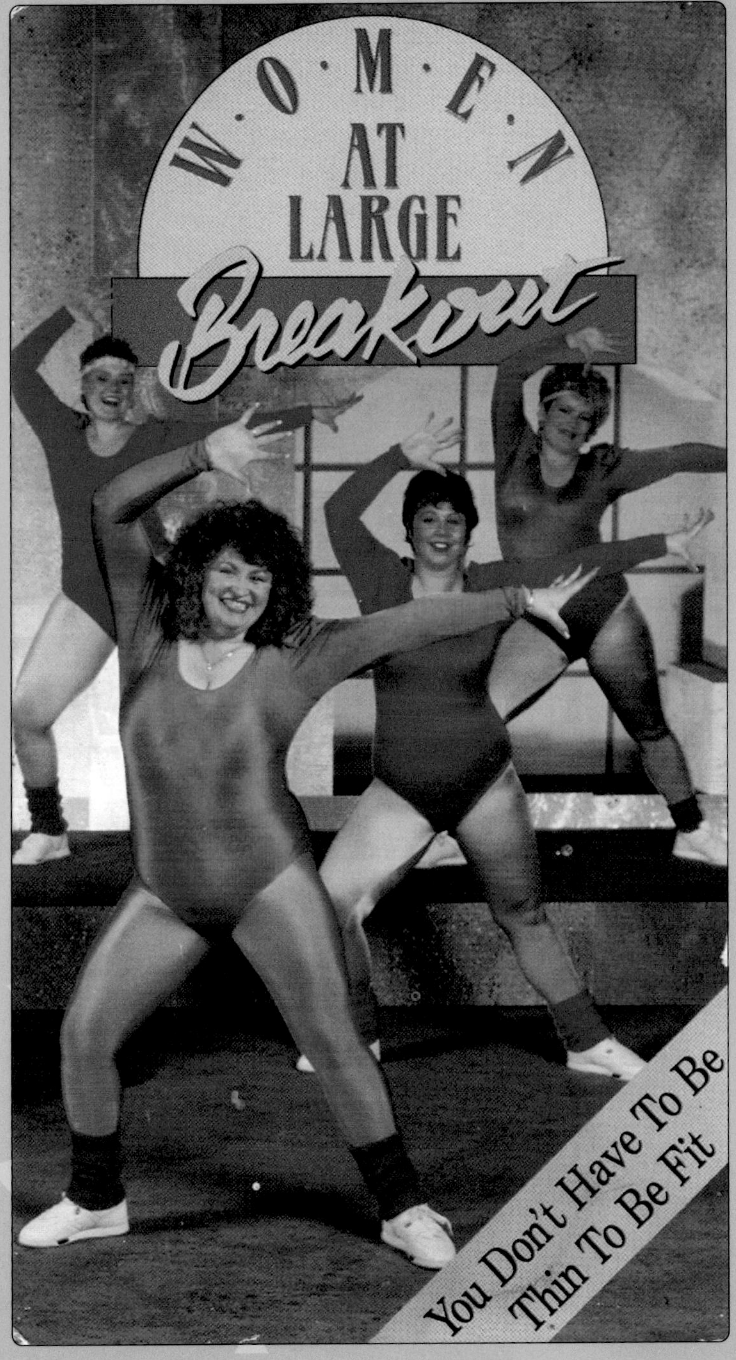
W·O·M·E·N
AT
LARGE
Breakout
You Don't Have To Be
Thin To Be Fit

They broke out of their suburban Minnesota living rooms.

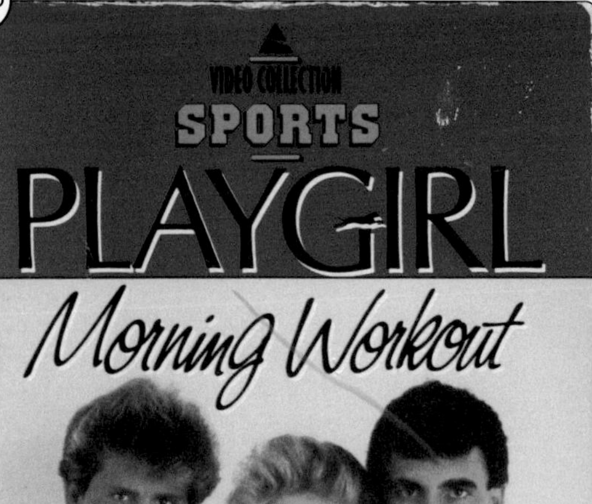
VIDEO COLLECTION
SPORTS
PLAYGIRL
Morning Workout
A FANTASTIC FITNESS, TONING, AND EXER
PROGRAM THAT'S PERFECT FOR EVERYD

They take sexy fitness very seriously.

PLAYGIRL
Super Toner
The ultimate body contouring and sculpting workout!
PRISM

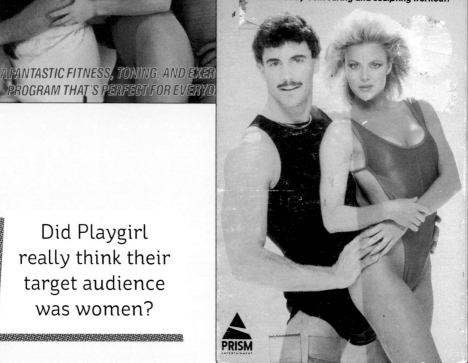

Did Playgirl really think their target audience was women?

VIDEOCASSETTE

HOW TO PICK UP MEN

Dr. Elliott Jaffa teaches you how to play the dating game . . . and win!

Step 1: Have a pulse.

CALIFORNIA
big hunks

EROTIC MALE DANCERS

Big hunks are California's leading export.

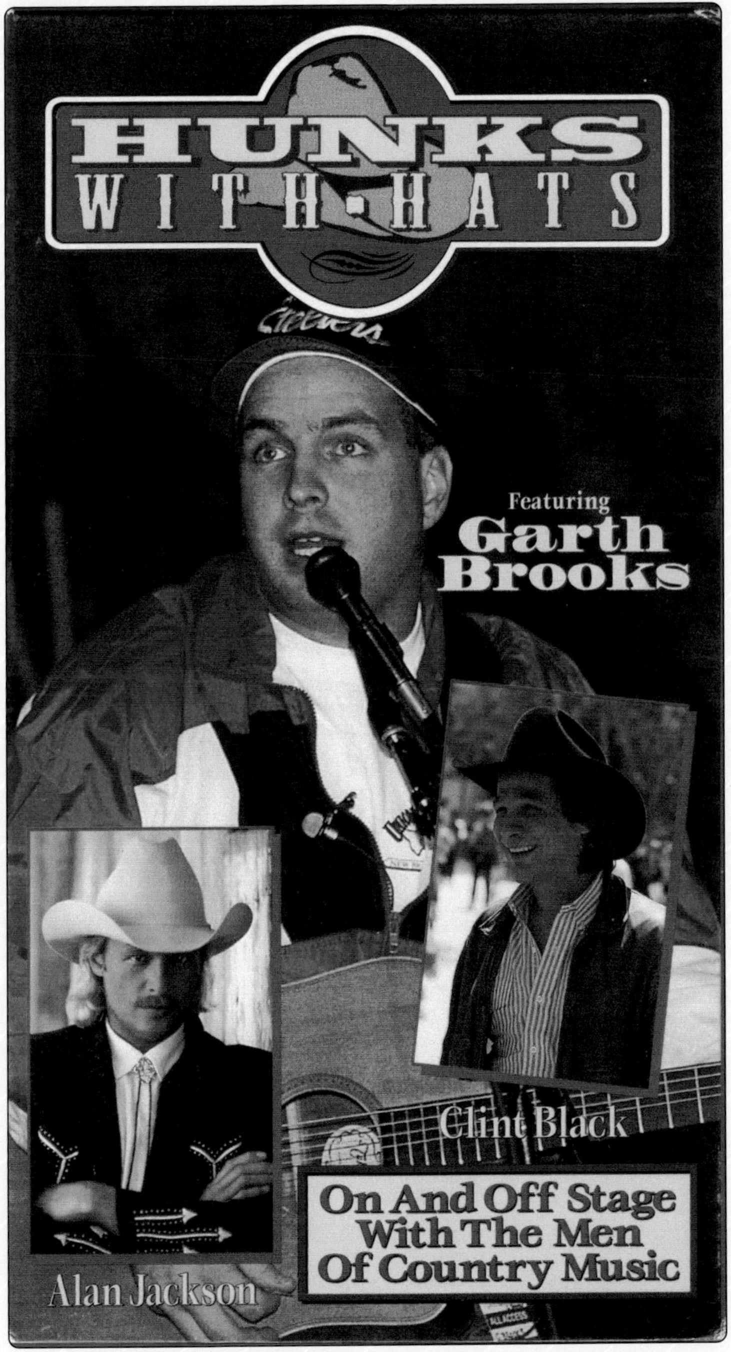
HUNKS
WITH·HATS
Featuring
Garth
Brooks
Clint Black
Alan Jackson
On And Off Stage
With The Men
Of Country Music

A hunk? Garth Brooks looks more like a high school football coach.

95

STRAIGHT TO VIDEO

While Hollywood blockbusters stole away all the attention at video stores in the 80s and 90s, the vast majority of movies found their way onto VHS with little fanfare. There's no way anyone could have missed the 1,000 copies of *Cliffhanger* on Blockbuster's New Release wall the day it came out, but you had to dig deep to find the movies left to rot in the 5-day rental wasteland. In this chapter, we roll out the red carpet and give these cinematic treasures the gala premiere they so richly deserve.

F.A.R.T.
THE MOVIE
THE MOVIE THEY SAID
COULD NEVER BE MADE!

They knew it *could* be made; they meant it *should* never be made.

HAWK JONES

THE MOVIE WITH THE KIDS IN IT!

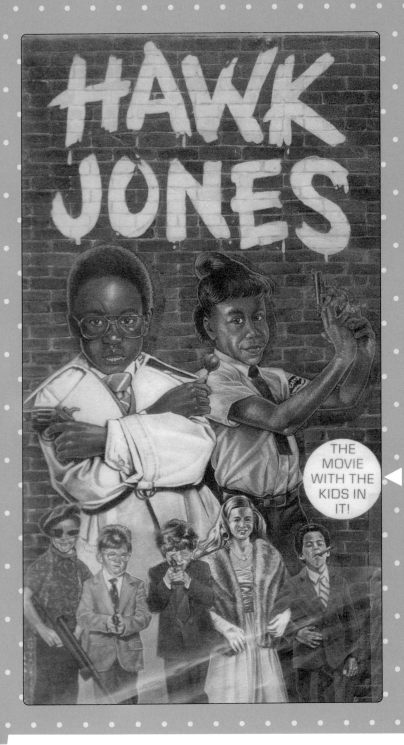

The movie with the kids in it? Doesn't this describe just about every movie?

Shades of Love
ROMANCE VIDEO NOVELS
Lilac Dream
STARRING DACK RAMBO
KLV-TV
KARL LORIMAR VIDEO

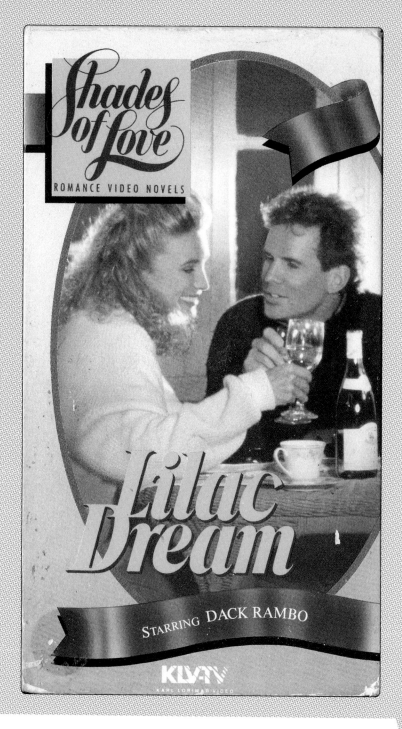

Mr. and Mrs. Rambo took one look at their baby boy and said, "Let's name him Dack."

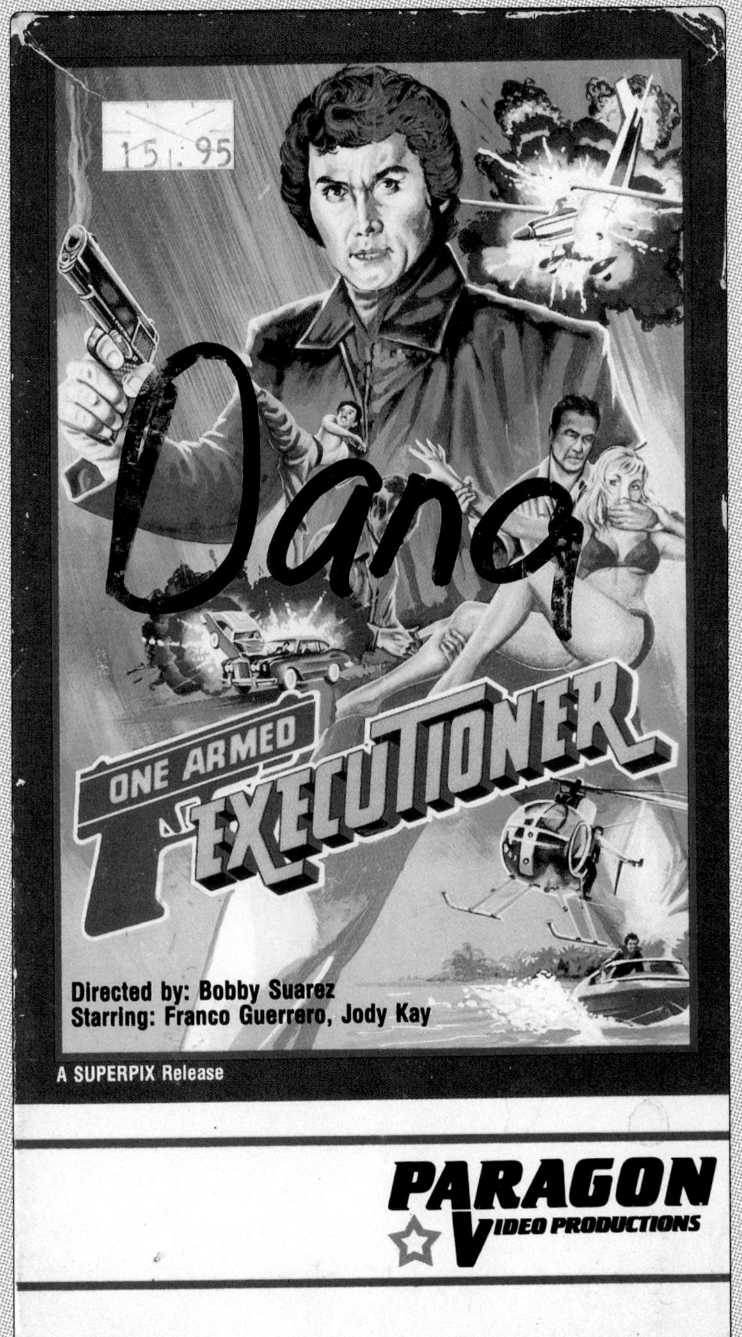
15 95
Dana
ONE ARMED
EXECUTIONER
Directed by: Bobby Suarez
Starring: Franco Guerrero, Jody Kay
A SUPERPIX Release
PARAGON
VIDEO PRODUCTIONS

"Dana, is this my copy of *One Armed Executioner* or yours? Oh, nevermind. I see."

YOU'VE NEVER SEEN A KARATE MOVIE LIKE THIS!
No one knows what a man will do until he's...
PUSHED TOO FAR
Starring
CLAUDE AKINS
&
HERB JOHNSON

See what happens when a tiny, floating ninja pushes an orange-ish cop too far.

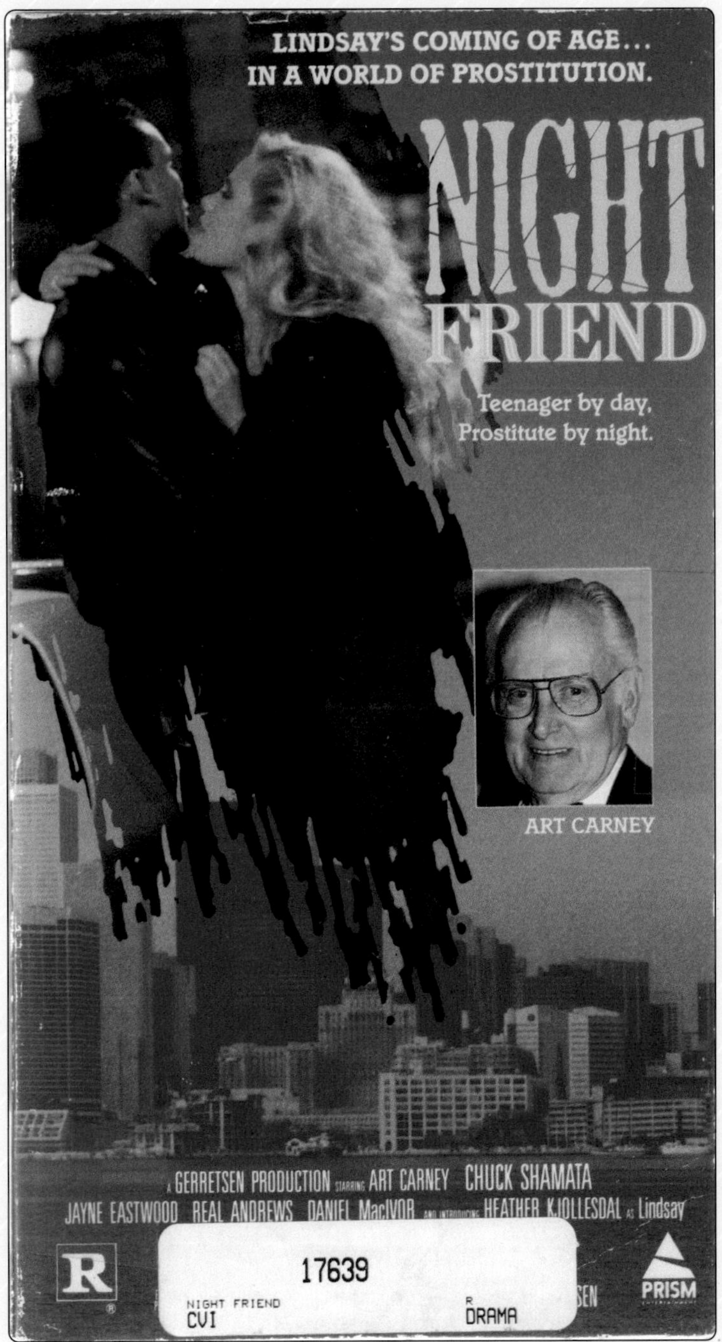
LINDSAY'S COMING OF AGE...
IN A WORLD OF PROSTITUTION.
NIGHT
FRIEND
Teenager by day,
Prostitute by night.
ART CARNEY
A GERRETSEN PRODUCTION STARRING ART CARNEY CHUCK SHAMATA
JAYNE EASTWOOD REAL ANDREWS DANIEL MacIVOR AND INTRODUCING HEATHER KJOLLESDAL AS Lindsay
R
17639
NIGHT FRIEND
CVI
R
DRAMA
PRISM

Please say Art Carney
plays her pimp.

BEEZBO's
ADVENTURES
HOW TO BEHAVE
LIKE A HUMAN BEING
An
Entertaining
Guide to
CHILDREN'S
MANNERS
IVI
HOME
VIDEO

Why does everything always have to be an adventure? Can't kids learn manners without the aid of a fey blonde alien?

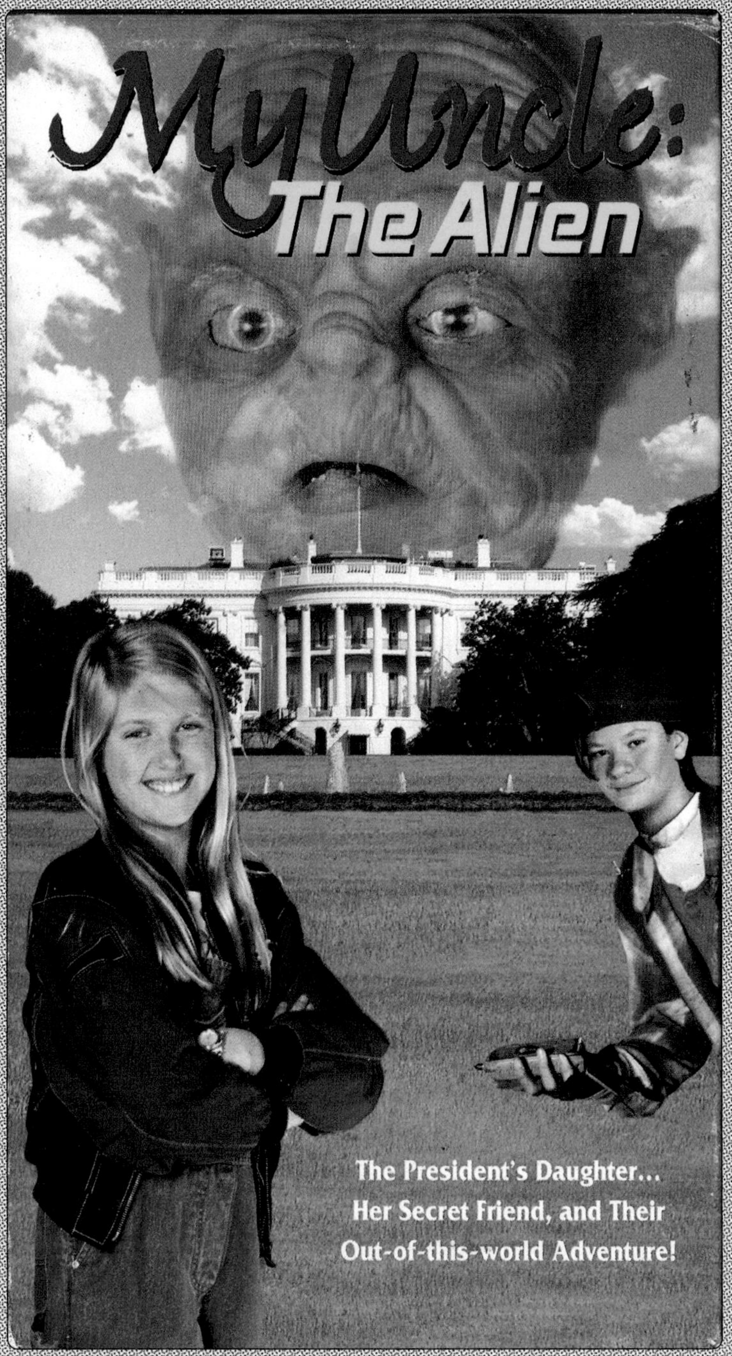
My Uncle:
The Alien
The President's Daughter...
Her Secret Friend, and Their
Out-of-this-world Adventure!

We haven't watched this one yet, but we're willing to bet that at some point the alien puts on sunglasses and raps.

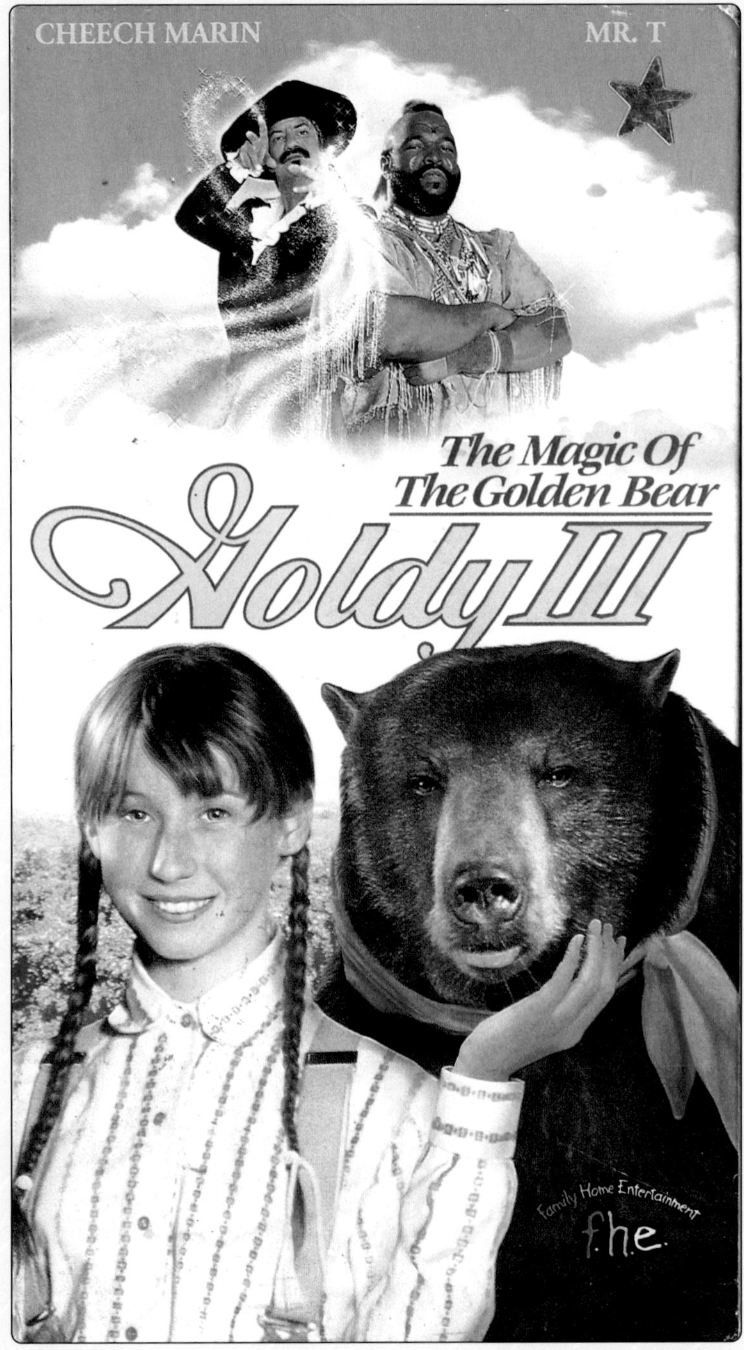
CHEECH MARIN
MR. T
The Magic Of
The Golden Bear
Goldy III
Family Home Entertainment
f.h.e.

The third and final chapter in the fucked-up "Goldy" trilogy.

WHISKERS
The Cat with
a Magical
Attitude.
"An engaging, cornball
(or should I say furball) comedy."
NEW YORK DAILY NEWS

This cover is two little pairs of yellow Chuck Taylors away from perfection.

TDK HS

☐SP ☐LP

AMERICA'S FUNNIEST HOME VIDEO COVERS

Apart from commercially released videos, the VHS era also offered the unparalleled ability to record your favorite shows and movies right off TV. Switch to EP mode and you could fit a half season of *M*A*S*H* reruns—commercials and all—on one 160-minute tape. When discovered at junk shops, these videos not only offer a voyeuristic glimpse into somebody else's private video collection, they provide a chilling look at the state of penmanship in America.

TDK HS
SP LP EP
VHS
Bonion sergery
TDK
VHS
SUPER AVILYN

We found this one in a Dumpster and the scrawled penmanship caught our eye. That and the fact that both "bunion" and "surgery" are spelled wrong.

maxell HGX GOLD 120
EPITAXIAL VIDEOCASSETTE
SP →120min.
LP →240min.
EP →360min.
Stereo Mono
Noise Reduction ON OFF
Everybuddy's Dancing
West Coast Swing #1
June 7, 1988
Bill MuiR

Dance like nobuddy is watching.

TDK
ICE CUBE
SP LP EP

This tape looks like it's literally been on the streets of South Central.

#1. THE EXSTERMERNATOR:
#2. ACROSS - 110TH STREET:
#3. BlACK SIX: - Please Rewind
V.M.
JVC
VHS
VIDEO CASSETTE
T-120

Her spellchecker must've been exstermernated.

This side in
VHS
WIZARD OF OZ
UNDER The umbrella TREE
Gumby Bears
CAUTION • This Video Cassette Tape cannot be
• Break the Tab on the rear side
accidental erasure of

Everybuddy loves "Gumby Bears."

Insert this side into recorder
Do not touch the tape inside
VHS
SONY
VHS
WALTON'S
MARATHON
PART TWO
This was Borrowed
From
Bob Potter

Does the world really borrow that much stuff from Bob Potter that it warrants a sheet of printed stickers?

TDK
HS HIGH STANDARD
VHS
Backstreet
December 16, 1991
Time 7:00
Parrish
(Ghost Dad Part 2)
a Good Picture
TDK
HS HIGH STANDARD
SUPER AVILYN TECHNOLOGY

"Ghost Dad Part 2" is in pencil and parentheses, almost as if it's embarrassed to share the label with "Backstreet."

LeRSuRe Time - nudity
HeTeROL WHiTe

Handwritten labels don't get much sketchier than this one.

Pretty elaborate drawing for a tape of *Seinfeld* reruns

THAT'S ENTERTAINMENT

Why go out and see live entertainment when the entertainment can come to you? With concerts and comedy on VHS, it wasn't the next best thing to being there, it was better than being there. There's no way to hit STOP when you're in the audience in Branson. Forget the two-drink minimum and heckle all you want, it's showtime!

Yeah, we can't miss you.

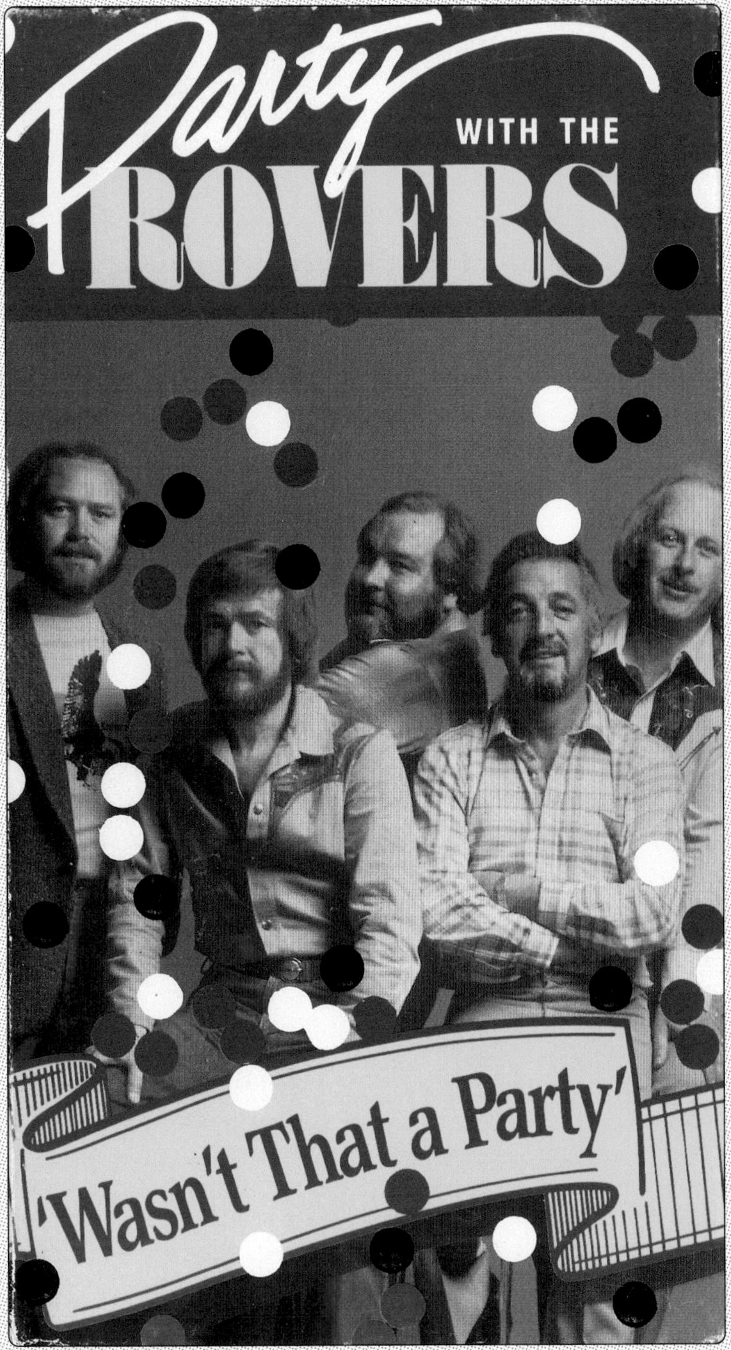
Party
WITH THE
ROVERS
'Wasn't That a Party'

The reason there isn't a question mark after "Wasn't that a party" is because the answer's no.

WILL THE REAL
SHOTGUN RED®
PLEASE STAND UP!

from forty dollars to fame
Country Music's
Best Kept Secret

Country music's best-kept secret is finally out at thrift stores all across the country.

Carl Hurley
Sunny Side Up
COMEDY VIDEO

This is the guy you get stuck at a table with on every cruise.

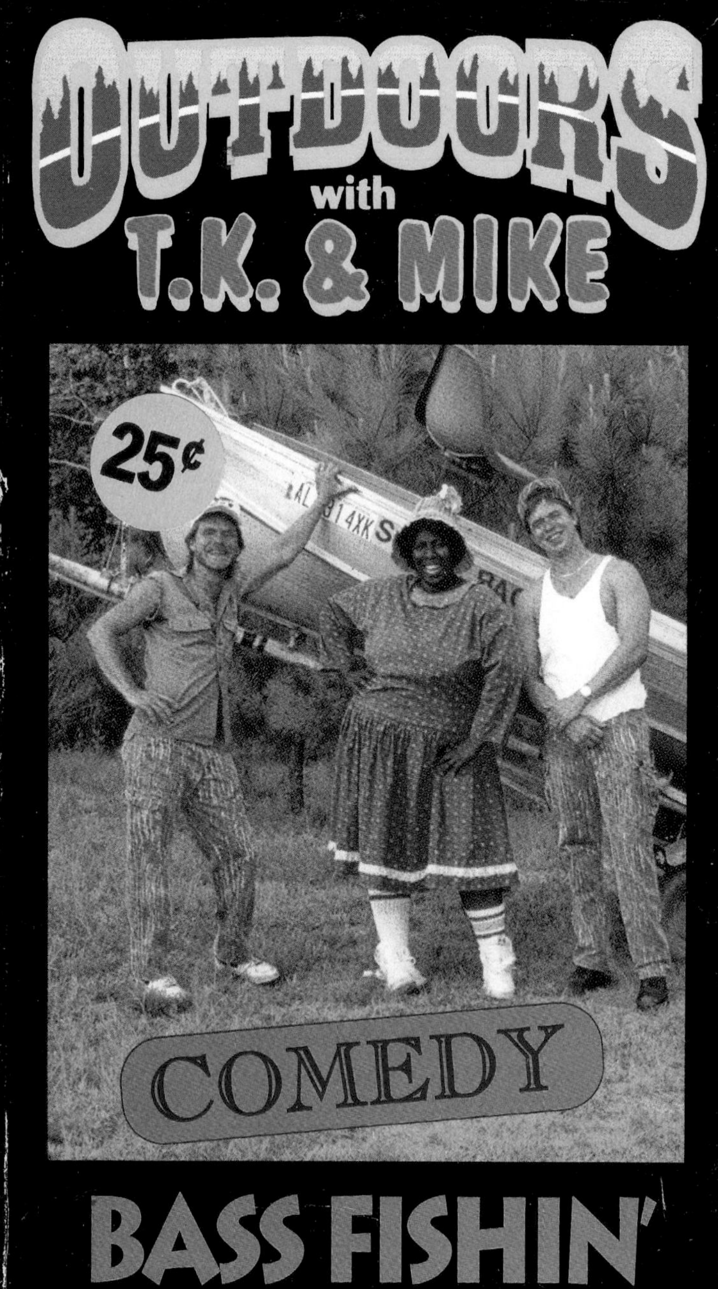
OUTDOORS
with
T.K. & MIKE
25¢
COMEDY
BASS FISHIN'

This video cost us a quarter, and we still paid too much.

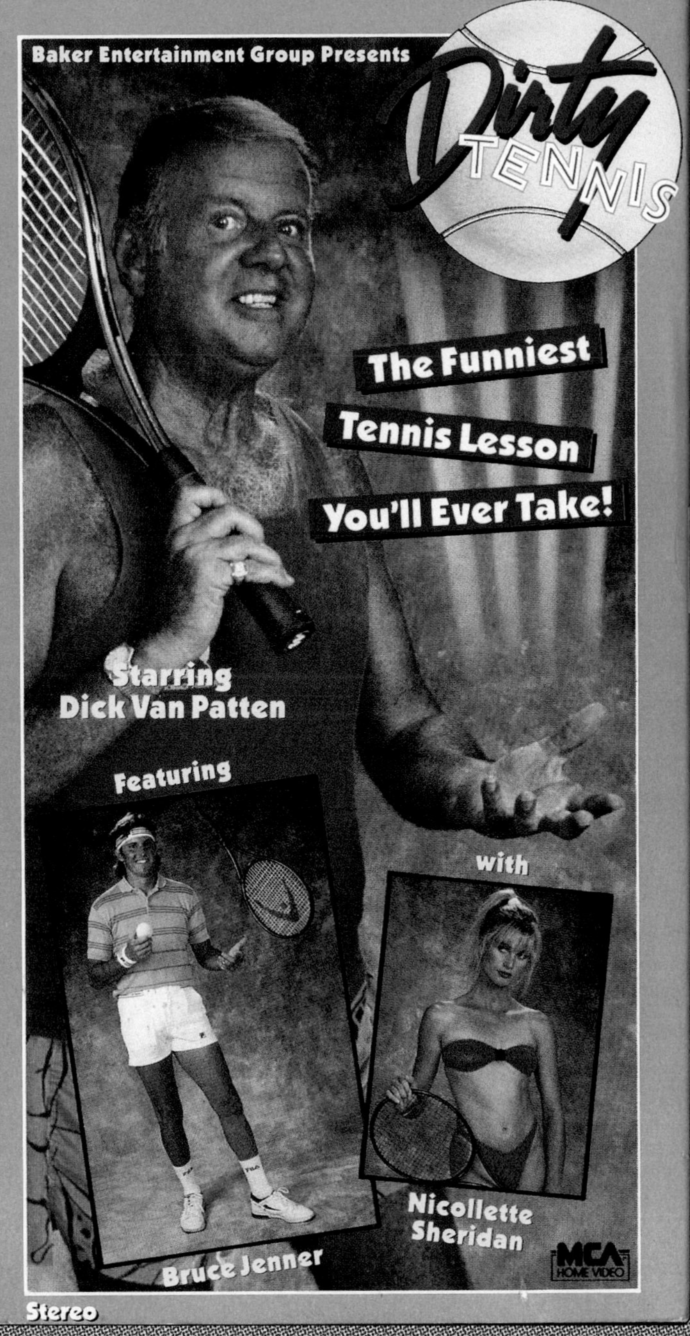
Baker Entertainment Group Presents
Dirty
TENNIS
The Funniest
Tennis Lesson
You'll Ever Take!
Starring
Dick Van Patten
Featuring
with
Nicollette
Sheridan
Bruce Jenner
MCA
HOME VIDEO
Stereo

The words "dirty" and "Dick Van Patten" should never appear this close together.

CATS

Before the Internet made cats into superstars, they were lighting up the small screen on VHS tapes everywhere. And let's face it, during the precious few moments they're awake each day, cats are furry little balls of hilarity. In this chapter, we've sifted out the nuggets from the thrift store litter box to present the best in feline footage.

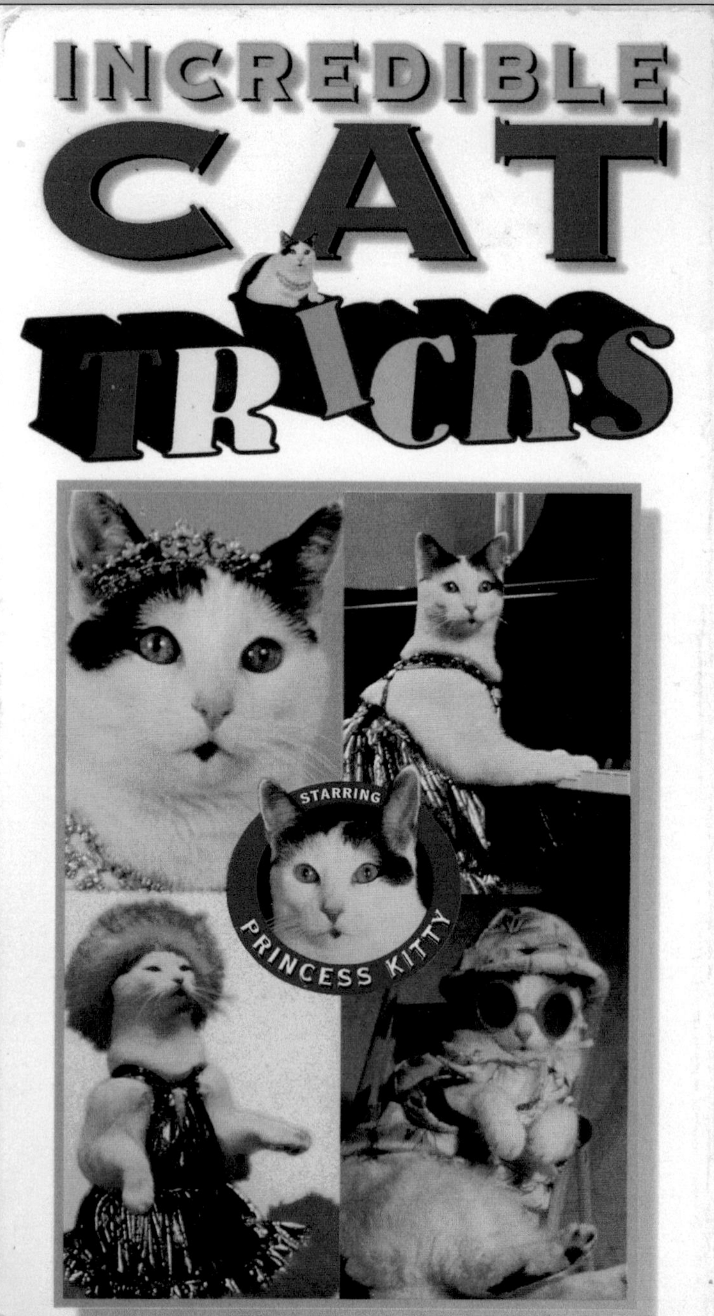
INCREDIBLE
CAT
TRICKS
STARRING
PRINCESS KITTY

It's not hyperbole when we say that this cover is the answer to the world's problems.

CAT ENTERTAINMENT VIDEO

Here Kitty Kitty

A MAGICAL TRIP TO THE PET STORE, ESPECIALLY FOR CATS.

Pornography for cats.

CAT
ADVENTURE
VIDEO
The Video Cats
Love To Watch!

Look at those intrepid cats, fearlessly embarking on another adventure.

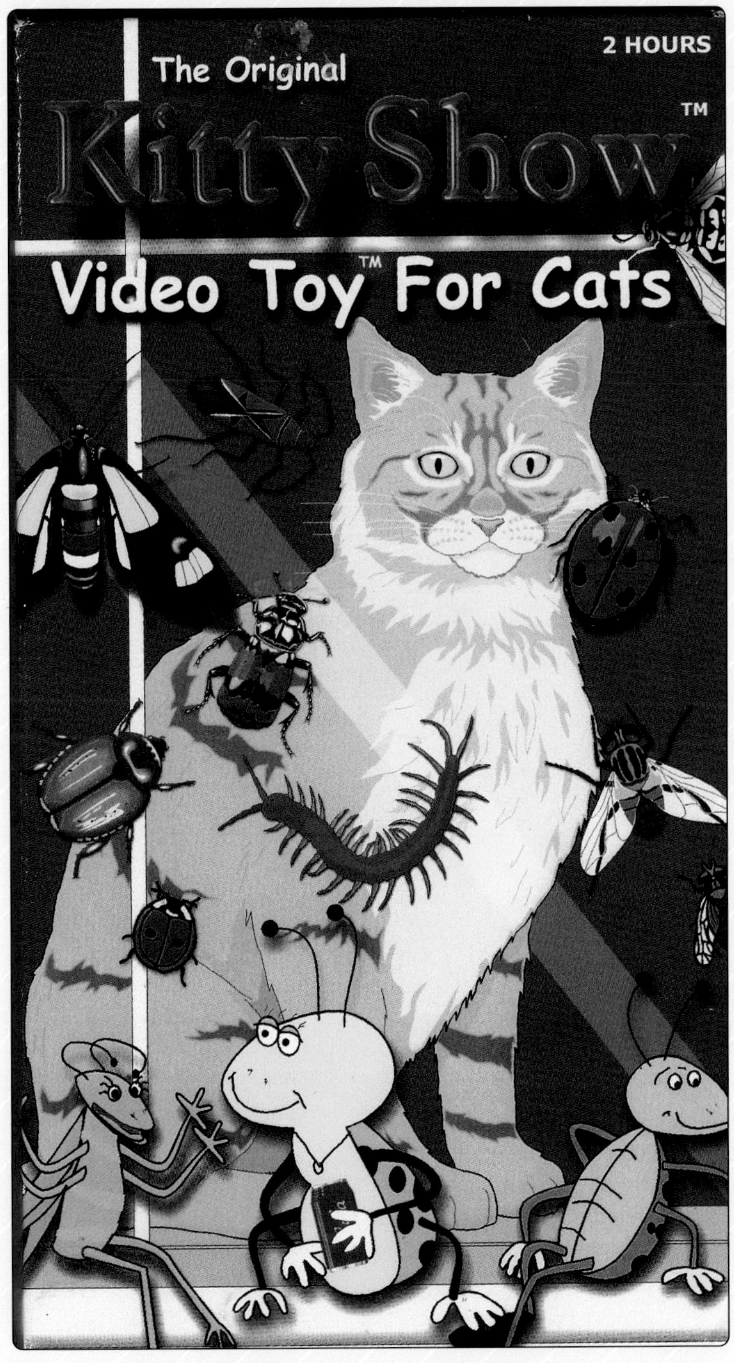
2 HOURS
The Original
Kitty Show
TM
Video Toy TM For Cats

This is what happens when there's a clearance sale on insect clip art.

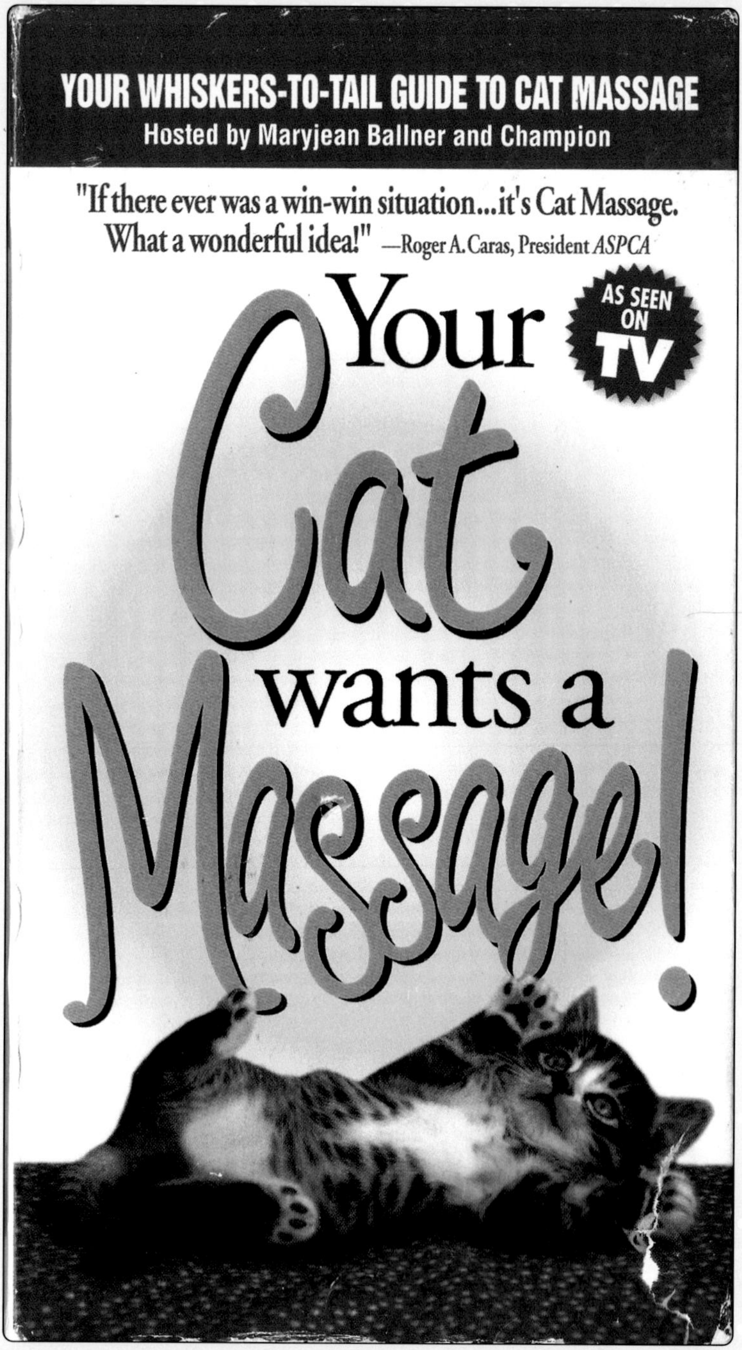

YOUR WHISKERS-TO-TAIL GUIDE TO CAT MASSAGE

Hosted by Maryjean Ballner and Champion

"If there ever was a win-win situation...it's Cat Massage. What a wonderful idea!" —Roger A. Caras, President *ASPCA*

AS SEEN ON TV

Your Cat wants a Massage!

Really helps relieve the tension in your cat's stressful life.

Grooming and Bathing Your Cat

Common Sense Cat Care

Volume 1

Starring this pissed off cat.

"Toilet Training the Feline"

A step-by-step guide to conditioning your kitten or cat to use the flush toilet.

Veterinarian Approved

Because cats just love cooperating.

The Original World Famous
JiNGLE CATS®
REAL KITTENS SING HOLIDAY CLASSICS!

Putting the "Christ, is this for real?" back in Christmas.

UNUSUALLY SPECIFIC

There's a hobby for everybody, and in the Golden Age of VHS, there was a video for every hobbyist. These videos went all but unnoticed by the general public, but if you happened to be a woman who was really into identifying machine-made marbles, you couldn't live without your copy of *How To Identify Machine-Made Marbles.* This chapter focuses on the esoteric videos that beg the question, "Who the hell bought these?"

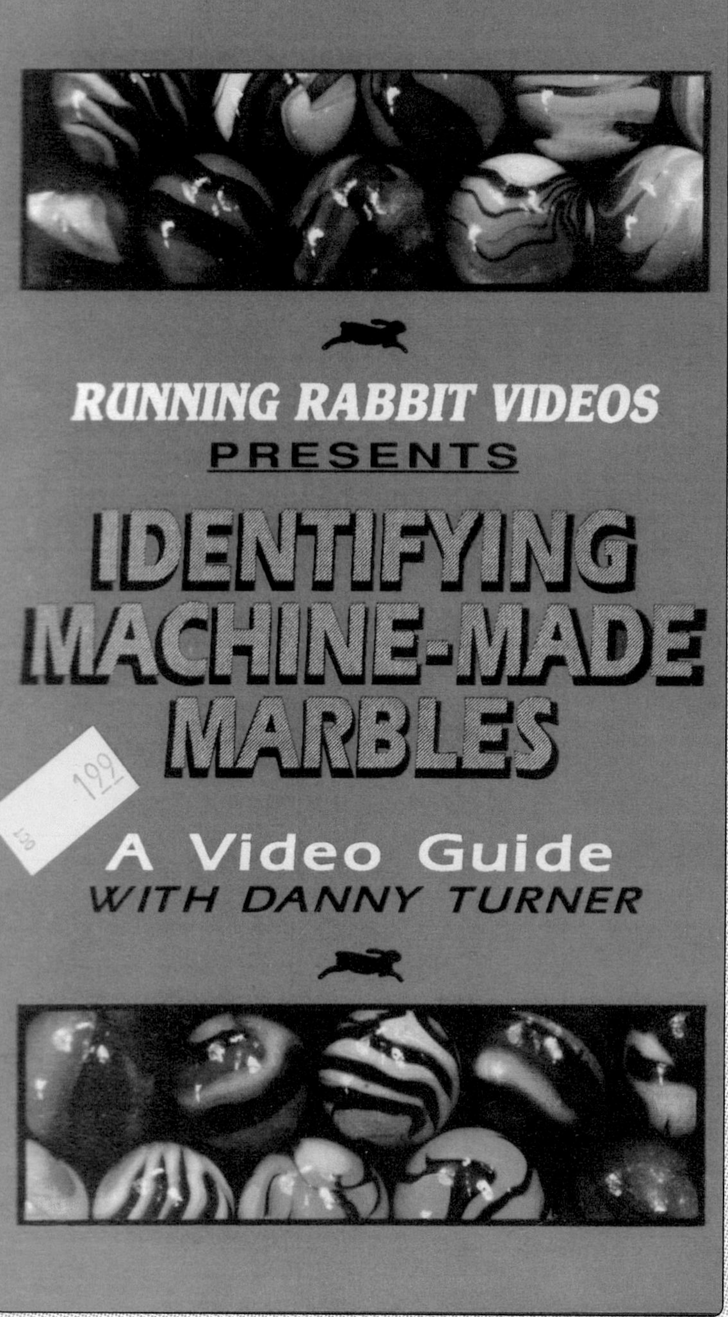
RUNNING RABBIT VIDEOS
PRESENTS
IDENTIFYING
MACHINE-MADE
MARBLES
A Video Guide
WITH DANNY TURNER

We identify with
machine-made marbles.

HOW TO BUILD & PAINT MILITARY FIGURES

08.18.06
CLEARANCE
$1.00

Great for Diorama Builders!

Featuring Kevin Golden's "Macbeth" and Other Award-Winning Figures

Video Workbench®
Your How-To Video Guide for Building Scale Models

Great for diorama builders!
Horrible for meeting women.

DELUXE EDITION

Painting Wizard's Workshop 1 with Scott Jensen

Learn to paint miniatures the fast and easy way!

This might be the sexiest wizard of all time.

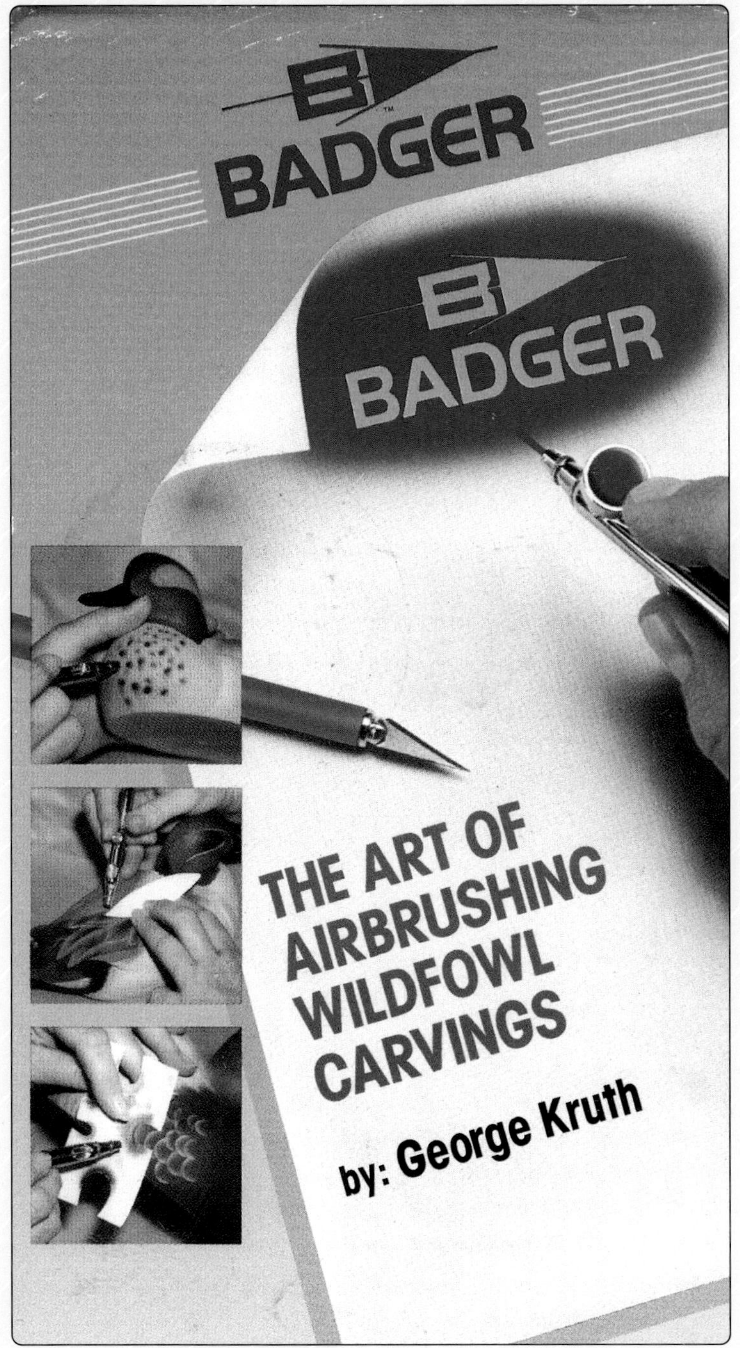
BADGER
BADGER
THE ART OF
AIRBRUSHING
WILDFOWL
CARVINGS
by: George Kruth

With this video and a little practice, you could get really good at airbrushing wildfowl carvings. Not George Kruth good, but still . . .

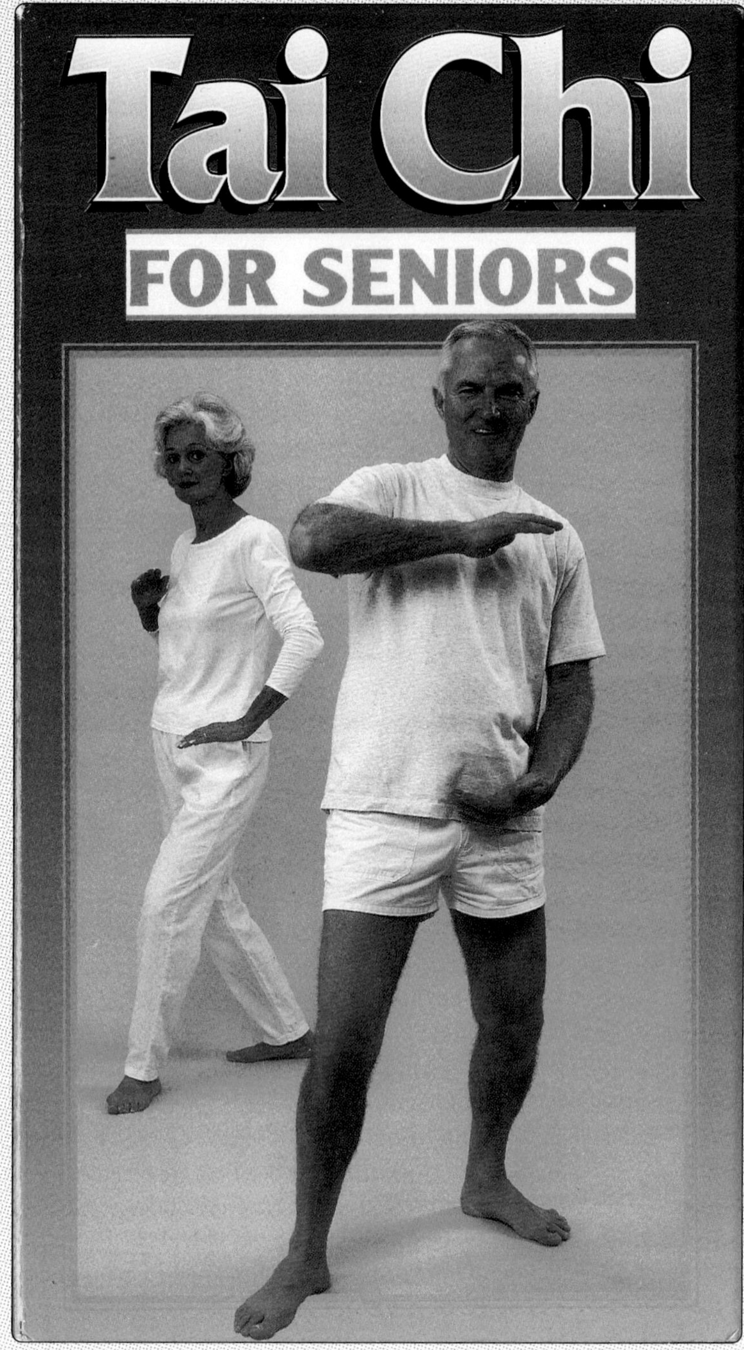
Tai Chi
FOR SENIORS

“I know this much Tai Chi.”

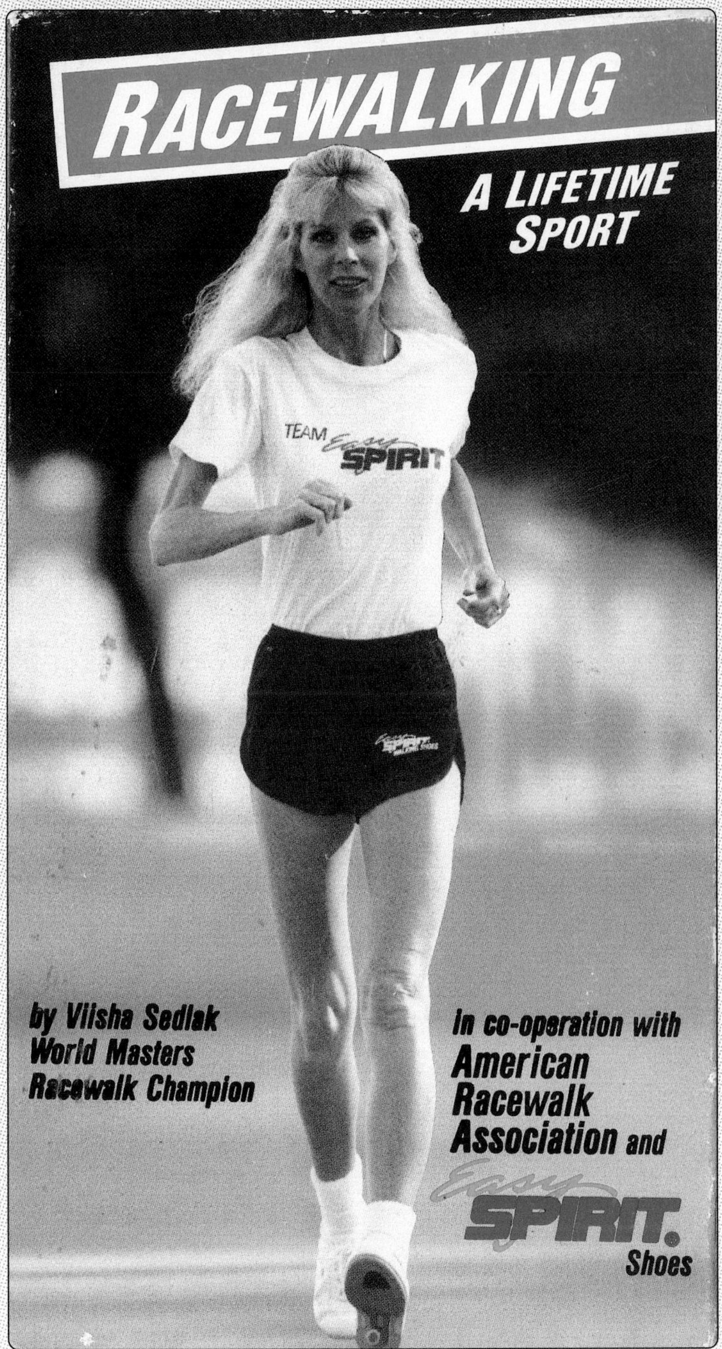
RACEWALKING
A LIFETIME SPORT
TEAM Easy SPIRIT
by Viisha Sedlak
World Masters
Racewalk Champion
In co-operation with
American
Racewalk
Association and
Easy SPIRIT
Shoes

Look out! She's briskly walking right for us!

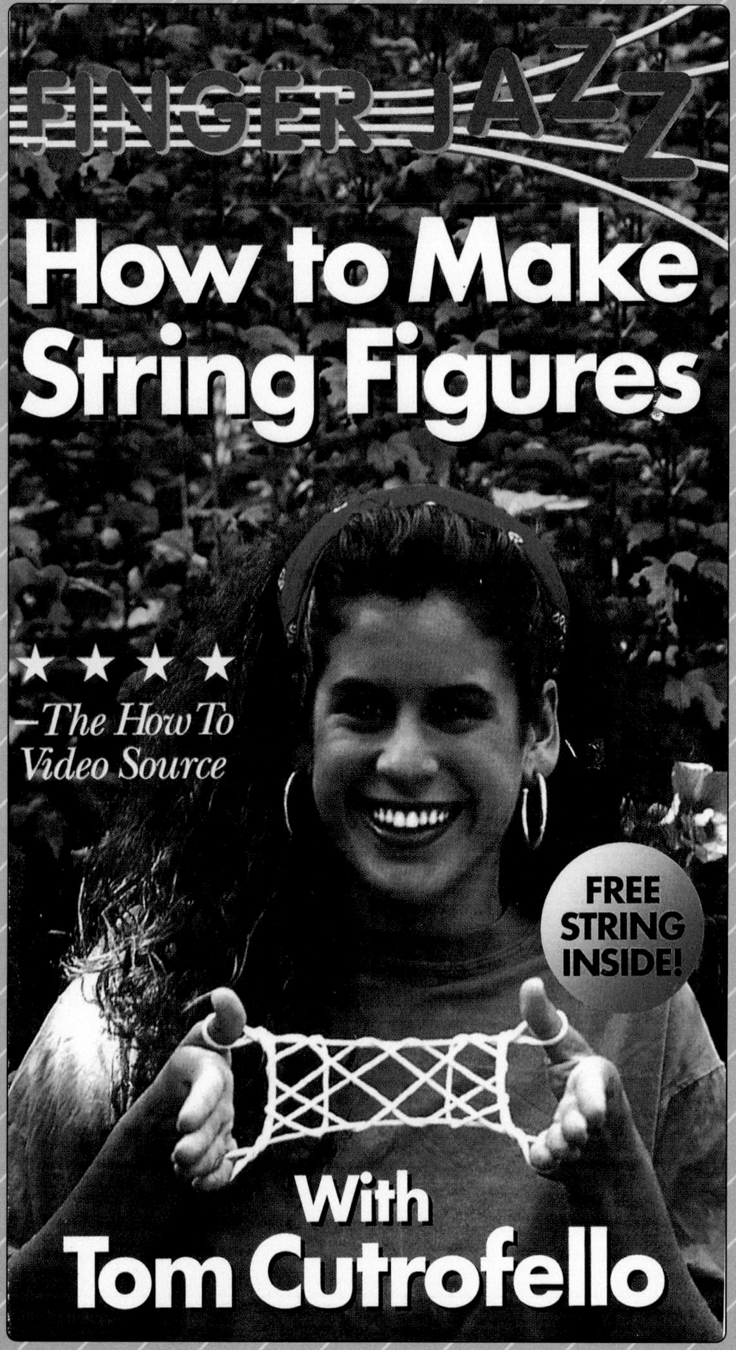
FINGER JAZZ
How to Make String Figures
★ ★ ★ ★
–The How To Video Source
FREE STRING INSIDE!
With
Tom Cutrofello

Free string inside? This tape practically pays for itself!

A Tangent Toy Company
Production
TANGENT TOY CO.
Lights...
Camera...
Bubbles!
A wild romp through the world of bubbles. Good clean fun for kids of all ages!

"No, Mom. Listen. I'm making a bubble video and I need to borrow a thousand dollars. What part of that don't you understand?"

Balloons For The Restaurant Worker

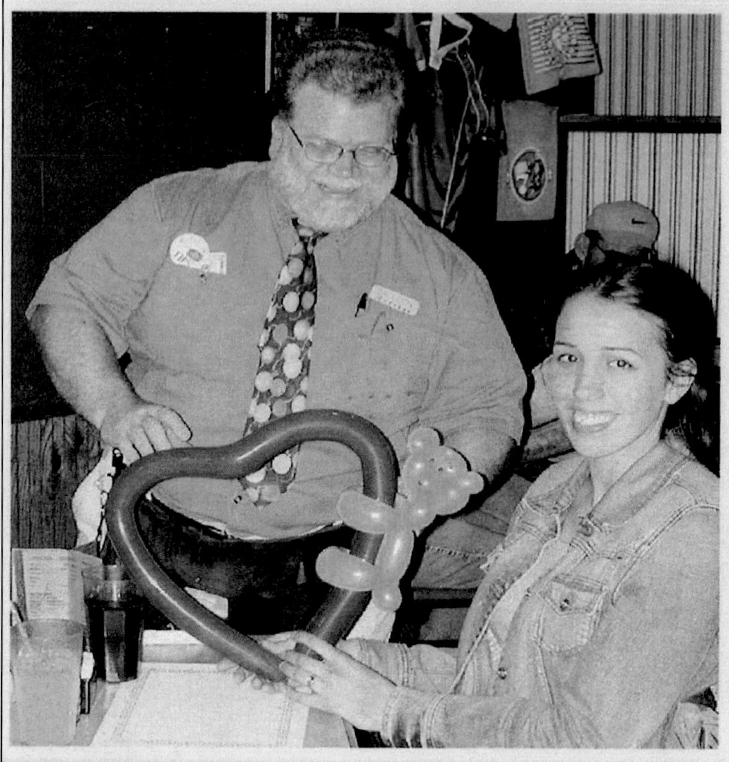

Dennis Regling

America's #1 Strolling Balloon Artist

As ranked by *Strolling Balloon Artist Digest.*

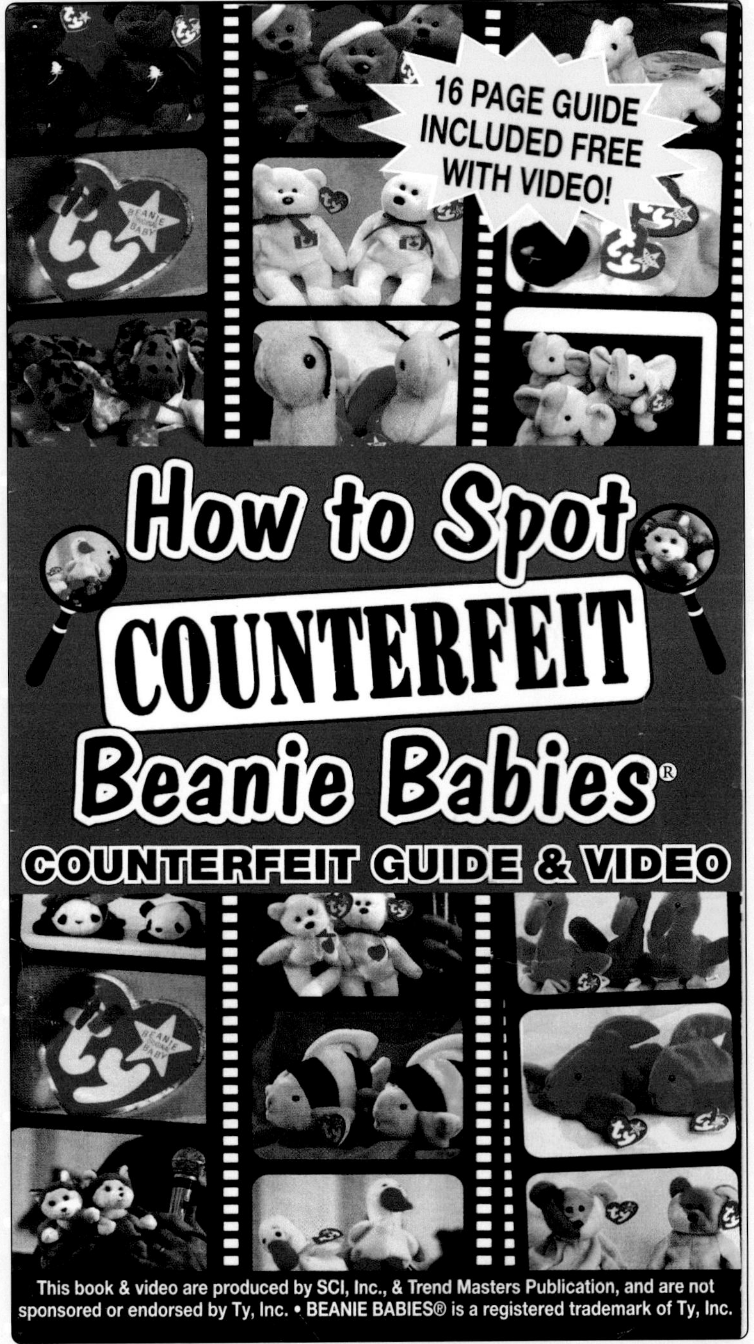
16 PAGE GUIDE
INCLUDED FREE
WITH VIDEO!
How to Spot
COUNTERFEIT
Beanie Babies®
COUNTERFEIT GUIDE & VIDEO
This book & video are produced by SCI, Inc., & Trend Masters Publication, and are not sponsored or endorsed by Ty, Inc. • BEANIE BABIES® is a registered trademark of Ty, Inc.

The FBI is working around the clock to put a stop to this adorable crime.

MILESTONES

As VHS camcorders became more affordable, consumers finally had the tools to document all of life's extraordinary moments which, based on our findings, were almost exclusively birthdays and anniversaries that were divisible by ten. We're not sure how these videos ended up at thrift stores—some were found inside used camcorders, others were perhaps carelessly thrown out with the rest of the VHS tapes—but we can almost guarantee the original owners don't miss them.

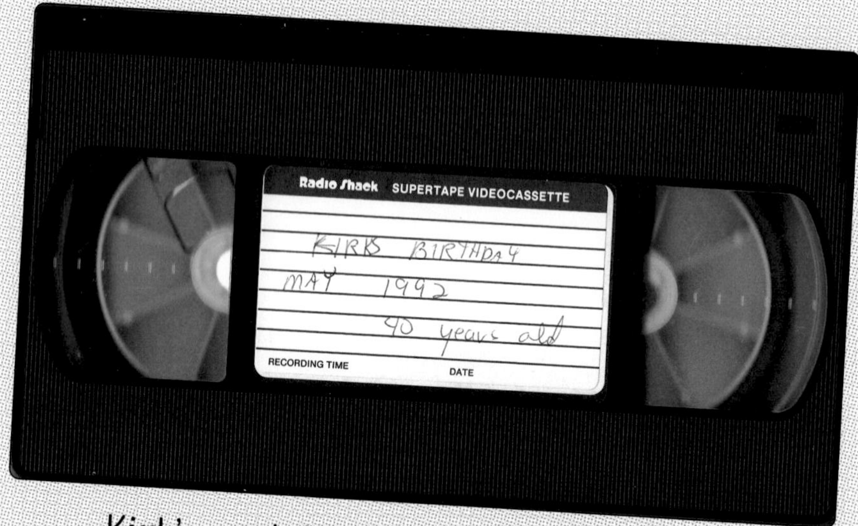
Radio Shack SUPERTAPE VIDEOCASSETTE
KIRKS BIRTHDAY
MAY 1992
40 years old
RECORDING TIME
DATE

Kirk's 40th birthday was special.
RadioShack Supertape special.

Master
VHS
Bob's 50th Birthday
FUJI
BGR
SERIES

Behold, the master tape
of Bob's 50th Birthday!

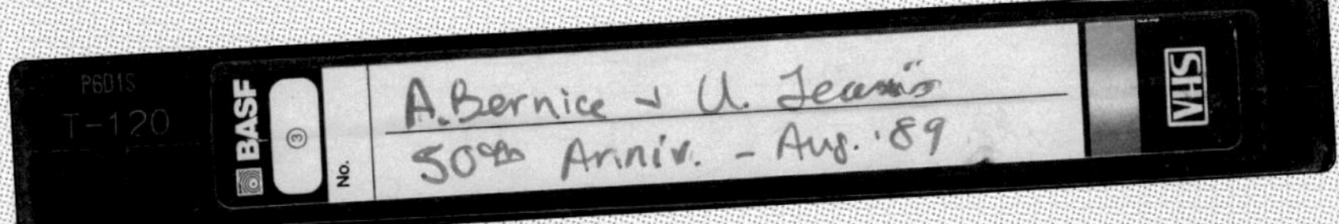
T-120
BASF
No.
A. Bernice + U. Jeans
50th Anniv. - Aug. '89
VHS

Hard to believe it was only 50 years ago that U. got down on one knee and said, "A., will you marry me?"

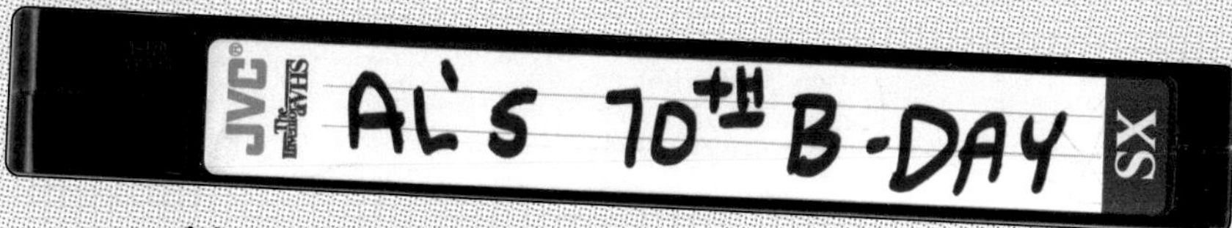
JVC
AL'S 70th B-DAY
SX

Al lived his life like this VHS label: boldly, and in all caps.

It looks like these tapes have been around as long as these ladies were.

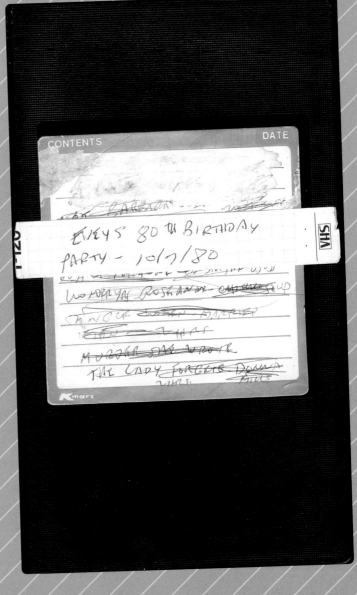

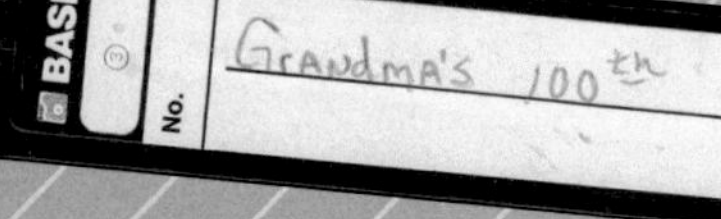
BASF
No.
Grandma's 100th

VHS

Our Wedding Day

Those wedding rings are getting a head start on the consummation.

BAD IDEAS

There came a time during the Golden Age of VHS when it felt like we finally ran out of ideas. But that didn't stop us. We persevered and managed to crank out more. And more. Once videos became cheap and easy to produce, even the most inane ideas could still find the funding, the camera crew, the talent and maybe, just maybe, the audience. More than likely, however, they found their way onto a dusty shelf at Value Village.

CREATED EXCLUSIVELY FOR GIFT-GIVING BY
Cardsettes
GIFTVIDEO GREETINGS
Congratulations
Western Express-A-Gram
Congratulations!
You did it!
Featuring the song: "(This Is Your) Celebration"
COMPLETE AND READY-TO-GIVE
CONTENTS INCLUDE
• MUSIC GIFTVIDEO.
• CONTEMPORARY GIFTCARD AND ENVELOPE.
• ILLUSTRATED GIFTBOX MAILER.
SEE BACK

When you care about someone enough to hand them a congratulatory VHS tape.

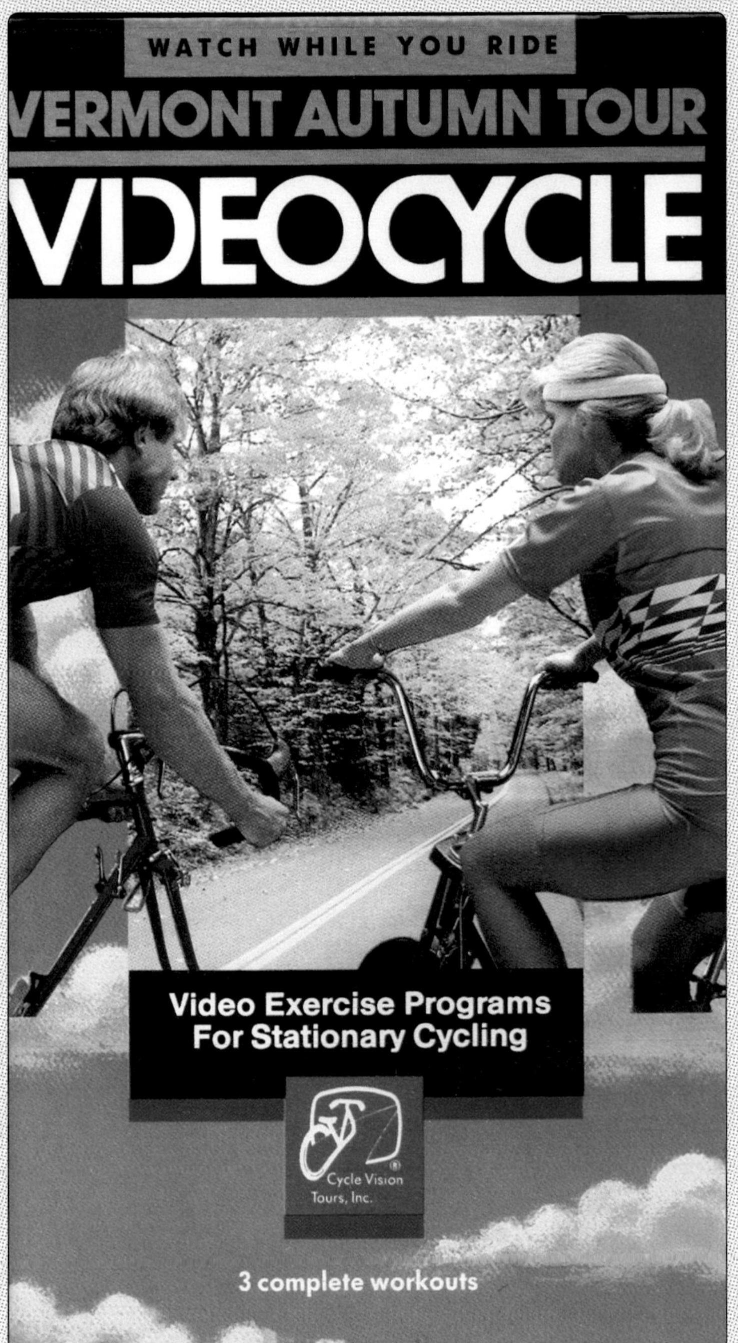
WATCH WHILE YOU RIDE
VERMONT AUTUMN TOUR
VIDEOCYCLE
Video Exercise Programs
For Stationary Cycling
Cycle Vision
Tours, Inc.
3 complete workouts

All it requires is a stationary bike, a TV, and a strong suspension of disbelief.

Hi!
I want to be
YOUR friend
Meet
RENT-A-FRIEND™
the Original Video Companion
He talks to you • He listens to you • He drinks with you
HE EVEN LENDS YOU MONEY!
Get-Acquainted
Action Workbook
Enclosed!

If you're lonely and you have a VCR, say hello to your new best friend

Therapeutic Massage
for Dogs
Step-by-Step Instruction
by the founder of Equissage®
Mary Schreiber

Even the dog thinks
she's going too far.

Face Aerobics

EXERCISES FOR A NATURAL FACELIFT

Discover the deep muscle facial exercise program that will give you a beautiful, firm face

PROVEN FAST RESULTS

Includes demonstration of The Beautiful Skin Kit

Why do you have to be topless for face aerobics?

Baby-n-Momerobics

As seen on "Live with Regis and Kathie Lee"

Traumatize your baby the fun and healthy way!

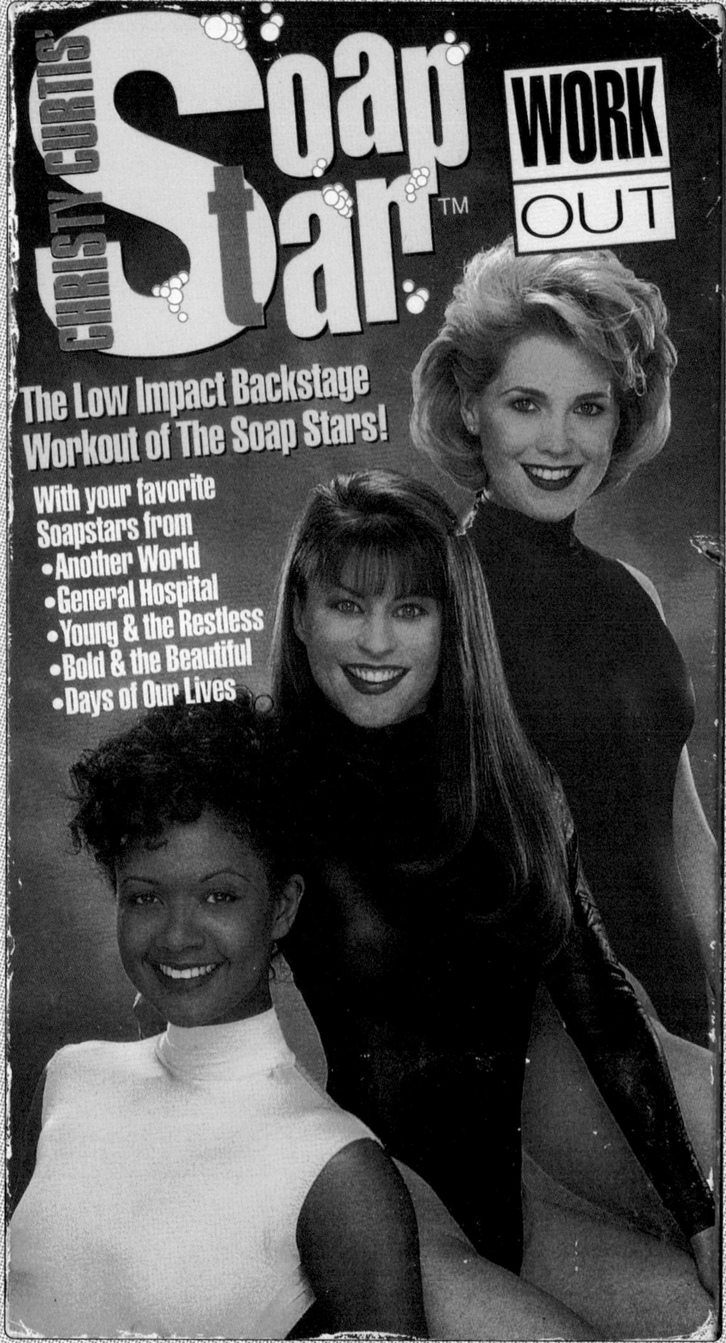
CHRISTY CURTIS'
Soap Star™
WORK OUT
The Low Impact Backstage Workout of The Soap Stars!
With your favorite Soapstars from
•Another World
•General Hospital
•Young & the Restless
•Bold & the Beautiful
•Days of Our Lives

Now we can spend even more time with those people in the TV.

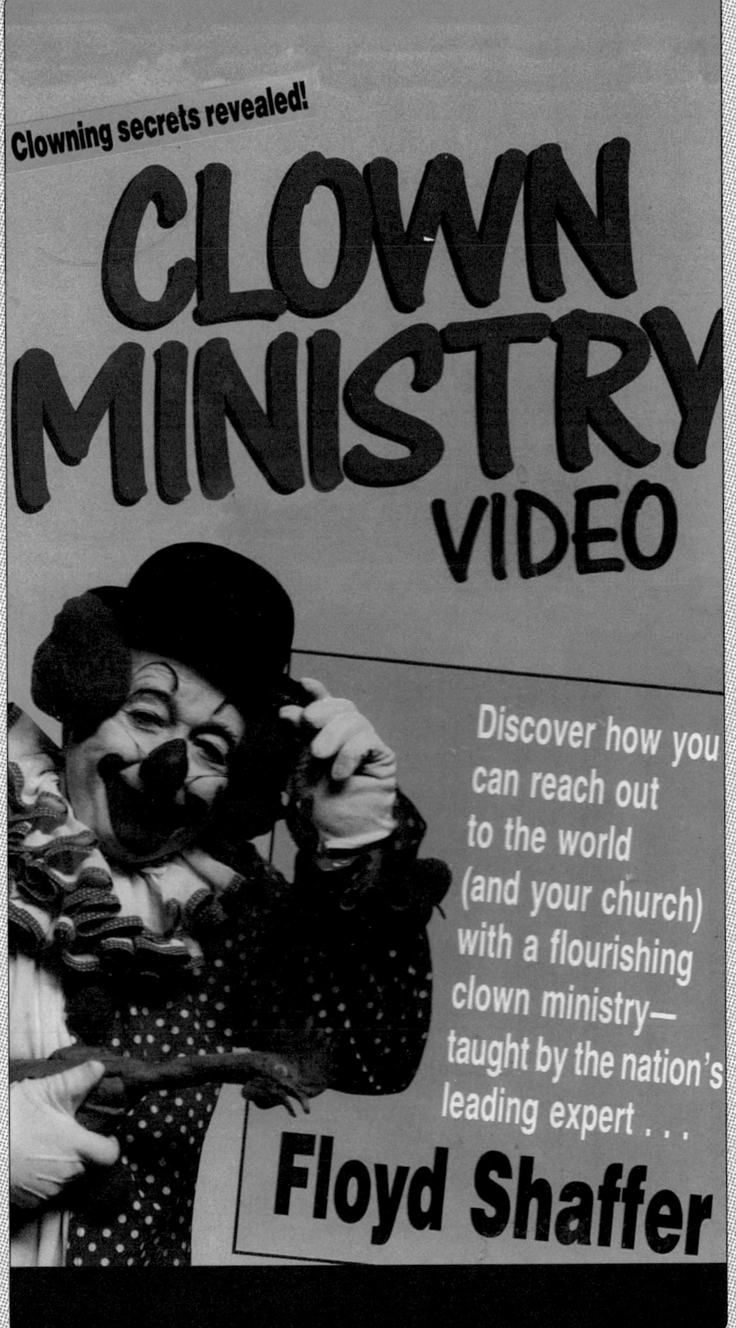
Clowning secrets revealed!
CLOWN MINISTRY VIDEO
Discover how you can reach out to the world (and your church) with a flourishing clown ministry— taught by the nation's leading expert . . .
Floyd Shaffer

Rubber chickens help teach Christ's love.

Hosted by
Leonard
Nimoy
What you,
your family and
community
need to know
about Y2K.
Y2K
FAMILY
SURVIVAL
GUIDE
> Exactly What Y2K Means <
> Worst Case Scenarios <
> Responsible Action <
> Personal Survival <

This video single-handedly prevented the world from exploding in the year 2000.

THE
PET ROCK
VIDEO™
A REAL ROCK VIDEO
BY
A REAL ROCK STAR

After a journey of more than four billion years, this rock suddenly found itself wearing headphones.

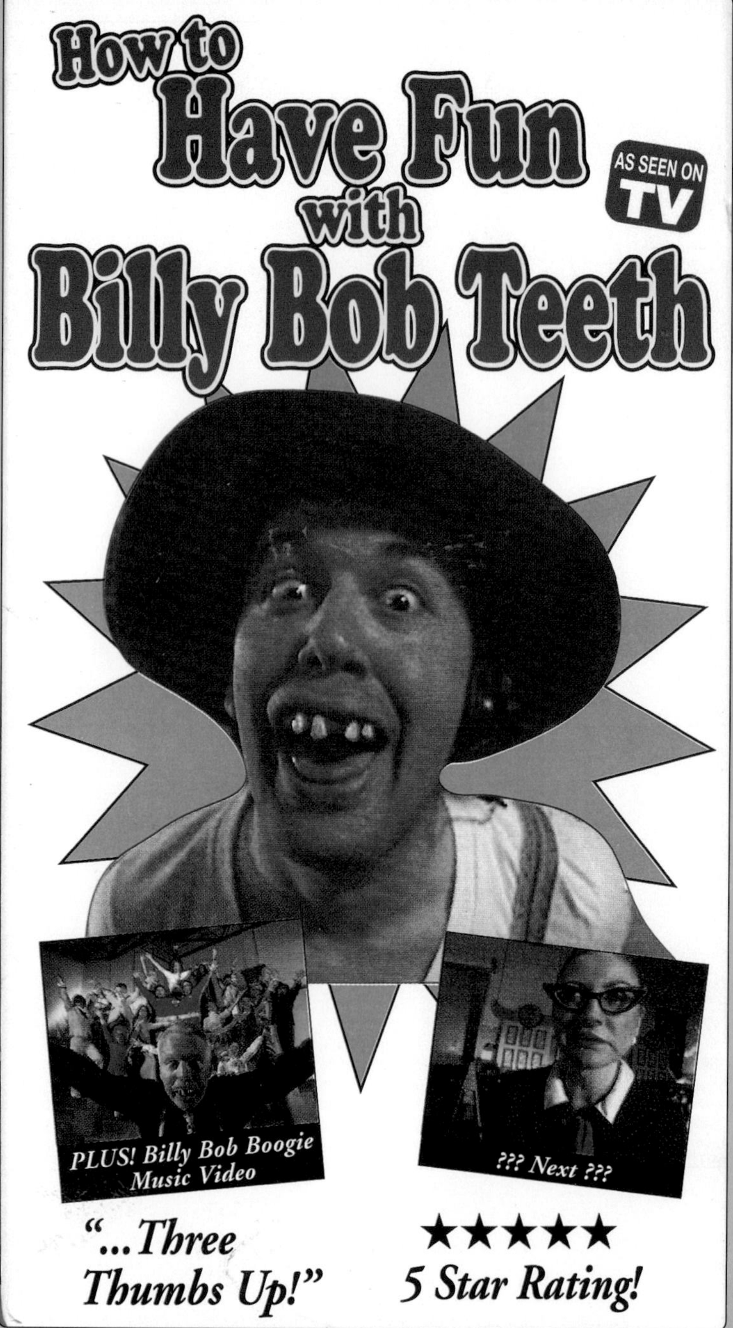
How to
Have Fun
with
Billy Bob Teeth
AS SEEN ON
TV
PLUS! Billy Bob Boogie
Music Video
??? Next ???
"...Three
Thumbs Up!"
★★★★★
5 Star Rating!

This video all but announces, "Prepare to be irritated."

HOW TO
SEDUCE WOMEN
THROUGH HYPNOSIS

We hope to one day hypno-seduce a girl we're proud to introduce to our parents.

SCARE TACTICS

Warning: The video covers you are about to see cannot be unseen.

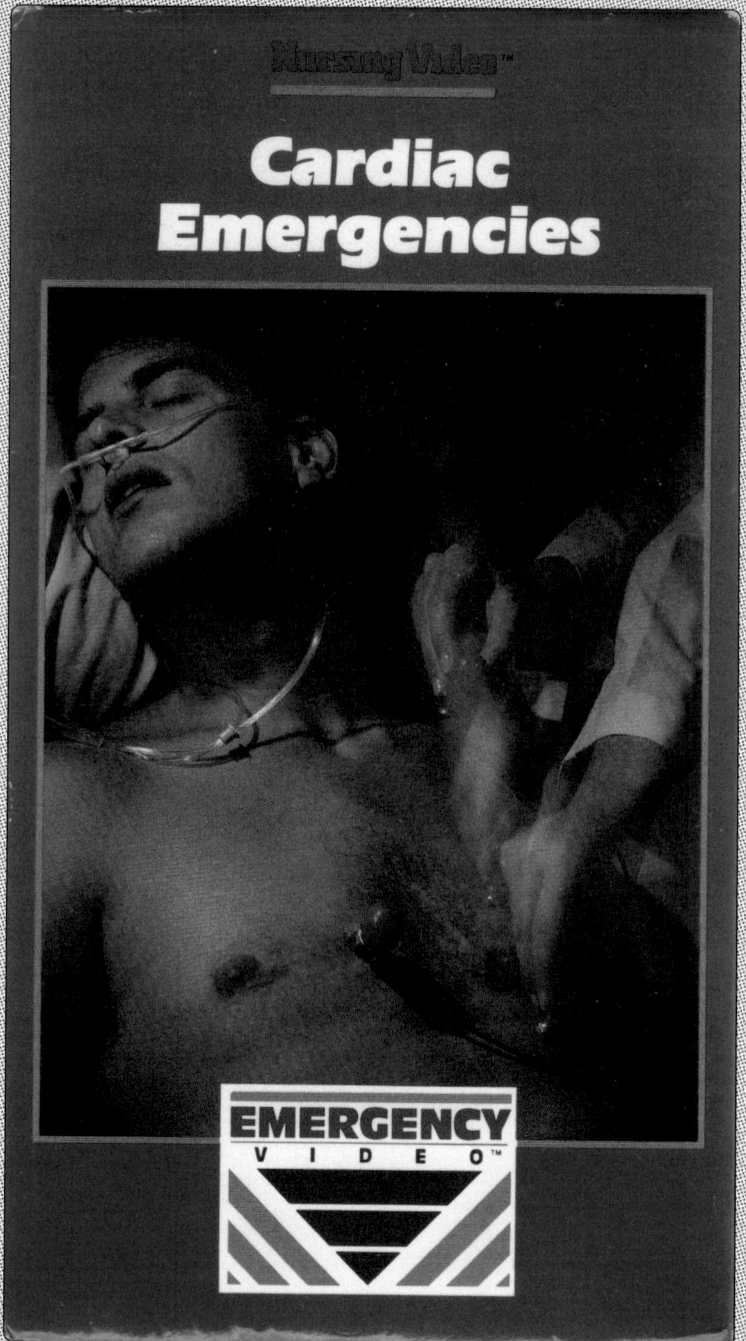

Nursing Video™

Cardiac Emergencies

EMERGENCY VIDEO™

This cover has caused more heart attacks than it's treated.

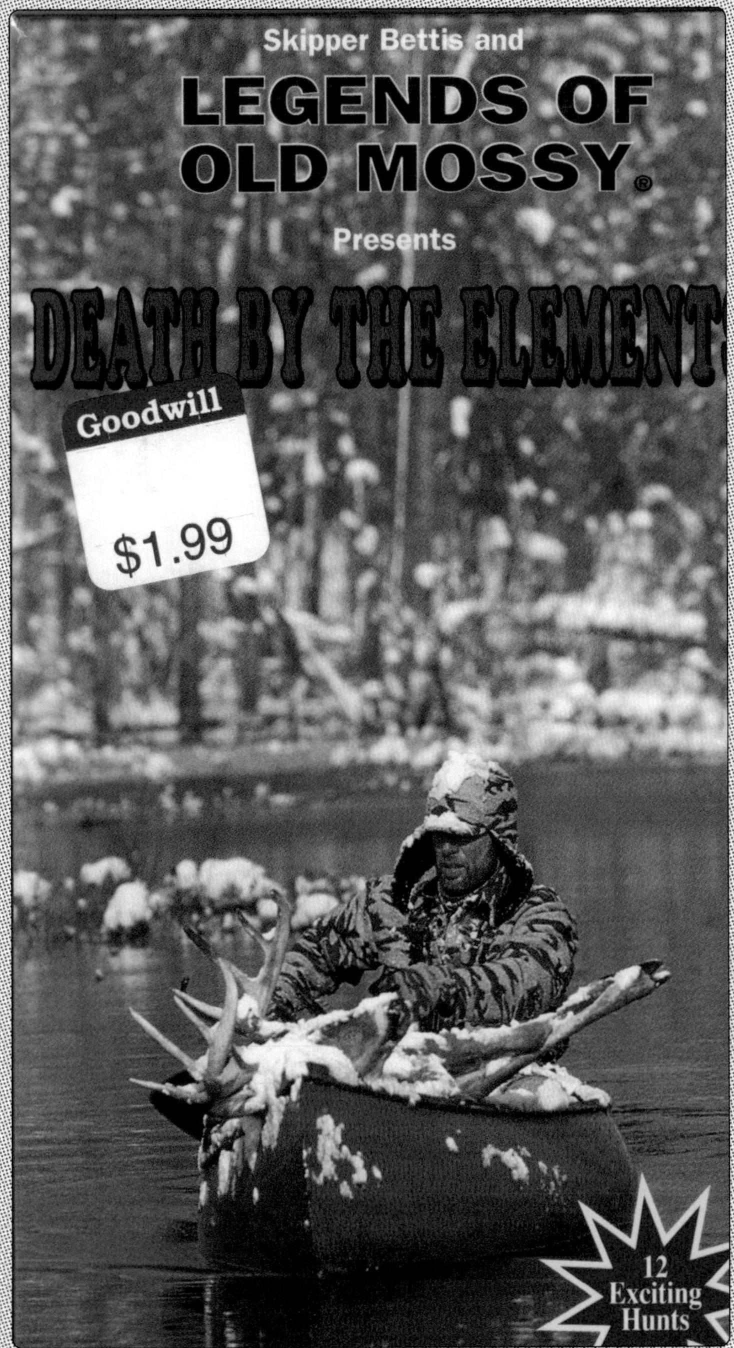
Skipper Bettis and
LEGENDS OF OLD MOSSY®
Presents
DEATH BY THE ELEMENTS
Goodwill
$1.99
12 Exciting Hunts

Is it still considered hunting when you're just out looking for frozen deer?

ALMOST HOME

Living With Suffering & Dying

The key is to do it with a smile on your face.

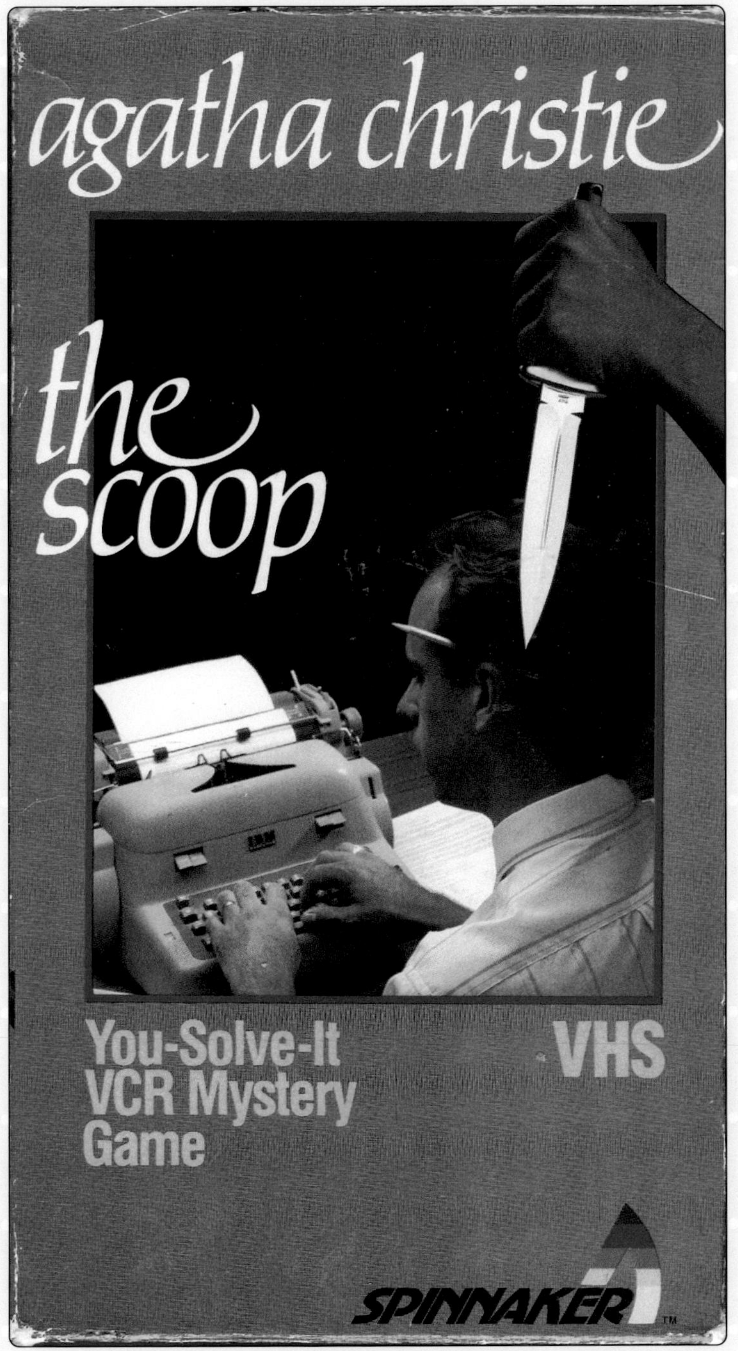
agatha christie
the scoop
You-Solve-It
VCR Mystery
Game
VHS
SPINNAKER

VCR games: The price of a real board game, all the entertainment of an awful movie, and you only get to play it once.

Who's Really Behind the Terrorist
Attack on the World Trade Center
Osama bin Laden or Osama bin Bush?
Anthony J. Hilder's
Illuminazi 9-11

Looks like it was somebody's first day at Photoshop.

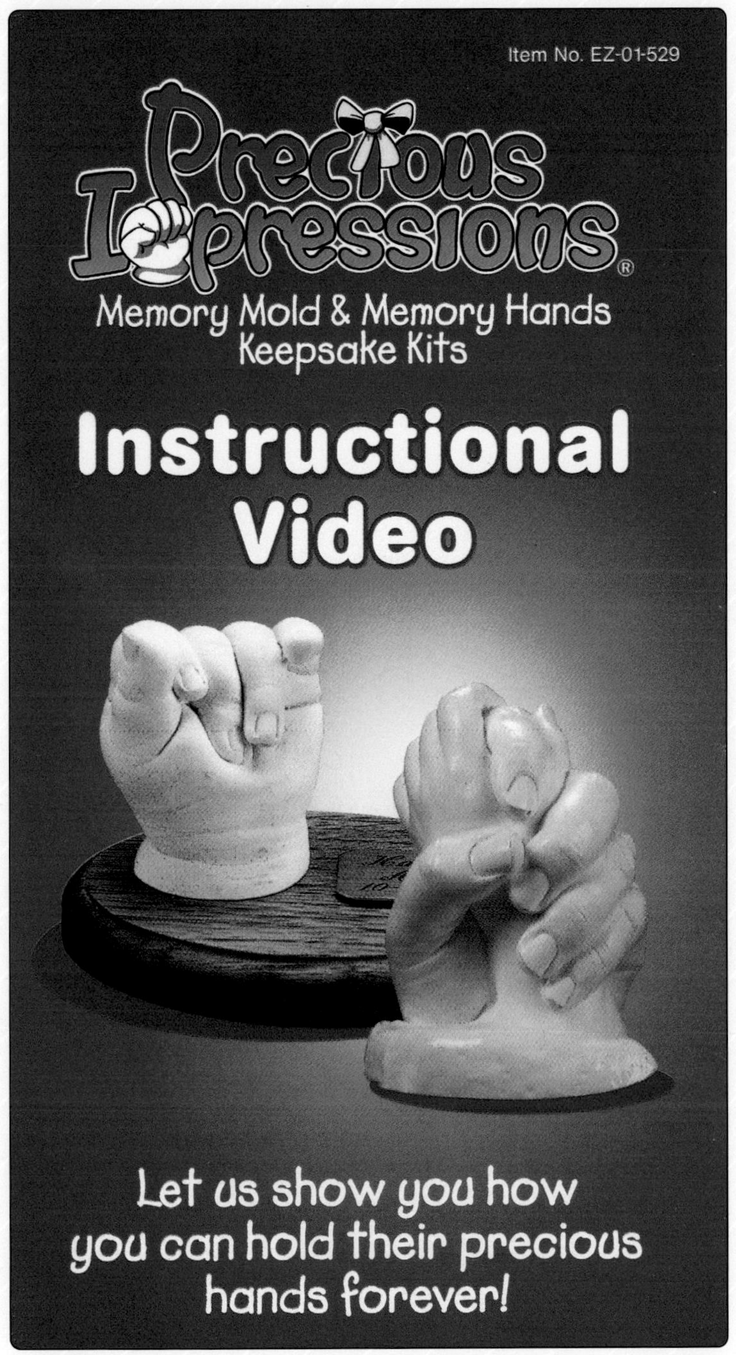
Item No. EZ-01-529
Precious Impressions®
Memory Mold & Memory Hands Keepsake Kits
Instructional Video
Let us show you how you can hold their precious hands forever!

Brighten up your mantel with a severed baby hand.

Kudos to this cover for inventing a new form of punctuation: the crucifix exclamation point†

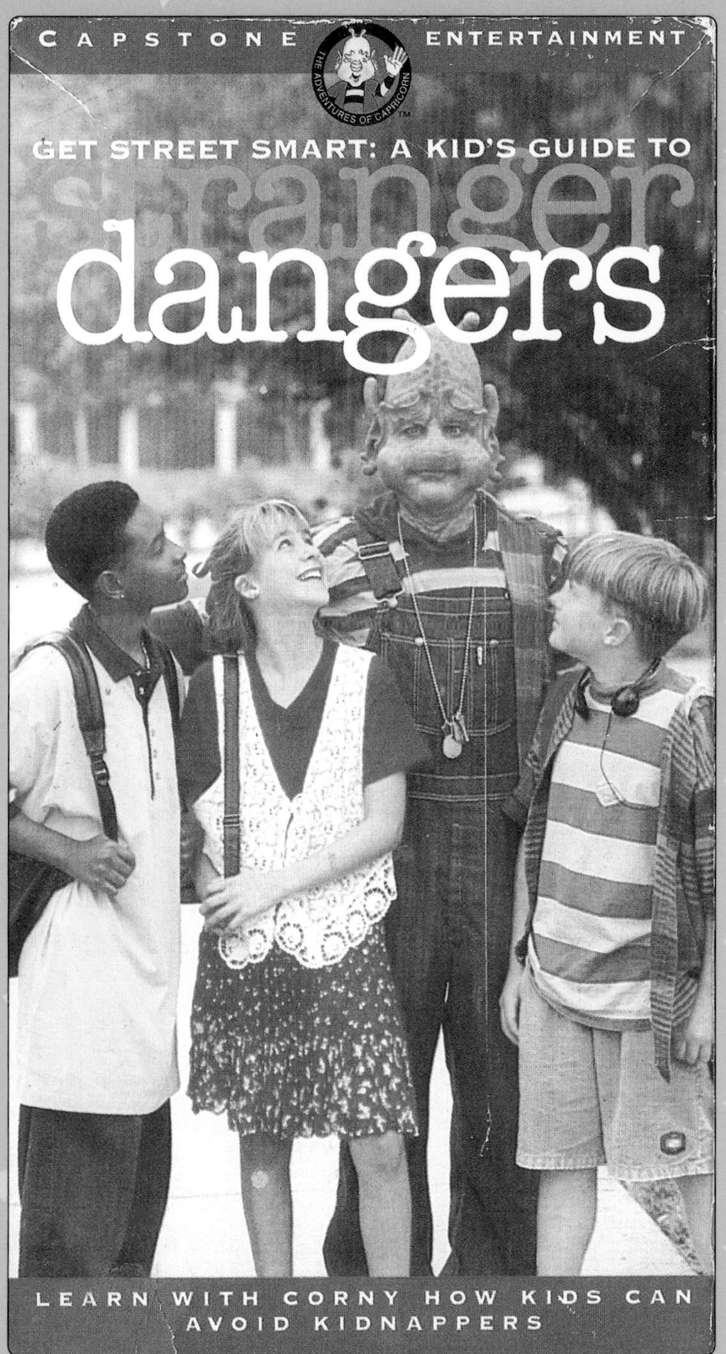
CAPSTONE ENTERTAINMENT
THE ADVENTURES OF CAPRICORN
GET STREET SMART: A KID'S GUIDE TO
stranger
dangers
LEARN WITH CORNY HOW KIDS CAN
AVOID KIDNAPPERS

It would suck if you were being kidnapped. It would suck even more if this alien popped into your head while it was happening.

MEN WE LOVE

Every man needs a role model, and for us, it's the fine gentlemen on the next video covers. These are men's men, dudes who know the score, guys who'd offer you a firm handshake and a glass of scotch. With apologies to our own fathers, these are the dads we always wanted. These are the men we love.

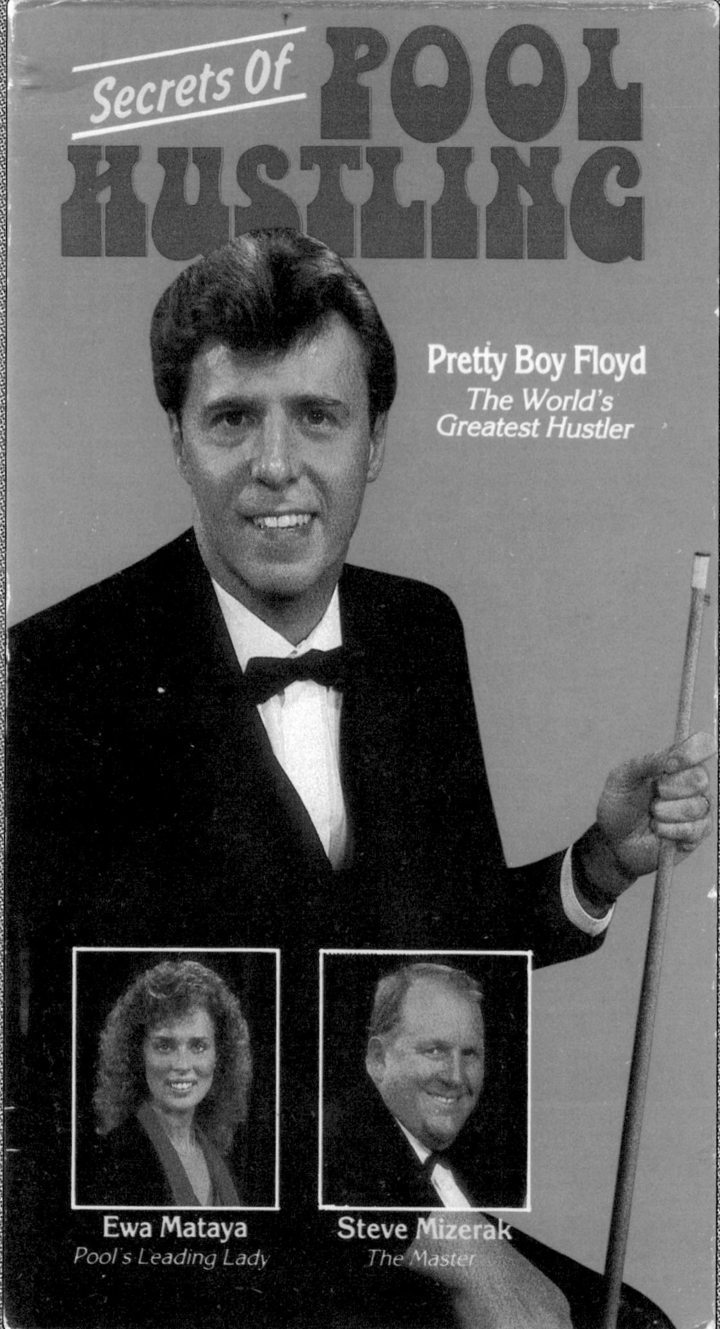
Secrets Of
POOL
HUSTLING
Pretty Boy Floyd
The World's
Greatest Hustler
Ewa Mataya
Pool's Leading Lady
Steve Mizerak
The Master

These pool hustling secrets
don't leave this room.

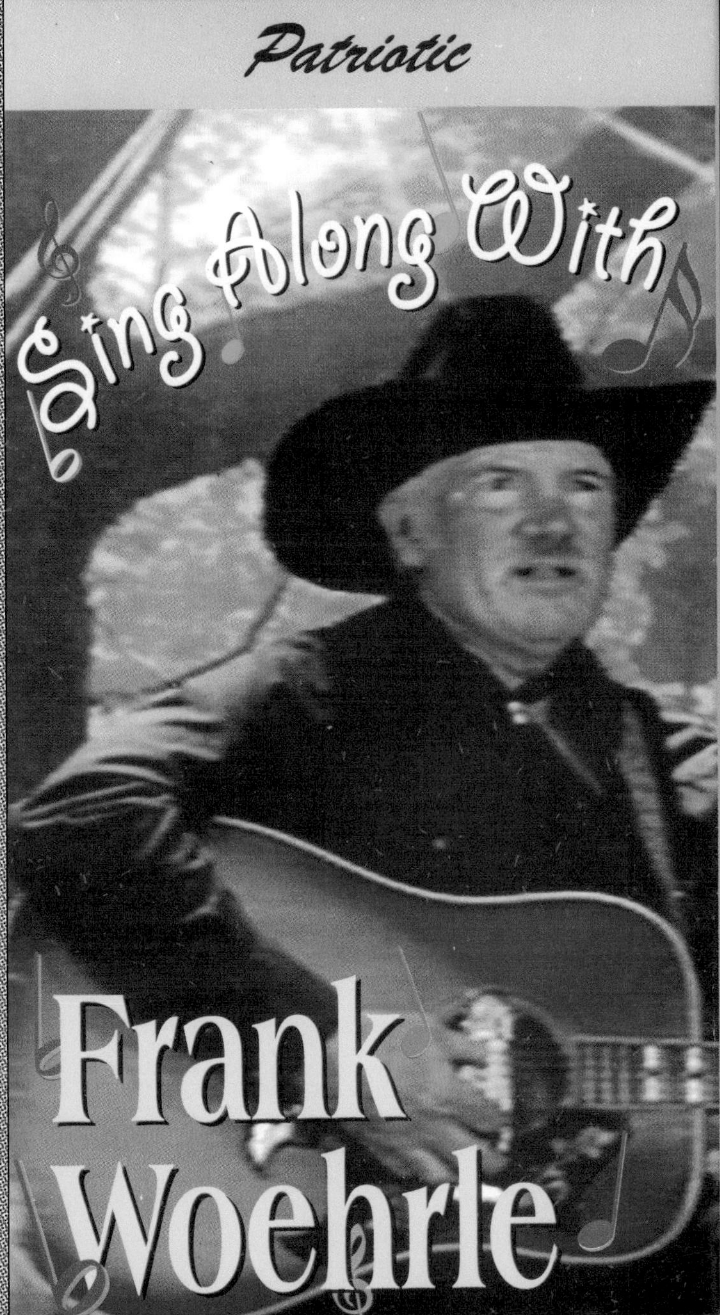
Patriotic
Sing Along With
Frank
Woehrle

We've sung along with a lot of different men in our time, but none as wonderful as Frank.

DENNIS AWE
NEAR YOU

We love you, Dennis, but you might be a little too near.

AMERICA'S
JUDGMENTS
WHAT LIES AHEAD?
1. LACK OF FOOD (Famine)
2. ENEMY TROOPS (Evil Beast)
3. MILITARY EQUIPMENT (Sword)
4. BIO-CHEM WARFARE (Pestilence)
(A Must See Video)

That's a bold parenthetical statement.

MARK ROTHSTEIN'S
WORLD OF ROPE JUMPING

BEST OF
#6 in the series

It's Mark Rothstein's world of rope jumping. We just live in it.

Master Arts Video
TM
REFUSE TO BE A
VICTIM!

$3.00 BOOKSELLER 2 NIGHT
11219 $ 48.90 NON FICT
RAPE: A CRIME OF VIOLENCE
A Docudrama Written and Produced by Bob Chaney

We watched this tape and found out the guy on the cover is actually the host of the video. That's right, the man wearing no shirt and a jean jacket is the host of the anti-rape video.

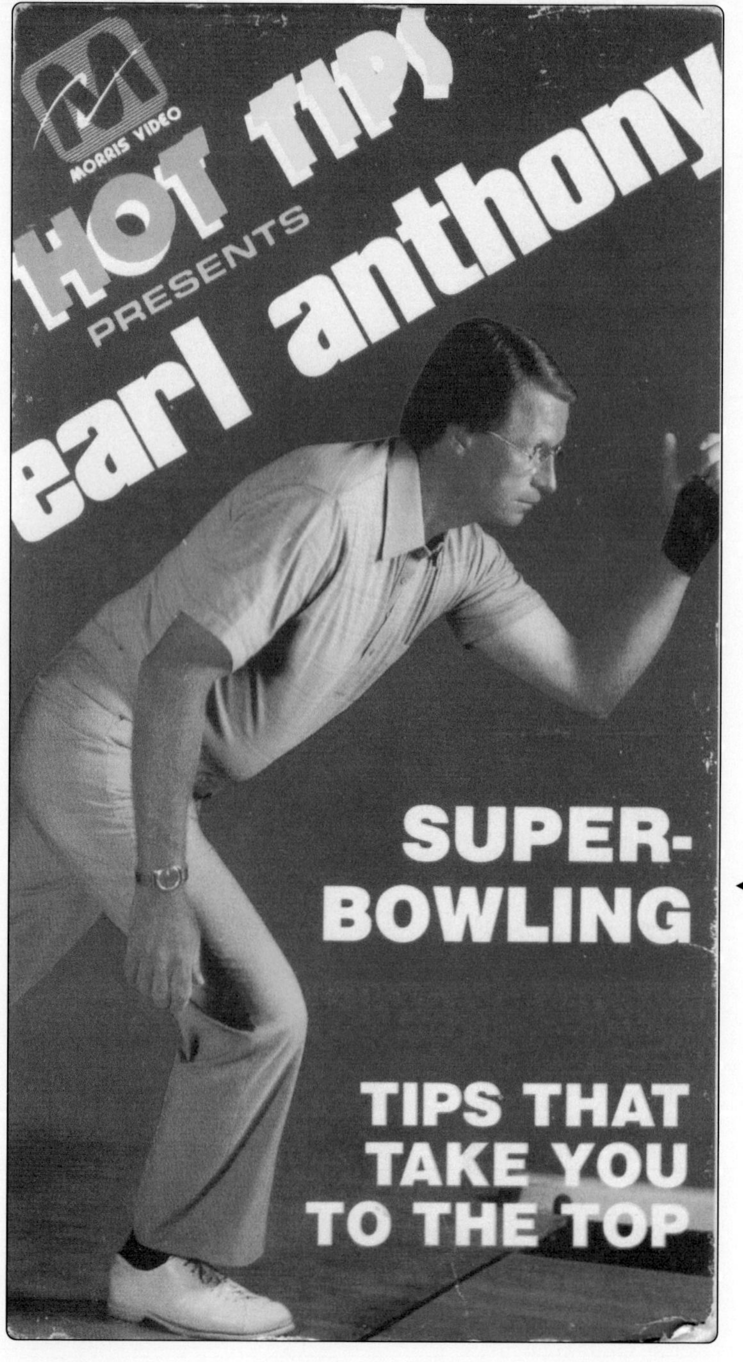
MORRIS VIDEO
HOT TIPS
PRESENTS
earl anthony
SUPER-
BOWLING
TIPS THAT
TAKE YOU
TO THE TOP

"Super-Bowling" is hyphenated? And to think, all these years we've been spelling it as two words.

WINNING
LOTTO
LOTTERY
STRATEGIES
David Wilhite Gaming Expert for over 15 years will show you how to increase your odds just by playing smart.

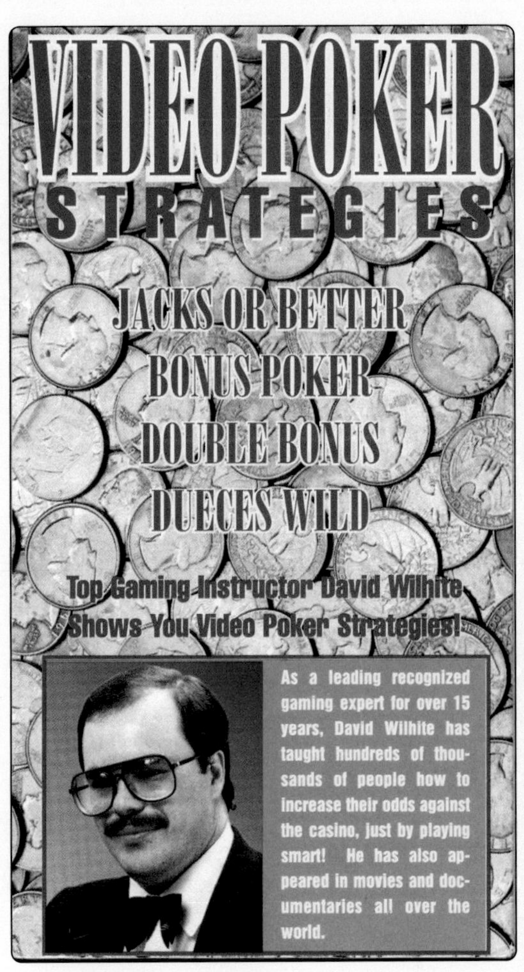
VIDEO POKER
STRATEGIES
JACKS OR BETTER
BONUS POKER
DOUBLE BONUS
DUECES WILD
Top Gaming Instructor David Wilhite Shows You Video Poker Strategies!
As a leading recognized gaming expert for over 15 years, David Wilhite has taught hundreds of thousands of people how to increase their odds against the casino, just by playing smart! He has also appeared in movies and documentaries all over the world.

Never question a man
with glasses this thick.

On our first trip to Vancouver, we found a video called *Hank's Christmas Glitter 2005*. It turned out to be an hour-long video of this enthusiastic guy, Hank, videotaping Christmas lights around various Vancouver neighborhoods. We looked him up and found out he's released a new one every Christmas since 2004. Hank's last few were released on DVD, but we thought we would include them anyway. Here are some of his glitteriest.

Hank's
Christmas Glitter
2004

Hank's
Christmas Glitter
2005

HANK'S
CHRISTMAS GLITTER
2006
WIDESCREEN

Hank's
Christmas
Glitter
2009

BACKS, SPINES, AND LABELS

VHS covers get all the attention, but sometimes the best bits are hidden on other parts of the tape. Closer examination sometimes pays off, and rest assured, we've scoured our entire collection to dig up the secrets that can only be revealed by looking beyond the cover.

We've watched this movie and can assure you Tanglefoot is no less terrifying on-screen than he is here.

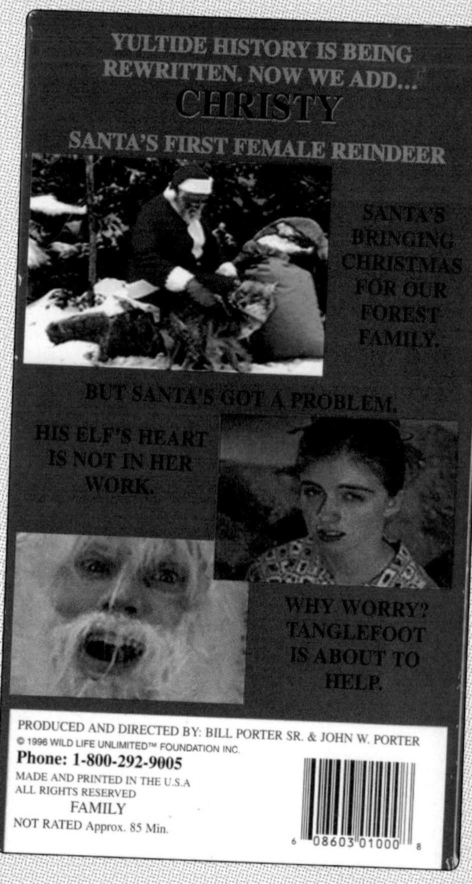
YULTIDE HISTORY IS BEING REWRITTEN. NOW WE ADD...
CHRISTY
SANTA'S FIRST FEMALE REINDEER
SANTA'S BRINGING CHRISTMAS FOR OUR FOREST FAMILY.
BUT SANTA'S GOT A PROBLEM.
HIS ELF'S HEART IS NOT IN HER WORK.
WHY WORRY? TANGLEFOOT IS ABOUT TO HELP.
PRODUCED AND DIRECTED BY: BILL PORTER SR. & JOHN W. PORTER
© 1996 WILD LIFE UNLIMITED™ FOUNDATION INC.
Phone: 1-800-292-9005
MADE AND PRINTED IN THE U.S.A
ALL RIGHTS RESERVED
FAMILY
NOT RATED Approx. 85 Min.
6 08603 01000 8

"*Jingle Bell Rockin' Christmas*"

With Bobby Helms

Wrap your presents, decorate the tree and enjoy all the legendary music of Bobby Helms. It wouldn't be Christmas without *Jingle Bell Rock*. You'll love watching and listening to Bobby Helms sing the greatest songs of Christmas. This is the only Christmas video you'll ever need to complete your holiday music library.

Jingle Bell Rock
White Christmas
Rudolph The Red Nose Reindeer
I Saw Mommie Kissing Santa Claus
Silver Bells
Here Comes Santa Claus
Christmas Time In My Home Town
Jingle Bells
Winter Wonderland
Santa Claus Is Coming To Town
I Wanna' Go To Santa Claus Land

Produced by John Kleiman and Kelly Hocker

Approximate Running Time: 35 Minutes

Color/ VHS

FBI Warning! Federal Law provides severe civil and criminal penalties for the unauthorized reproduction, distribution or exhibition or copyrighted video tapes. Criminal copyright infringement is investigated by the F.B.I. and may constitute a felony with a maximum penalty of five years in prison and/or a $250,000 fine.

This video is for private home exhibition only. Any public performance is strictly prohibited.

7 00431-0101-3 4

Chart Breaker Video
P.O. Box 29142
Indianapolis, IN 46229

Copyright © 1994 John Kleiman and Kelly Hocker, All rights Reserved.

Featuring the real life Popeye.

JVC
Highroller Craps
with
Low Risk
© Leonard Benson 2000

Highrollers endure enough risk while gambling. They should be able to crap in peace.

HOW TO GET GREAT RESULTS
WITH NAD'S

TRT 7:53

We think the word "nad's" is funny.

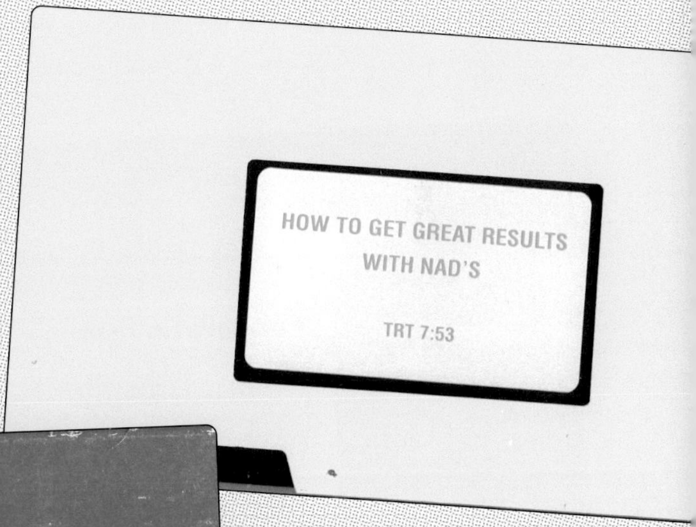

An Opportunity . . .
For
Your Future

An opportunity for what? The suspense is killing us! Oh, for our future.

TAI SENG
Video Marketing
PORKY'S MEATBALLS

We haven't watched this one yet, but it appears the Chinese have created the greatest 80s sex comedy of all time.

POOFDINI™ & CLIPDINI™
11 - Style Instructional Video
• Includes step-by-step techniques
• Shows 11 Styles
• Works with curly or straight, thick or fine hair
Running Time: 14 minutes 55 seconds
© 1998 HAIRDINI INVENTIVE PRODUCTS, INC. - ALL RIGHTS RESERVED

Good for people who like to wastedini their timedini.

Andersons
DESIGNER PORTRAITS
WEDDINGS - PORTRAITS - COMMERCIAL
Michael and Joannie Anderson
8350 Eastwood Road
Mounds View, MN 55112-4612
(612) 785-1177

But if the Andersons are in the portrait, who's taking the picture?

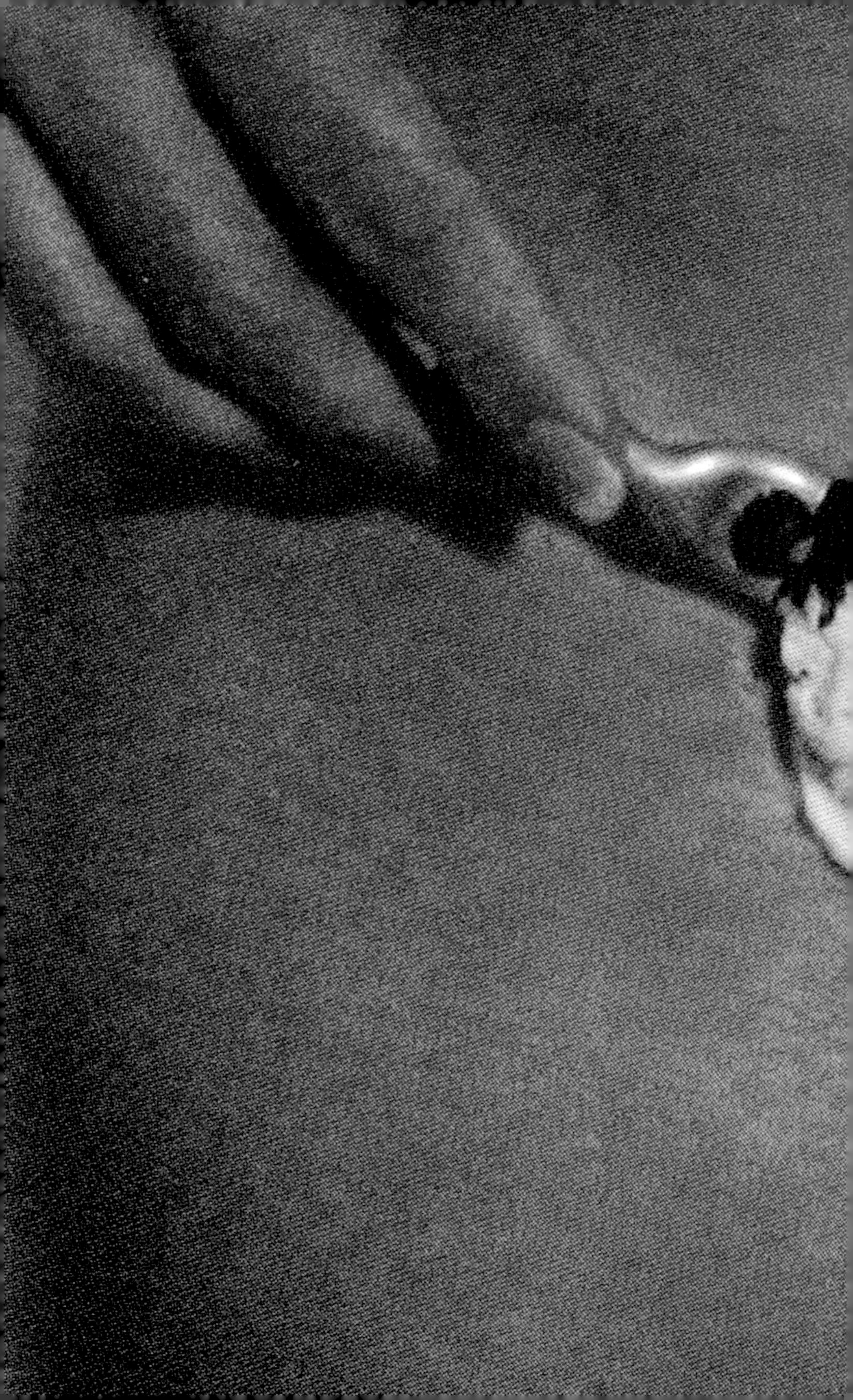

AFTER DARK

Putting a half-naked lady on a VHS cover doing anything, no matter how mundane or boring, sold tapes. That's why these softcore classics, apparently for people who were sort of horny and didn't have Cinemax, continue to litter thrift stores around the country. Come along with us on this trip through the saloon doors at the back of the video store, and we'll explore the world of VHS After Dark.

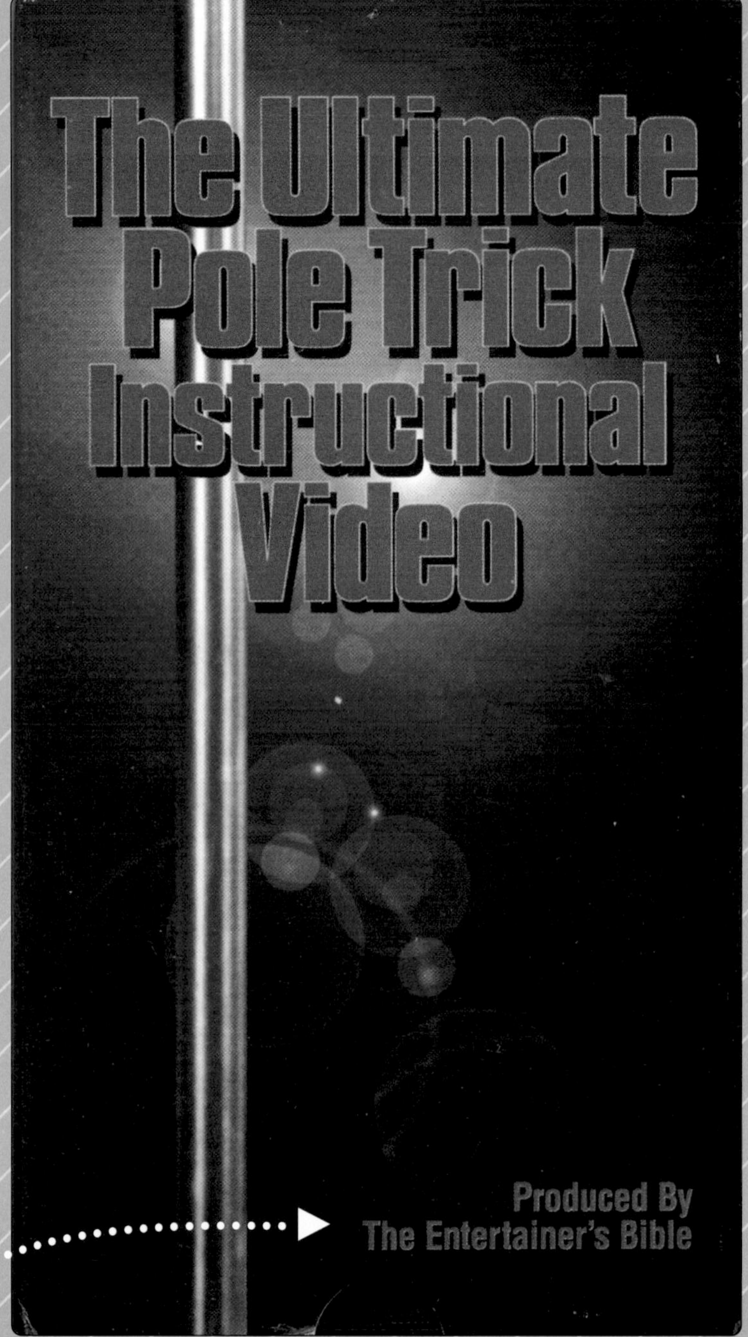
The Ultimate
Pole Trick
Instructional
Video
Produced By
The Entertainer's Bible

We bet this bible is almost as unsettling as the real one.

Erotic
Shaving
and
Sexual
Pleasures
Dare to Bare
SINCLAIR
Intimacy Institute®
Better Relationships, Better Sex.™

This video falls into a weird category: too sexy to be educational, too educational to get off to.

This was from a more innocent time before free agency and bloated salaries ruined the sport of topless arm wrestling.

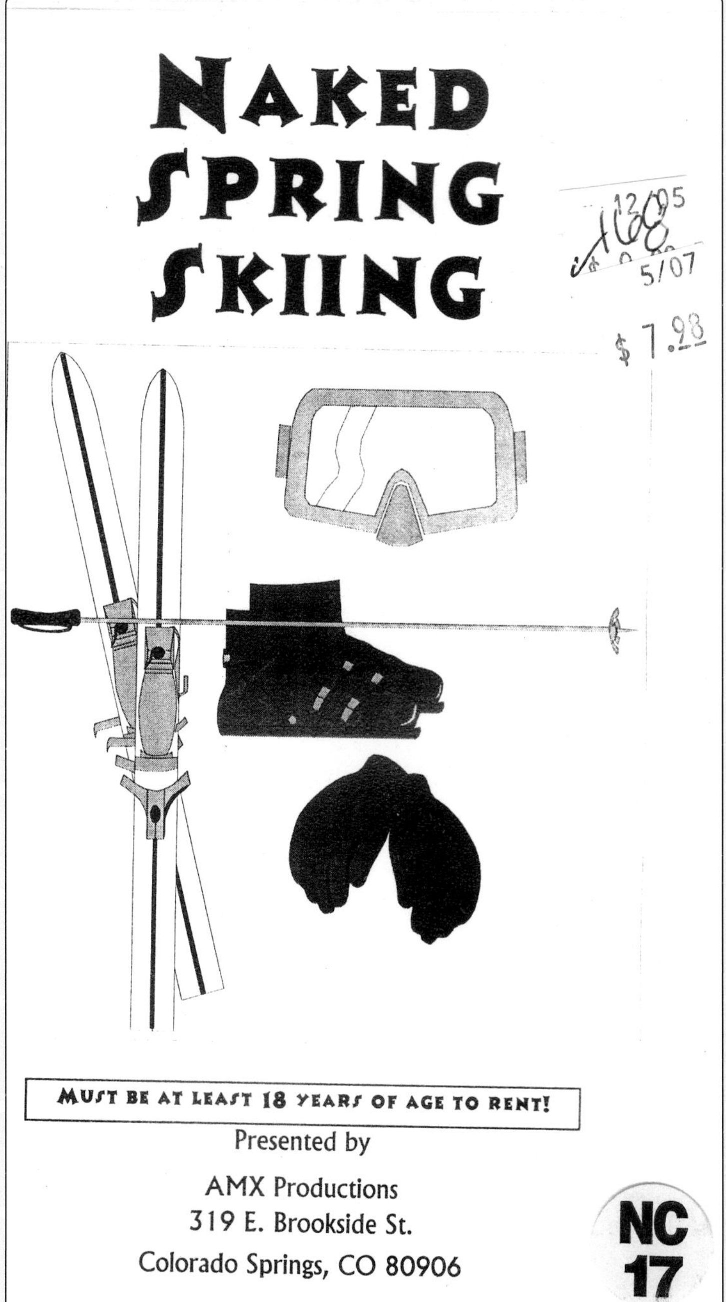
NAKED
SPRING
SKIING
12/05
5/07
$ 7.98
MUST BE AT LEAST 18 YEARS OF AGE TO RENT!
Presented by
AMX Productions
319 E. Brookside St.
Colorado Springs, CO 80906
NC
17

This video contains some of the most erotic clip art you'll ever see.

AN ORBIT COMEDY CLASSIC

"OUTRAGEOUS"

- *Ben Dover*

BUCK NAKED

LINE DANCING

MT

MT stands for mature. Make no mistake, Buck Naked Line Dancing is for mature audiences only.

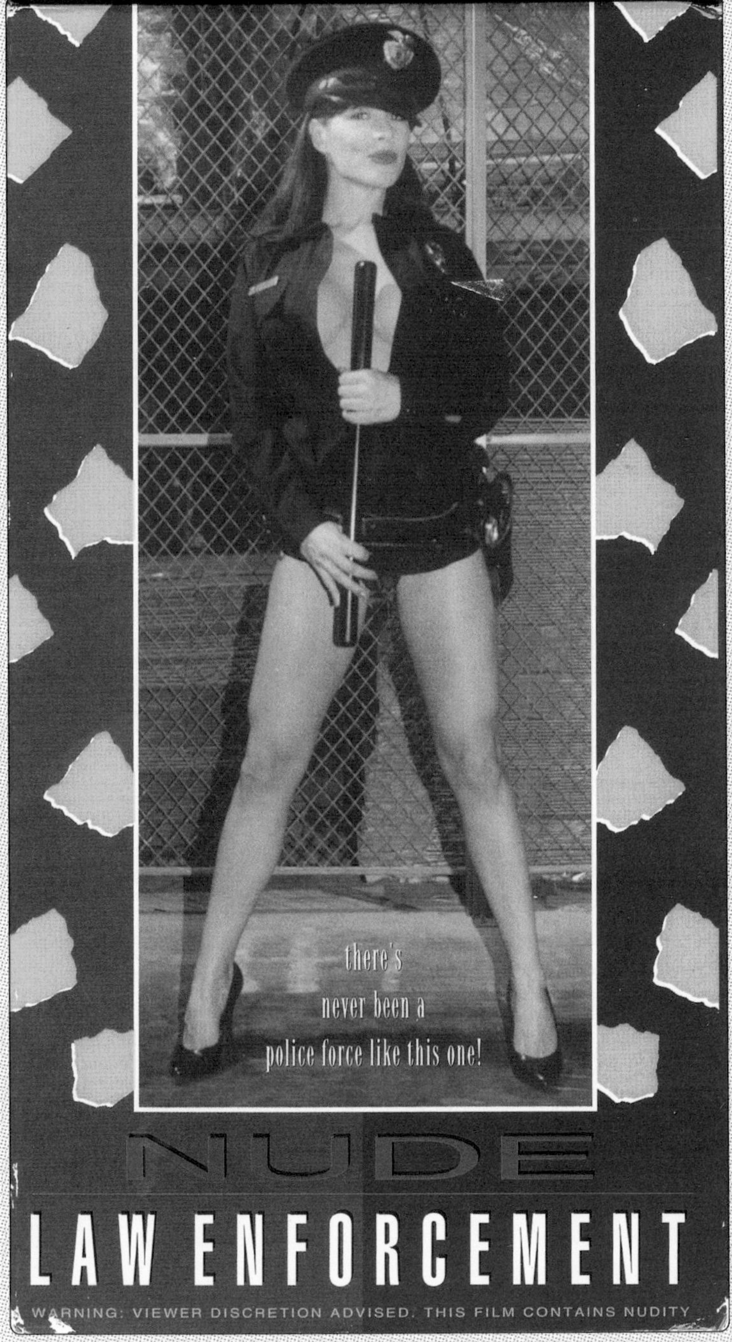
there's
never been a
police force like this one!
NUDE
LAW ENFORCEMENT
WARNING: VIEWER DISCRETION ADVISED. THIS FILM CONTAINS NUDITY

She fills out paperwork sexier than anyone on the force.

NUDE HOUSE WIVES OF AMERICA

TZ VIDEO PRESENTS "NUDE HOUSEWIVES OF AMERICA"
PRODUCED AND DIRECTED BY BOB SCOTT MUSIC BY BOB SCOTT
CINEMATOGRAPHY BY BILL EXECUTIVE PRODUCER U.C.C.C
SP STANDARD PLAY
WARNING: Viewer discretion advised. This film contains nudity and sexual situations.

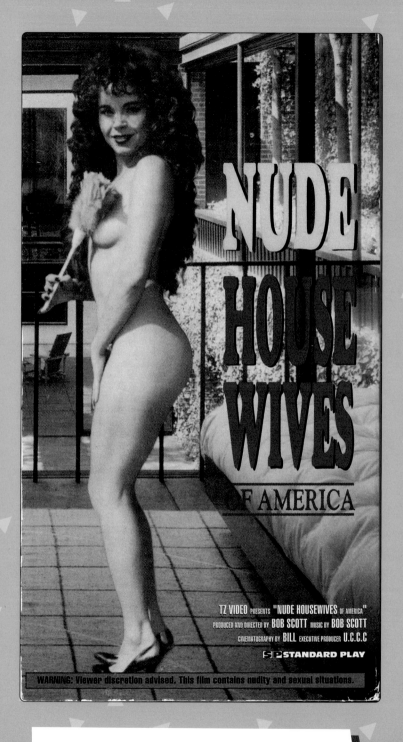

The NHA unionized shortly after the release of this video.

Do The
MACARENA
TOTALLY NUDE!
SIX BEAUTIFUL WOMEN SHOW YOU THE MOVES TO ITS ORIGINAL SOUND TRACK!

Timeless.

BOB KLEIN'S GREATEST HITS

If ever there was a man deserving of his own chapter in a book of VHS covers, it's Bob Klein. A tai-chi and kung fu master since 1975, Bob has released over 60 instructional videos, each one with a greater cover than the last. We love his eye for composition, we love his hair, and we love the fact that he's not afraid to be his own cover model. Plus, he's the only mystical martial arts master we know of named Bob Klein.

SHAOLIN SABRE (Mayflower Form)

太極拳功夫

太極拳功夫

with MASTER, BOB KLEIN
INSTRUCTIONAL

Bob Klein is so loyal, he'll defend the honor of his own drapes.

T'AI-CHI-CH'UAN
CHINESE MOVING MEDITATION

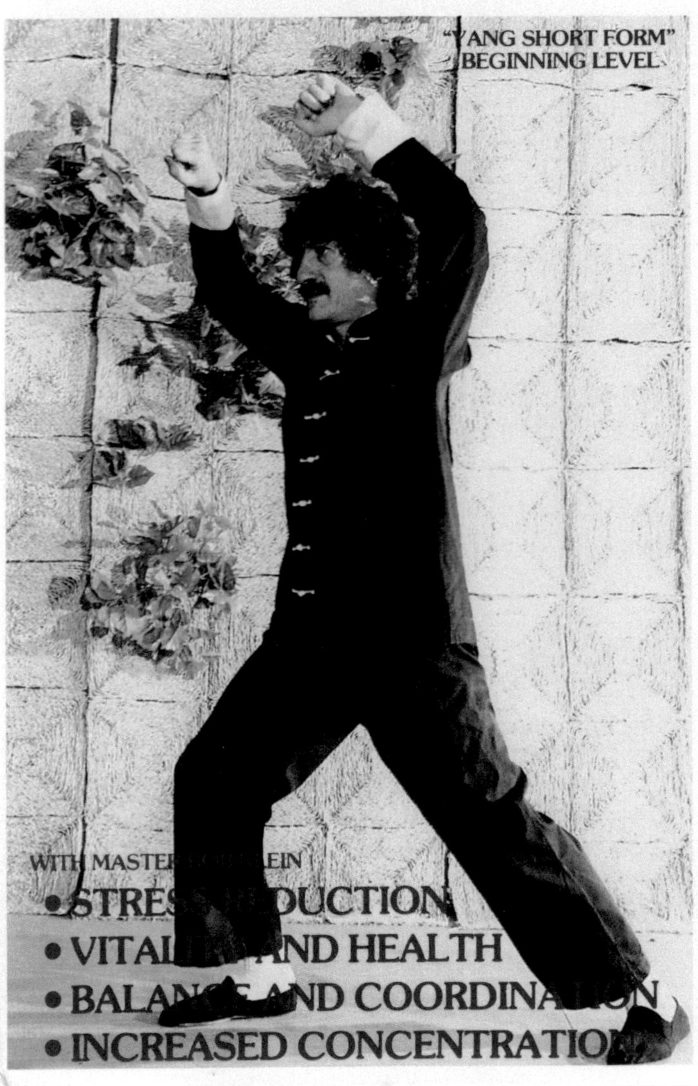
SHORT FORM”
BEGINNING LEVEL
• VITAL
ND HEALTH
• BAL
ND COORDINA
• INCREASED CONCENTRATIO

This is the pose Bob Klein makes just before he launches into flight.

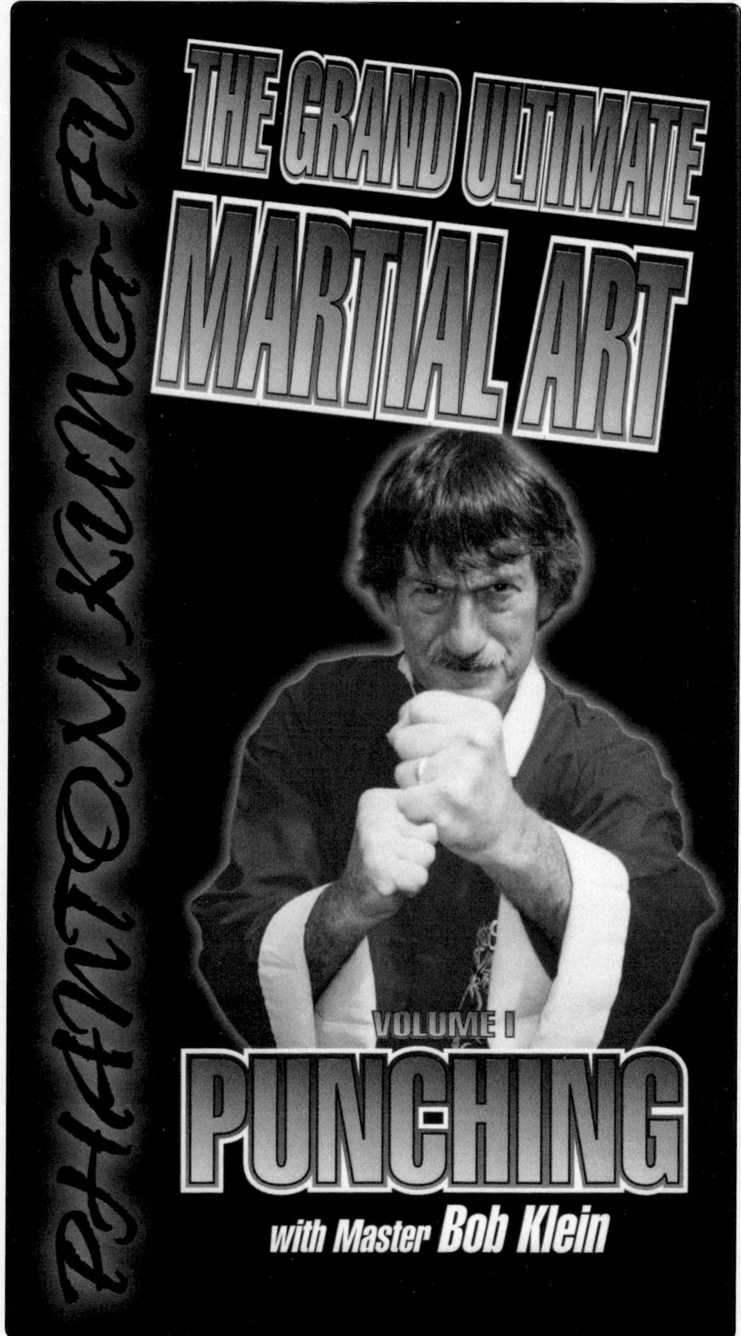
PHANTOM KUNG-FU
THE GRAND ULTIMATE
MARTIAL ART
VOLUME I
PUNCHING
with Master Bob Klein

If you haven't been punched by Bob Klein, you should seriously try it. It's like getting a sneak peek at death.

CHINESE
KICKBOXING

Artistic Video

VOLUME 1

太極拳功夫
太極拳功夫

• PUNCHING - KICKING - GRAPPLING AND GROUND FIGHTING

• ACTUAL CLASSROOM INSTRUCTION STEP BY STEP

with Master, Bob Klein

The last thing you want to stumble across while walking in the woods is a wild Bob Klein.

HOW TO SPAR AGAINST KARATE

HOW TO SPAR AGAINST TAE-KWON-DO

Bob Klein was the inventor of cockpunching. There's a statue on Long Island to commemorate it.

217

The benefits of Tai-chi and Yoga from a seated position.
CHAIR EXERCISES for seniors
With
The benefits of Tai-chi and Yoga from a seated position.
MORE CHAIR EXERCISES for seniors
With Tai-chi Master Bob Klein

The benefits of Tai-chi and Yoga from a seated position
CHAIR EXERCISES for FLEXIBILITY and STRENGTH

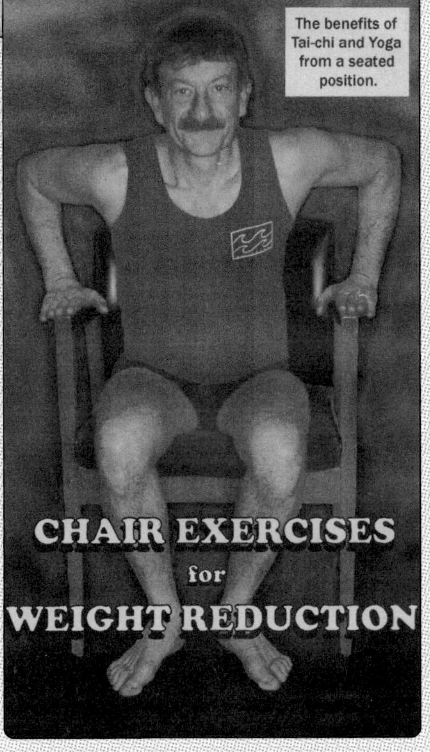
The benefits of Tai-chi and Yoga from a seated position.
CHAIR EXERCISES for WEIGHT REDUCTION

After a long day of kicking ass, Bob likes to take a load off and kick ass from his garden chair.

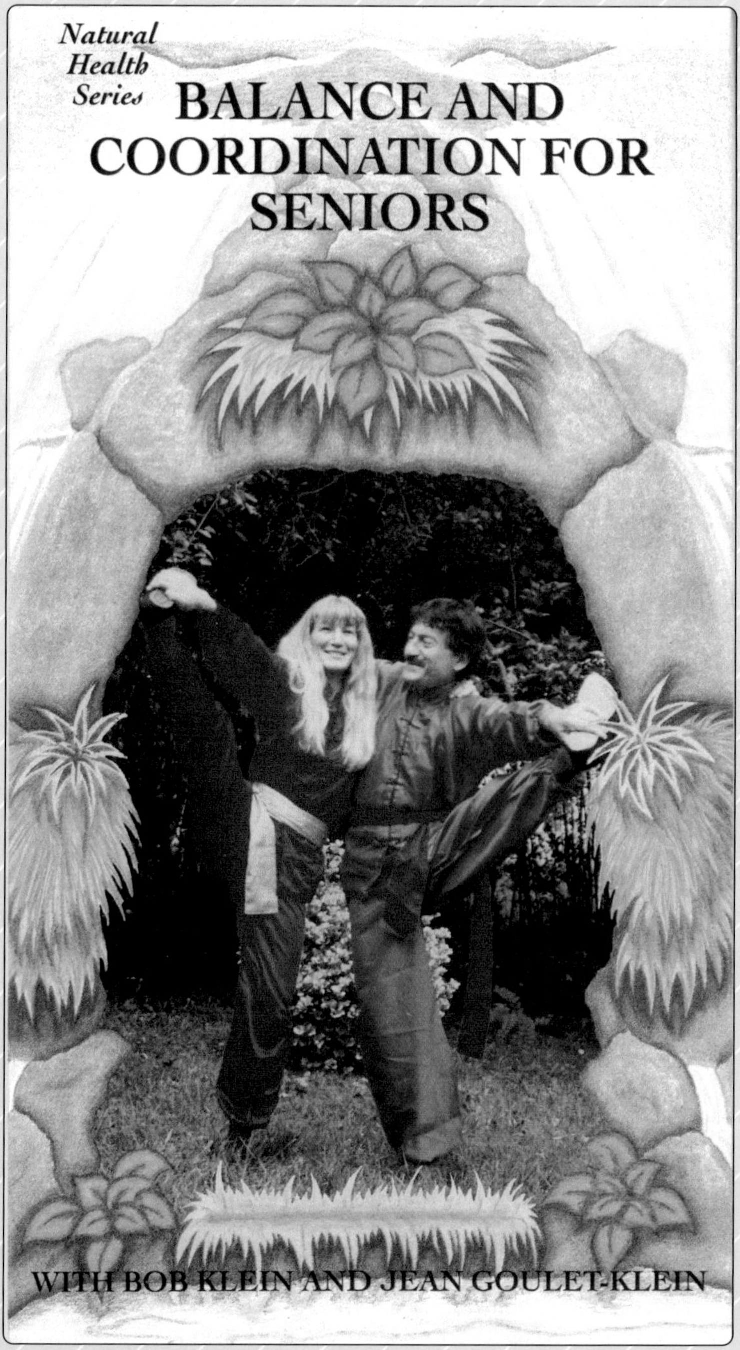

Natural Health Series

BALANCE AND COORDINATION FOR SENIORS

WITH BOB KLEIN AND JEAN GOULET-KLEIN

Bob knows that old people probably can't do this, but anything is possible inside the cartoon cave.

The
LAUGHING DRAGON
Exercises
For Seniors
With BOB KLEIN
Age Reversal Exercises

Bob Klein's age reversal technique works so well that he actually just celebrated his 15th birthday.

SELF DEFENSE
with
PRESSURE POINTS

with Master Robert Lyons

When you get your face caved in by Bob Klein, you feel around to find him afterward just so you can shake his hand.

PRACTICAL
SELF DEFENSE
With T'ai-chi-Ch'uan Master BOB KLEIN
HOW ORDINARY PEOPLE CAN PROTECT THEMSELVES AGAINST STRONGER ATTACKERS

We don't know what this little girl did to piss off Bob Klein, but she deserves whatever is coming to her.

CATFISH MAGIC

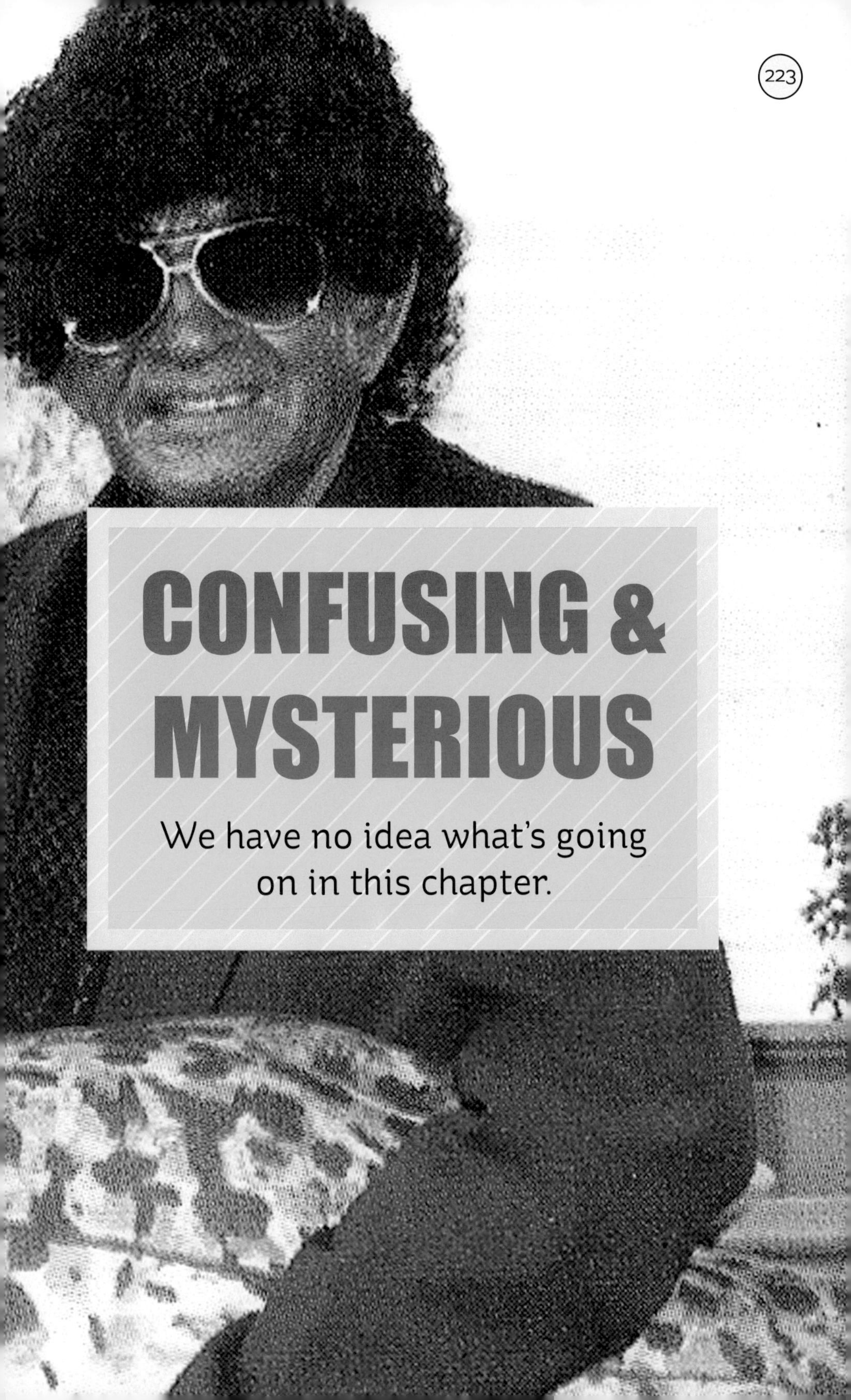

CONFUSING & MYSTERIOUS

We have no idea what's going on in this chapter.

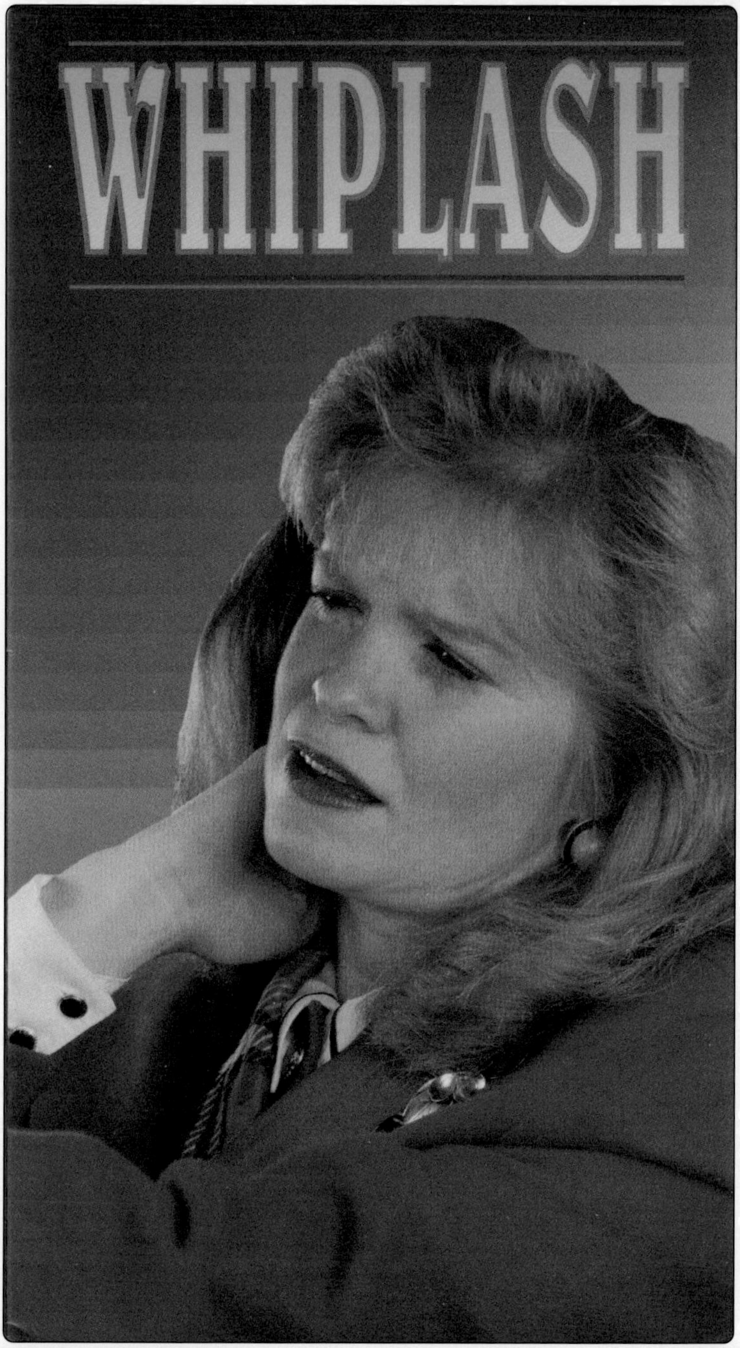

WHIPLASH

Now she's going to be late for her shift at Talbots.

MYSTERIOUS
DOINGS
339
COLOR
VHS

We don't approve of the way this cover depicts vegetable stereotypes.

Catfishin'

with

"The Phone Prankster"

Willie P. Richardson

and "Uncle Rassie" Richardson

WILLIE P. RICHARDSON'S
CATFISH MAGIC!™

CHEESE DOUGH BAIT

Catch 'em!
Clean 'em!
Cook 'em!
Eat 'em!

Most confusing ten bucks we ever spent.

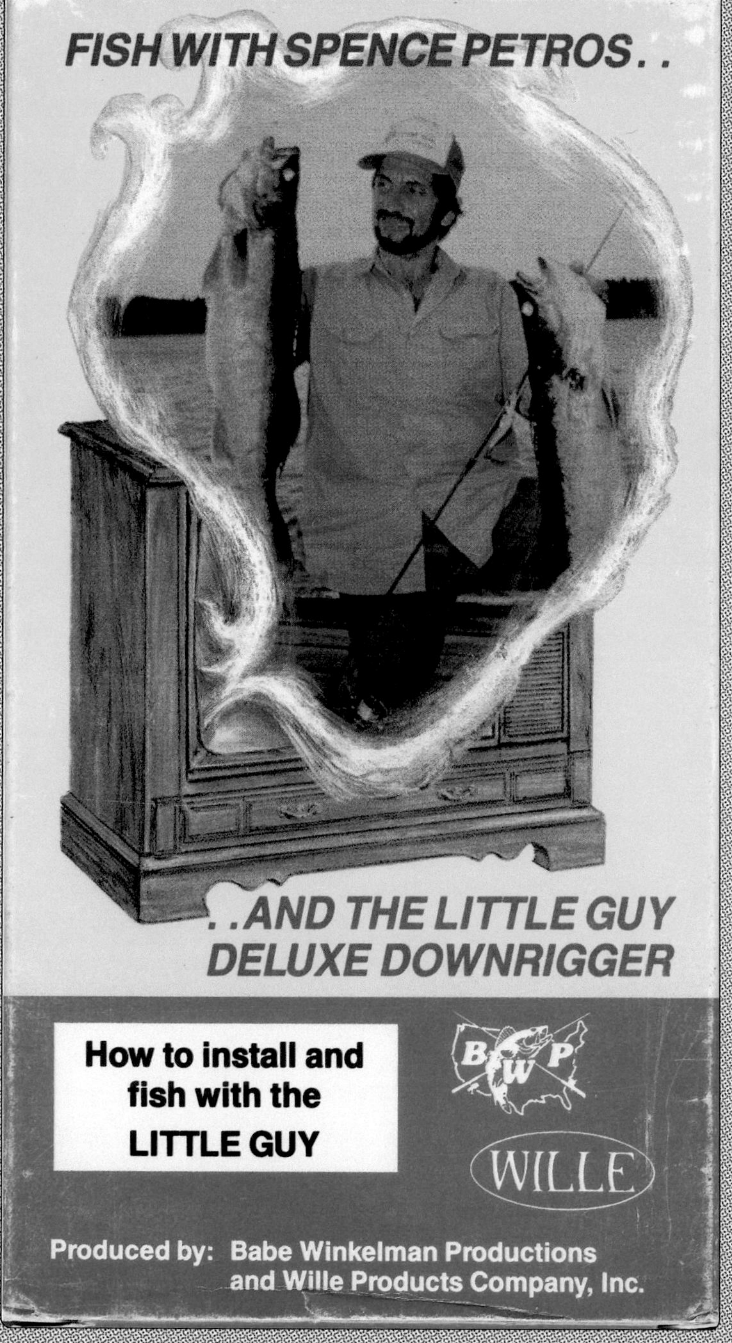
FISH WITH SPENCE PETROS. .
. .AND THE LITTLE GUY
DELUXE DOWNRIGGER
How to install and
fish with the
LITTLE GUY
B W P
WILLE
Produced by: Babe Winkelman Productions
and Wille Products Company, Inc.

Looks like that TV is having a Spence Petros–related nightmare.

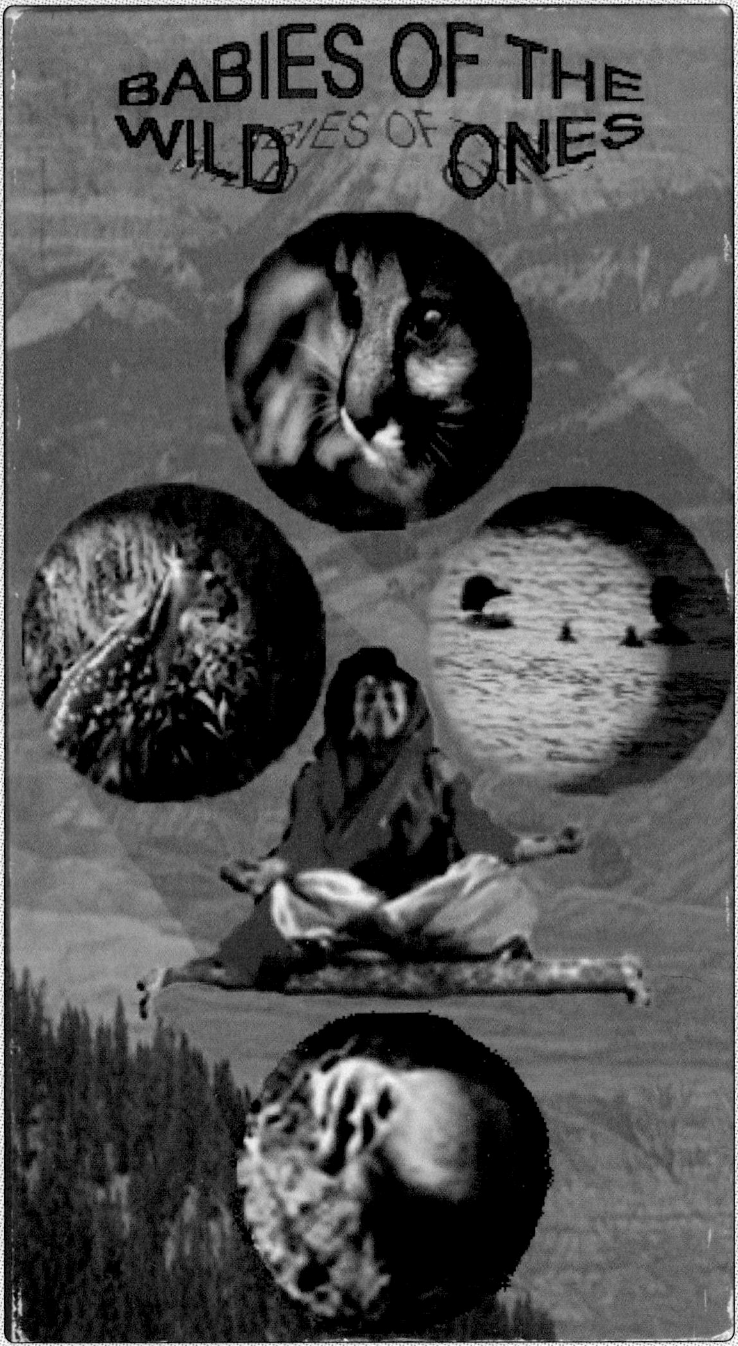

BABIES OF THE WILD ONES

Wildlife documentary or transcendental meditation tape? We're on board either way.

Marriage Insights™ Series
"Marriage in the Ring"
DIVORCE MANIA
Marriage Insights™
P.O. Box 4900
Akron OH 44310

Ah, the lighter side of divorce.

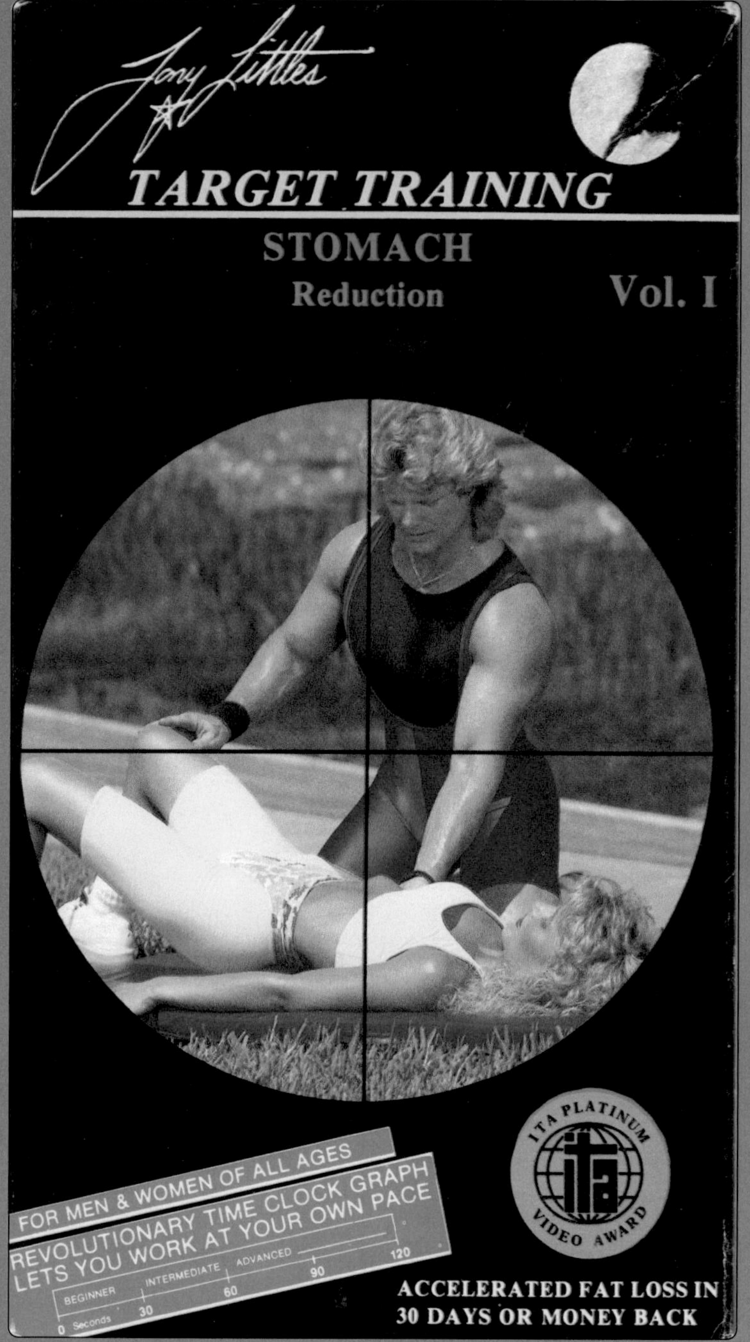
Tony Little's
TARGET TRAINING
STOMACH
Reduction
Vol. I
ITA PLATINUM
VIDEO AWARD
FOR MEN & WOMEN OF ALL AGES
REVOLUTIONARY TIME CLOCK GRAPH
LETS YOU WORK AT YOUR OWN PACE
BEGINNER
INTERMEDIATE
ADVANCED
0 Seconds
30
60
90
120
ACCELERATED FAT LOSS IN
30 DAYS OR MONEY BACK

Cover photo by Tony Little's assassin.

Sports Galaxy

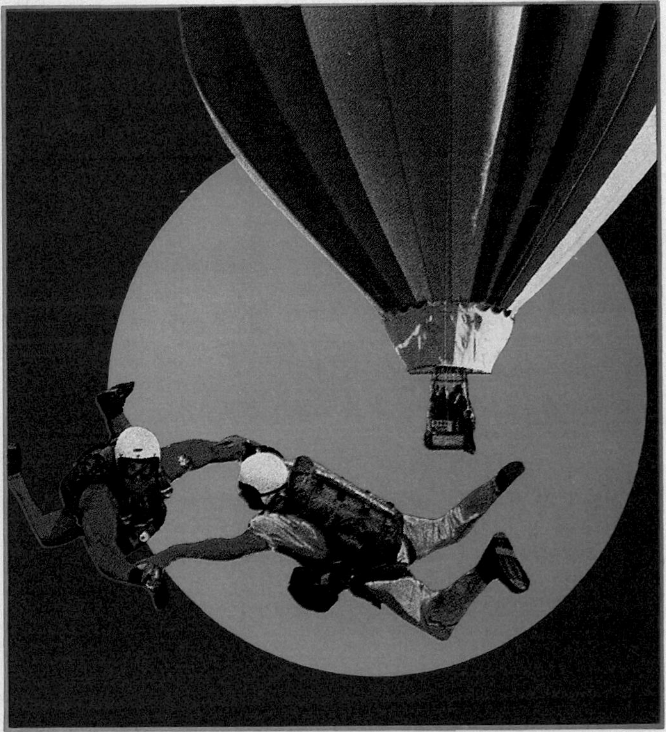

AN OUT-OF-THIS-WORLD
AERIAL SPORTS
SPECTACULAR!

OMEGA
Entertainment

In the Sports Galaxy, parachuters and hot-air ballooners live together in perfect harmony.

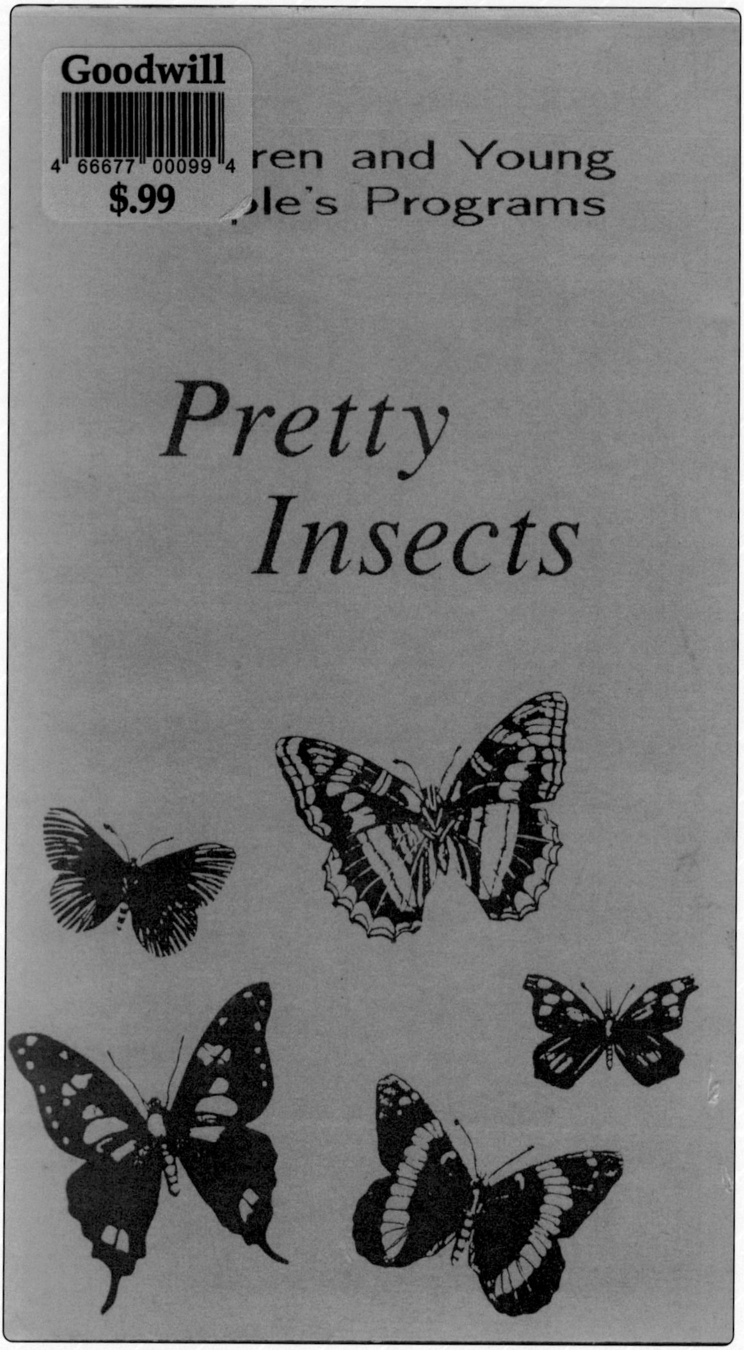

Goodwill

4 66677 00099 4

$.99

ren and Young

ple's Programs

Pretty Insects

This is a great post-lobotomy video.

LESS STRESS
IN 5
EASY STEPS
• Self Monitoring
• "Ventilation" Techniques
• Relaxation Exercises/Music Video
• Challenge & Creative Skills
• Self Appreciation
(WITH MUSIC VIDEO MEDITATION)
At last! A healthy, happy way
to get relief from everyday stress.
It's a natural.
Featuring
Ed Asner
AWARD WINNER
John Muir Medical Film Festival 1986

Why is Ed Asner an authority on stress again?

GRUPO
NICHE
94
VHS

* DUELE MAS
* LA GALLINITA DE LOS HUEVOS DE ORO
* LOS TRES SON CARIBE
* LA NEGRA NO QUIERE
* UNA AVENTURA
* HAGAMOS LO QUE DIGA EL CORAZON
* DROGA

"Grupo Niche" means
"little boy peeing" in Spanish.

As seen on
TV NEWS!
ULTRAVISION
INTERNATIONAL LIMITED
NO 2
VISION X
Just when you thought you'd seen everything...
With Guest Star TINA SMALL
SPECIAL PLATINUM EDITION
BRITISH
MADE
New Formula! Improved Quality!
Collector's Item Issue
18
COLOUR 1 HOUR STEREO HI-FI

As seen on TV news? We demand to know which TV news station aired this.

GRAPHIC DESIGN ATROCITIES

When you're working on a limited budget, the cover of your VHS tape is often an afterthought. That can be the only possible explanation for these bad, boring and just plain nauseating covers that, despite their total disregard for common decency, at least accurately warn you of what you're about to see on the tape.

HOW TO AVOID A BOZO

Jackie Kendall

Just because you can illustrate your cover on a computer doesn't mean you should.

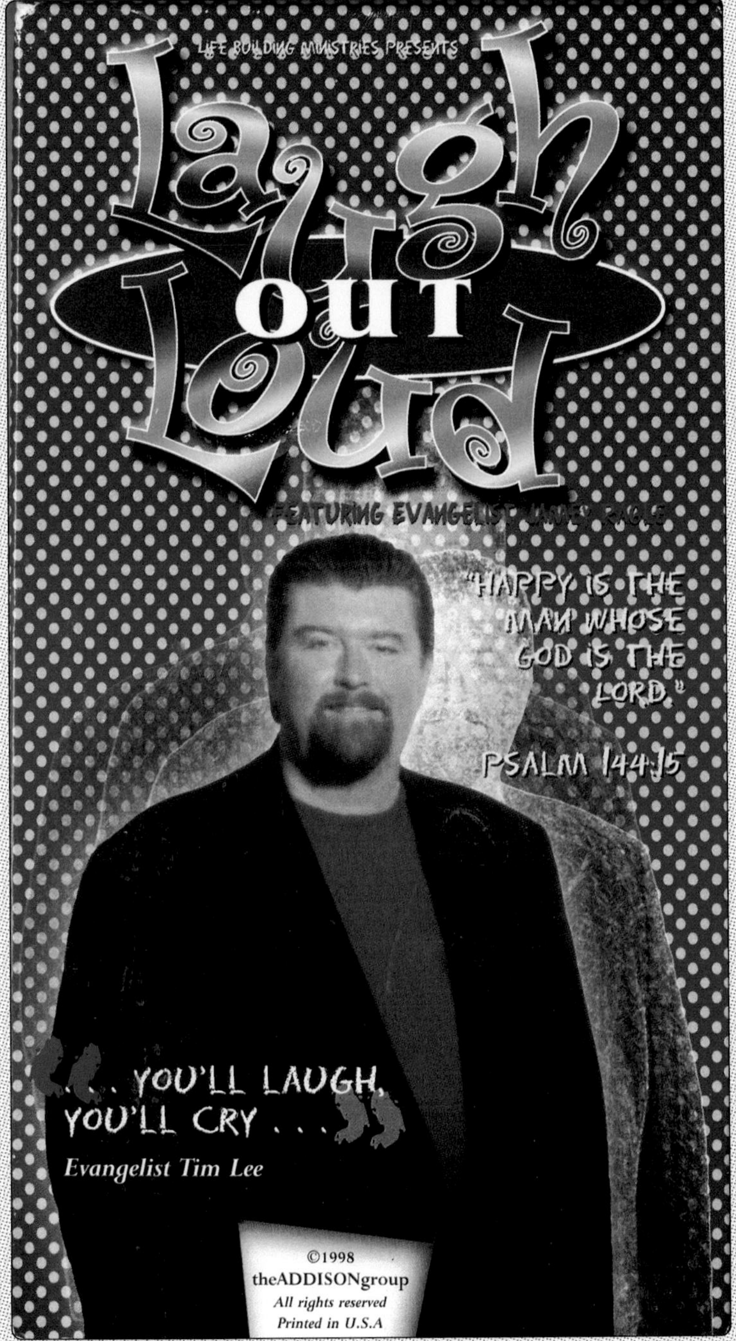
LIFE BUILDING MINISTRIES PRESENTS
Laugh OUT Loud
FEATURING EVANGELIST
"HAPPY IS THE MAN WHOSE GOD IS THE LORD."
PSALM 144:15
". . . YOU'LL LAUGH, YOU'LL CRY . . ."
Evangelist Tim Lee
©1998
theADDISONgroup
All rights reserved
Printed in U.S.A

This cover may cause seizures.

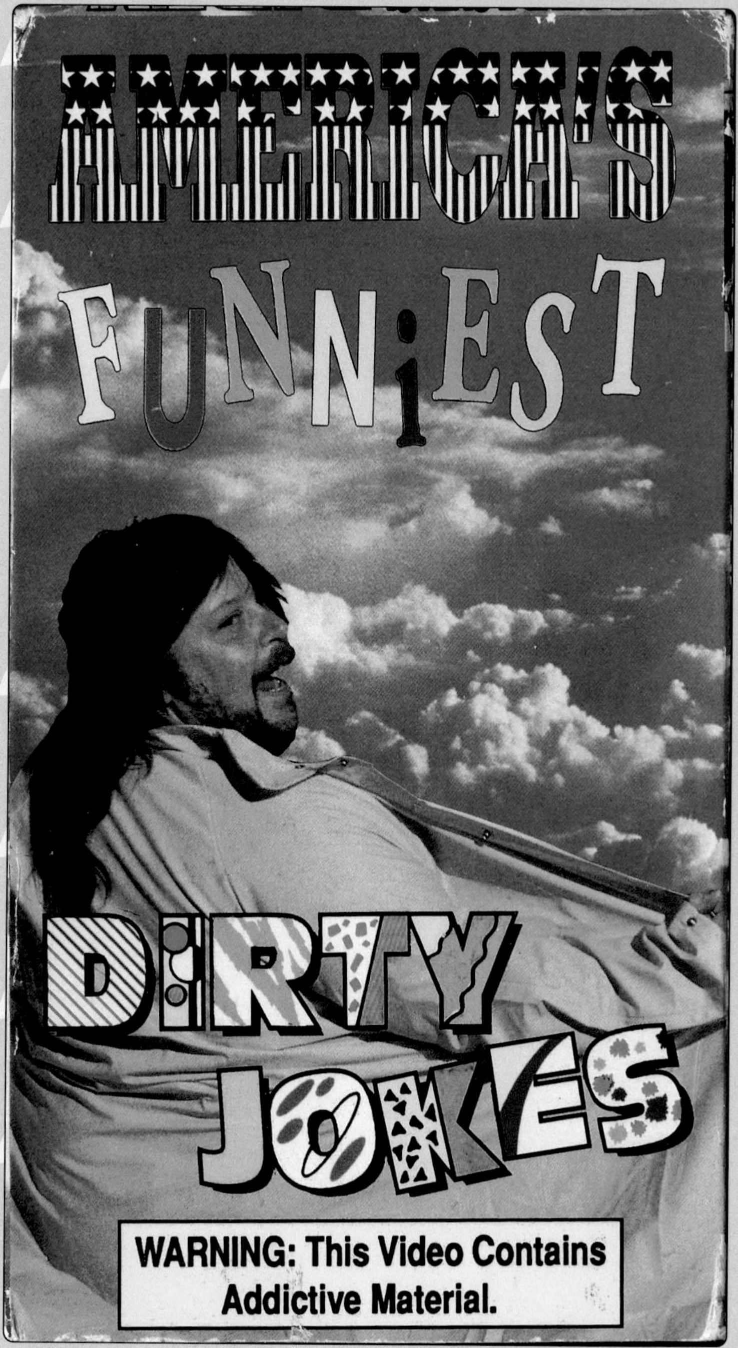

AMERICA'S FUNNIEST DIRTY JOKES

WARNING: This Video Contains Addictive Material.

WARNING: This cover will make you stupider if you look at it for too long.

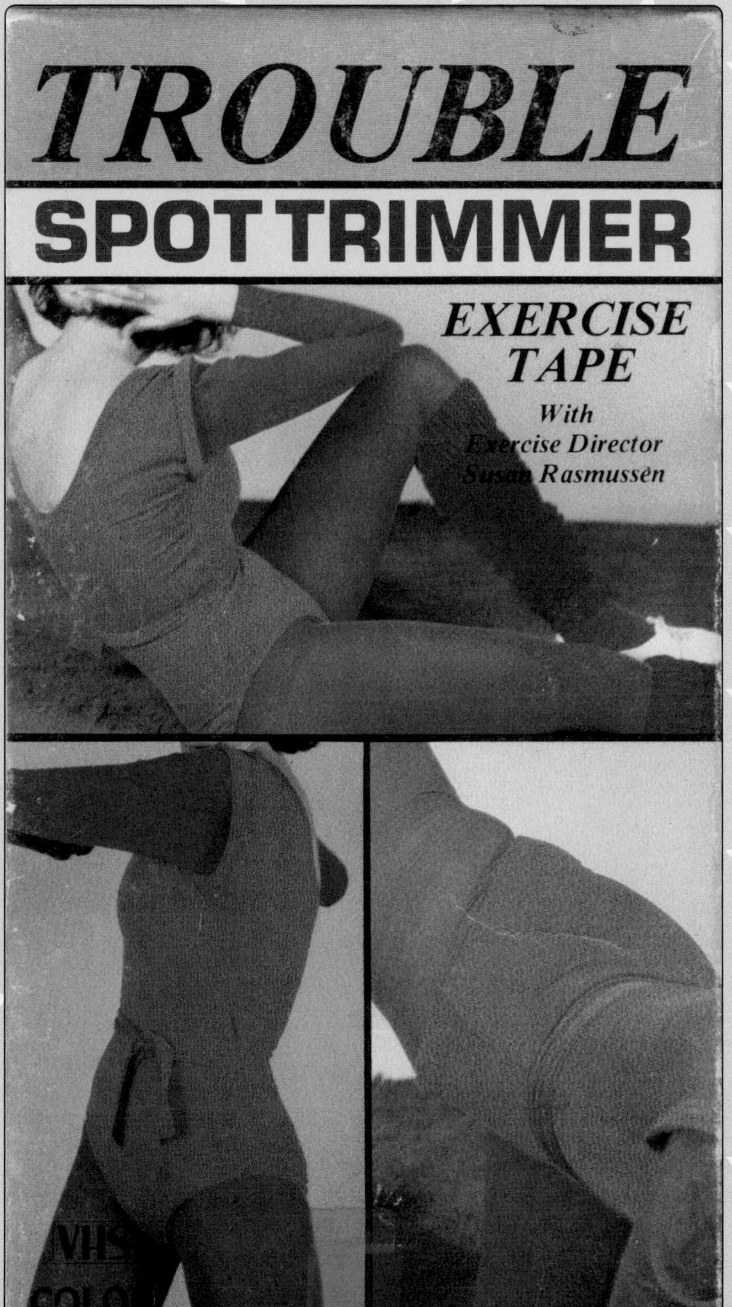
TROUBLE
SPOT TRIMMER
EXERCISE
TAPE
With
Exercise Director
Susan Rasmussen
VHS
COLOR

Get the disembodied torso you've always dreamed of.

WINNING

Slot Secrets

Now You Have A Fighting Chance

As the sun set slowly behind the slot machine,
we finally knew we had a fighting chance.

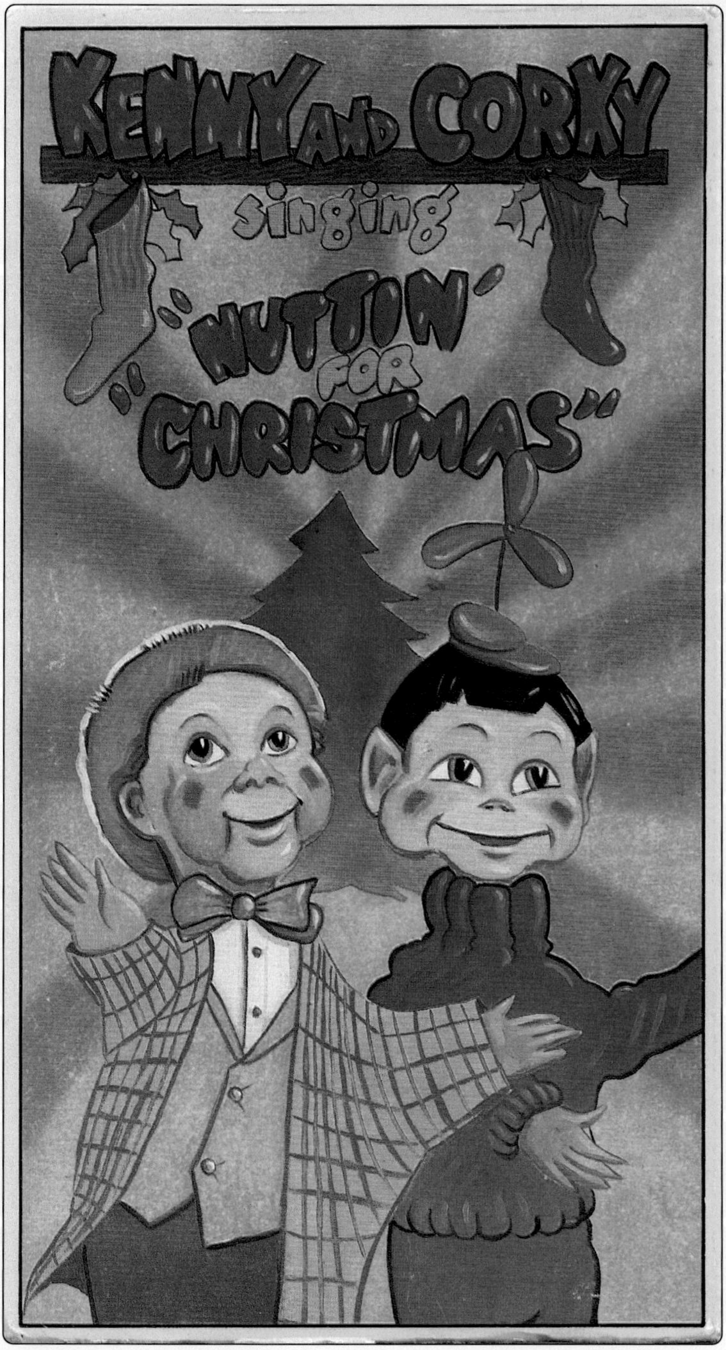

KENNY AND CORKY
singing
"NUTTIN FOR CHRISTMAS"

We've had nuttin' but nightmares ever since finding this video.

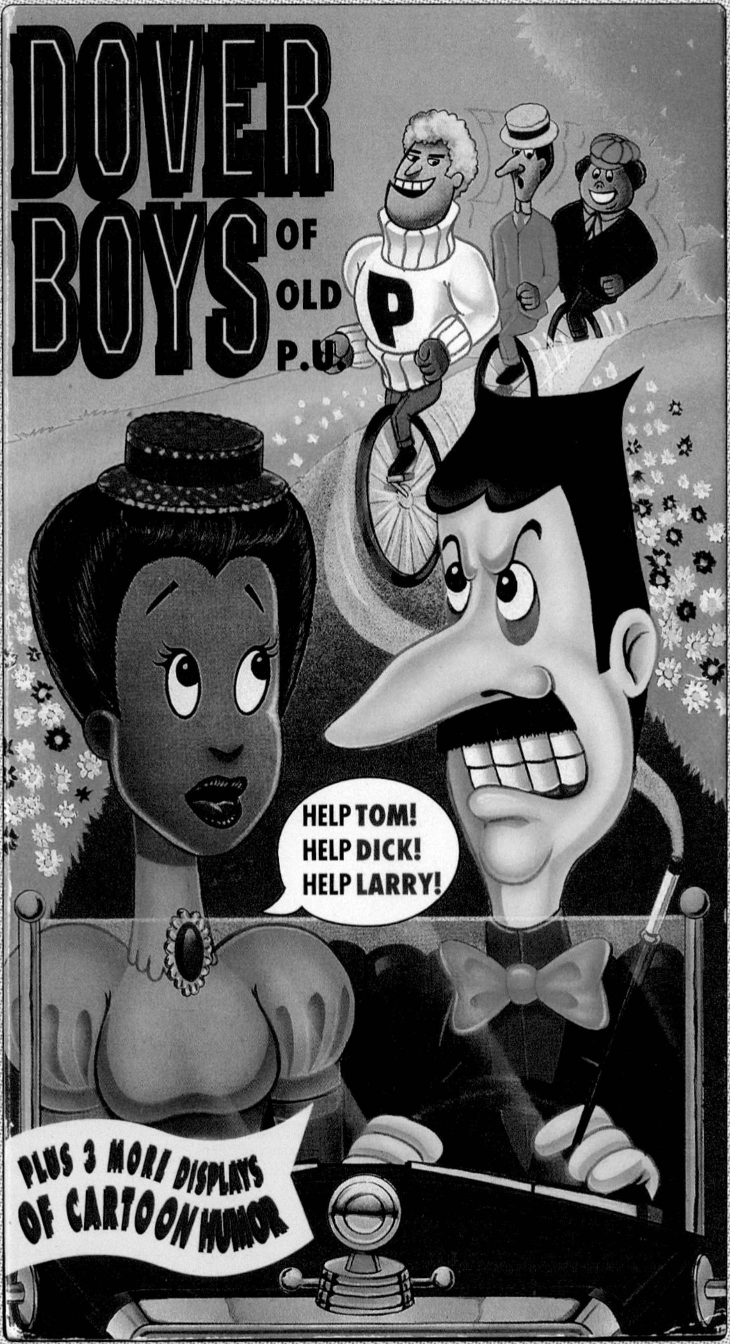

DOVER BOYS OF OLD P.U.

HELP TOM!
HELP DICK!
HELP LARRY!

PLUS 3 MORE DISPLAYS OF CARTOON HUMOR

Kids just love displays of cartoon humor.

MIGHTY SANITATION MACHINES

Kid Wise

No cover has ever waved at us this much.

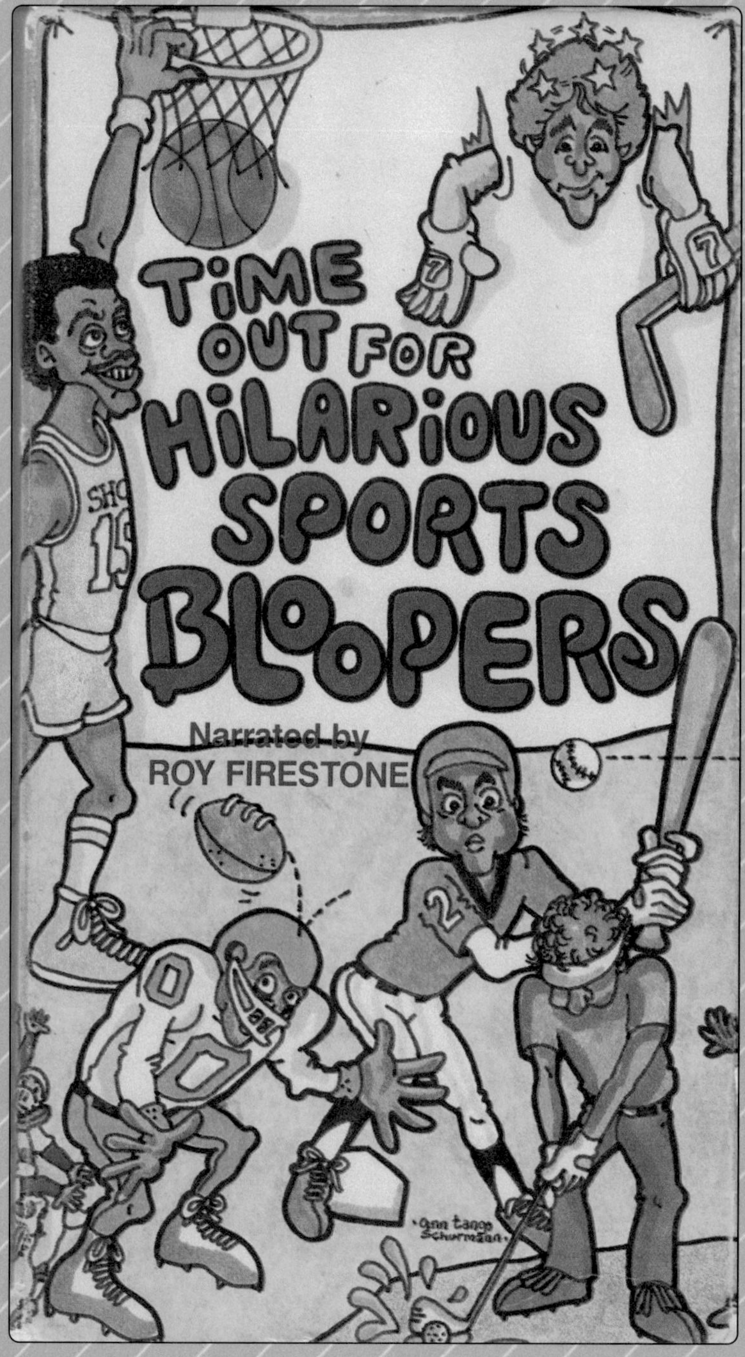
TiME OUT FOR HiLARiOUS SPORTS BLOOPERS
Narrated by
ROY FIRESTONE

If this video is half as funny as the cover, it won't be very funny at all.

SPORTS

SERIES

WATERSKIING FUN-DAMENTALS

Experience the thrills... Avoid the spills...
Experts show you how!

VHS

MORRIS VIDEO

We bet this clip art was titled, "handsome slalomer."

Ernie Rettino &
Debby Kerner Rettino
PRESENT
PSALTY'S
FUNTASTIC!
PRAISE PARTY!

Would it have killed them to anthropomorphize the balloons and confetti?

SMARKUS
AND COMPANY
IT'S... EDUCATIONAL! FUN! EXCITING!
FOR KIDS OF ALL AGES!
MINDY O'TOOLE • AMON RAPPAPORT • CORINA BENJAT
TROY ECKERT • MARK MENDONCO • TANNA THOMPSON
KELLY ANDERSON • AND R.D. GANZERT AS THE NASA GUARD
FEATURING THE VOICES OF RON HALL AS SMARKUS, GLITCH AND COMPUTER
SHANNON ORRICK AS PURGOYLE AND DOZIT
CREATED AND DIRECTED BY SASHA FERRER
WRITTEN BY RICHARD BEBAN AND JUDITH NIELSEN

"Bow before Smarkus, my children!"

VHS COVER HALL OF FAME

Every once in a great while, you come across a video that stops you in your tracks and makes you remember what it means to be alive. A video that slaps you across the face and demands to be noticed. A video so breathtakingly perfect that it blinds you with its beauty. In this chapter, we honor these esteemed tapes by inducting them into the VHS Cover Hall of Fame.

CHARLOTTE DIAMOND

10 Crunchy Carrots

Graphic designer to Charlotte Diamond:
"What about an orange drop shadow?"

Charlotte Diamond: (with a mouthful of carrot) "I love it!"

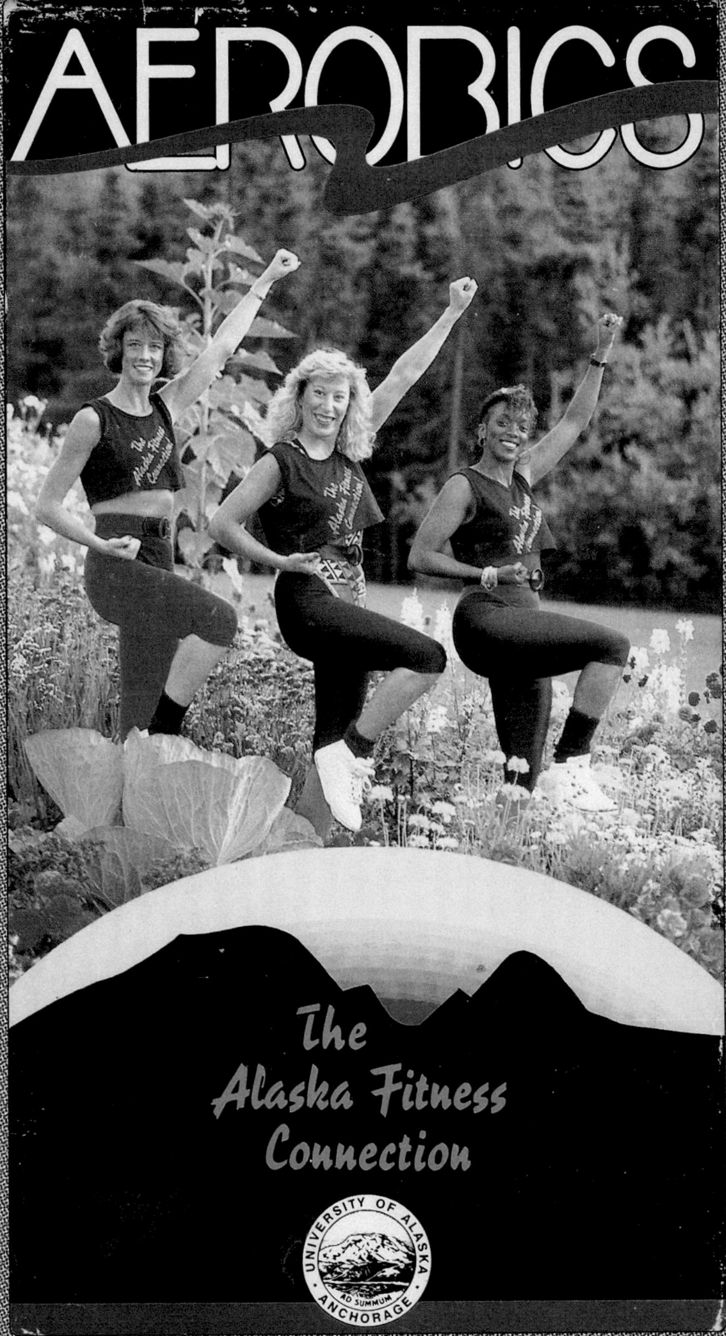
AEROBICS
The Alaska Fitness Connection
UNIVERSITY OF ALASKA
AD SUMMUM
ANCHORAGE

Containing all the latest flower trampling exercises for 1989!

Amaze your friends and family!

"Garbage Can Turkey"™

Cook a 12 to 14 lb Turkey in 1 hour

LEARN HOW IN JUST 8 MINUTES!

Storing trash *and* cooking meat? What can't a garbage can do?

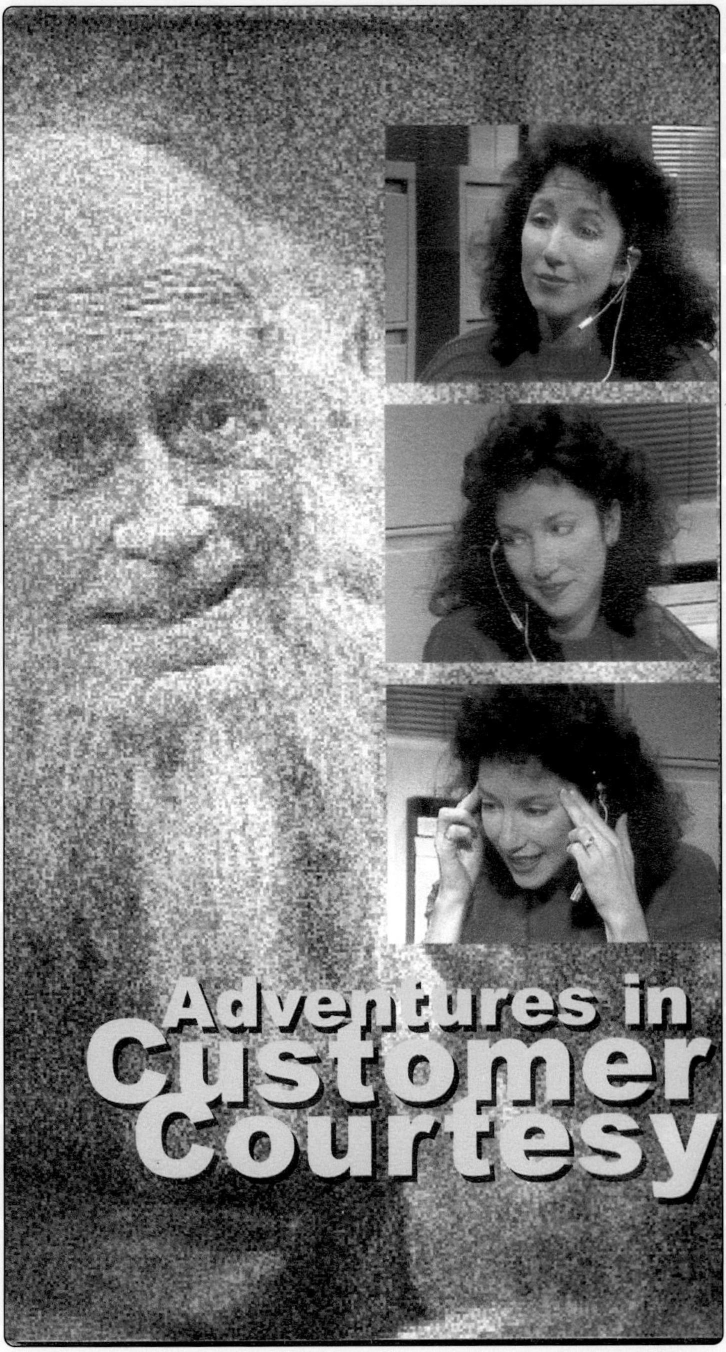

Adventures in
Customer
Courtesy

Customer courtesy is especially difficult when you're being menaced by an elderly leprechaun.

MEET A
REAL GIANTESS...
7'7¼" TALL

SANDY ALLEN
The World's Tallest Woman

"It's OK To Be Different"

"It's OK To Be Different!"

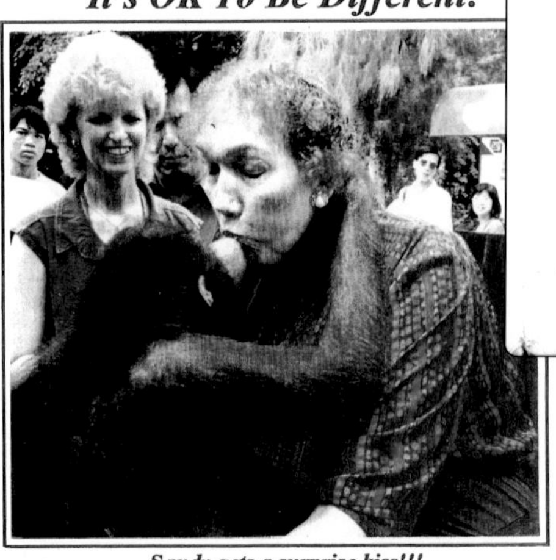

Sandy gets a surprise kiss!!!

Meet Sandy Allen...*The World's Tallest Living Woman* as she visits with kids and adults on her *"I'm Big On Books...You Can Be Too!"* tour to libraries and schools across the country. Why is she so tall? Was growing up fun? What's it like being different? Sandy answers these questions and more! See why Sandy is truly the world's tallest *"Gentle Giantess"* as she shares with you the humor and challenges of her life experiences...and that ***"It's OK To Be Different!"***

Produced by John Kleiman and Kelly Hocker
Approximate Running Time: 25 Minutes Color/VHS
Copyright 1995 John Kleiman and Kelly Hocker, All Rights Reserved
Chart Breaker Video P.O. Box 29142 Indianapolis, Indiana 46229
F.B.I. Warning! Federal Law provides severe civil and criminal penalties for the unauthorized reproduction, distribution or exhibition of copyrighted video tapes. Criminal copyright infringement is investigated by the F.B.I. and may constitute a felony with a penalty of five years in prison and/or a $250,000 fine. This video is for private home exhibition only. Any public performance is strictly prohibited.

CBV 9502

She was the world's tallest living woman. He was a frisky orangutan. Their love knew no bounds.

CHINESE YOGA

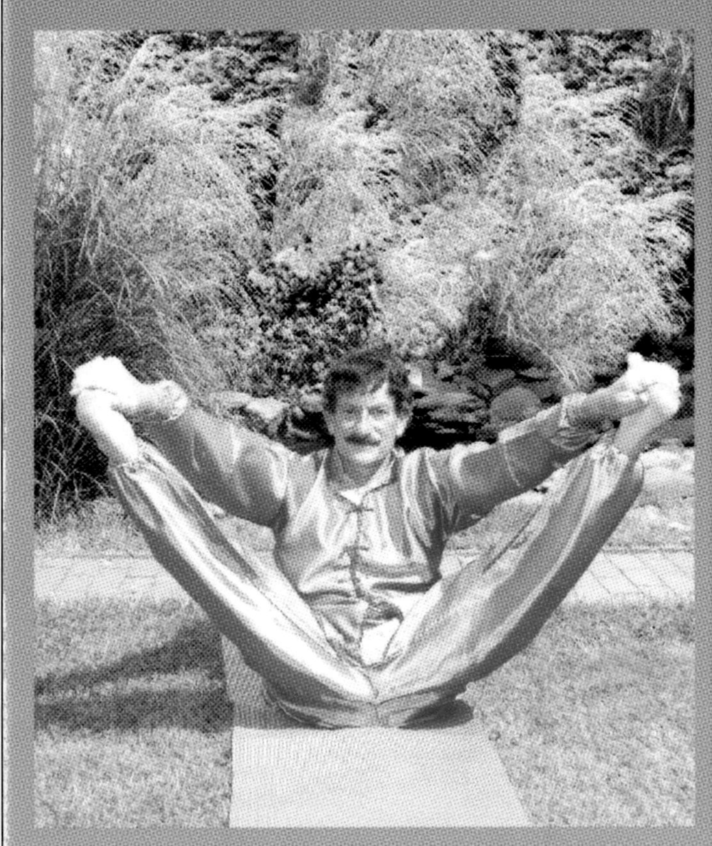

with Bob Klein

When Bob Klein does this,
it means he likes you.

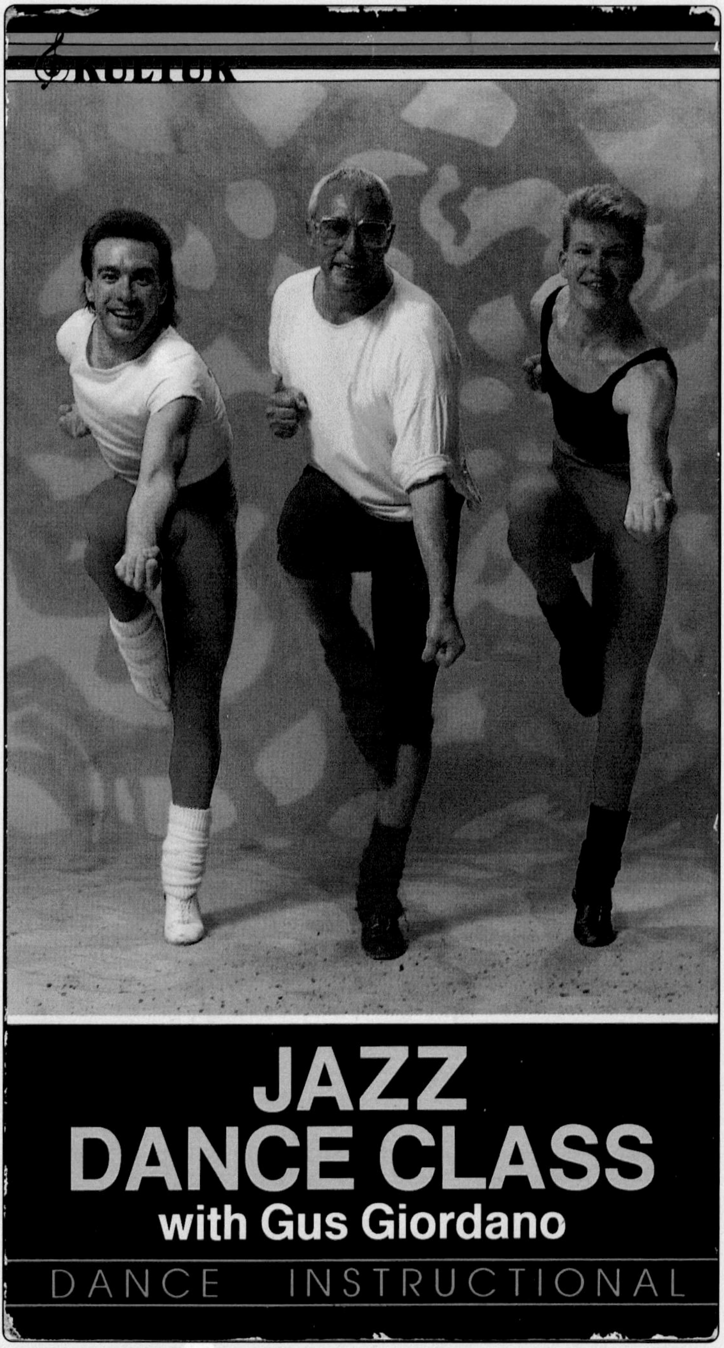

KULTUR

JAZZ
DANCE CLASS
with Gus Giordano

DANCE INSTRUCTIONAL

Coming out is never easy, but it's a little easier when you can just hand your parents this tape and say, "Yeah."

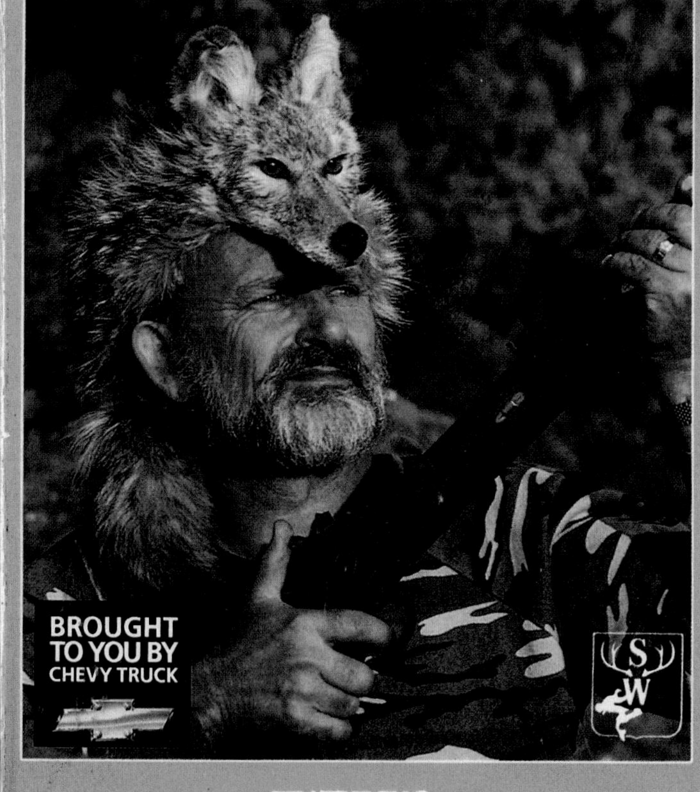
Introduction To
MUZZLE
LOADING
BROUGHT
TO YOU BY
CHEVY TRUCK
S
W
FEATURING:
DICK GASAWAY & JAY WARBURTON
Sportsman's Workshop Video Library

This coyote is wearing a very convincing middle-aged man costume.

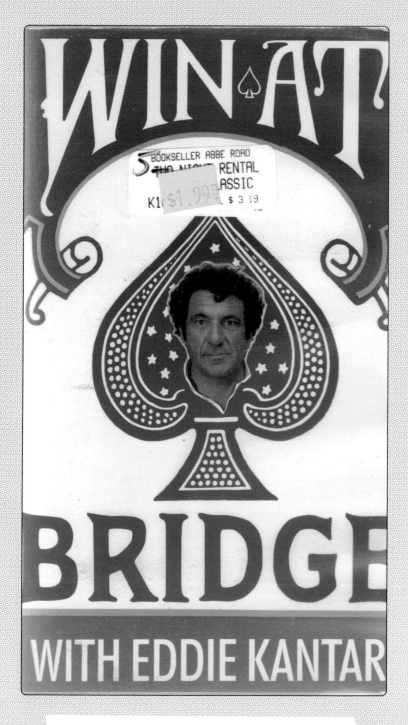

We had this one framed and hung above the mantel.

ACKNOWLEDGMENTS

First and foremost, we would like to thank Alex Pickett, who worked tirelessly on this book for little to no reward, partly because he's Joe's younger brother but mostly because that's the type of guy he is. Thanks also to Robert Austin, Mark Breese, Jacy Catlin, Greg DeLiso, Gary Lachance, Chris Pauls, Davy Rothbart, Glenn Severance and the other Found Footage Festival supporters who graciously donated their videos and talents to this project. Finally, thanks to William Clark and Jennifer Kasius for their professional guidance to a couple of unprofessionals.

MEET THE AUTHORS

Joe Pickett and Nick Prueher met in sixth grade and quickly bonded over their mutual appreciation for things that were so bad they were good. Since then, they have written for *The Onion* and *Entertainment Weekly* and directed the award-winning documentary, *Dirty Country*. While not sorting through dusty bargain bins for videos, Pickett directs short films and music videos. Prueher worked as the Head Researcher at the *Late Show with David Letterman* and, later, at *The Colbert Report*. In 2004, Pickett and Prueher founded the Found Footage Festival, which currently plays over 100 shows a year. Both men are yellow belts in karate.

CREDITS

(in order of appearance)

Body Break courtesy of Hal Johnson.

Silver Foxes II courtesy of David Krieff, Destiny Productions, LLC.

The Bottoms Up Workout courtesy of Gaiam, Inc. and Joyce Vedral.

Tight Assets Body Slide and *Yes, We're Walking* courtesy of John Sandy Productions, Inc. (jsptv.com and hotstockfootage.com), with thanks to John Santucci, Doug Darling, Phil Santucci, Richard Christiansen, King of the Hill Productions, Lee Speiker, and Fit Video Productions.

Bunnetics and *Learn to Dance* courtesy of Cal Pozo at Fitvid Productions, LLC.

Kids' Robics courtesy of Roy Kirkland and Doug Sebastian. The video is available at www.dspmovies.com.

Kid Fitness courtesy of Fenton Maxwell and Kid Fitness, Inc.

Shattered . . . If Your Kid's On Drugs courtesy of Eddie Kritzer, www.eddiekritzer.com.

How Can I Tell If I'm (Really) in Love and *Strong Kids, Safe Kids* courtesy of Paramount, with special thanks to Rick Hauser.

Teen Vid 2 and *Hunks with Hats* courtesy of Stuart S. Shapiro and Digital Download, Inc.

Learning Rock 'N Roll Piano courtesy of Happy Traum, Homespun Tapes, www.homespun.com.

Breaking into Hollywood courtesy of Bobb Hopkins.

Learn to Paint with Priscilla courtesy of Priscilla Hauser, www.priscillahauser.com.

Mr. Baby Proofer courtesy of Jonathan Bogner.

Jigs! and *Fish with Spence Petros* courtesy of Babe Winkelman, with special thanks to Donna Klimek.

C'mon Geese! courtesy of William Lishman.

Just Doing My Thang courtesy of Barry Youngblood, www.barryyoungblood.com.

The Magic of Squirrel Calling courtesy of Pradco Outdoor Brands.

Magical Rainbow Sponge courtesy of Warren Gruenig, Posh Impressions: www.poshimpressions.com.

Flirting with Magic courtesy of Michael Jeffreys, www.mjeffreys.com.

Line Dancing for Seniors courtesy of Brad Cole, Cole Media Group, Inc.

Dancin' Grannies 1, 2, and *3* courtesy of Beverly Gemigniani.

Chair Dancing courtesy of Jodi Stolove,
Chair Dancing® International Inc.,
www.chairdancing.com, 1-800-551-4386.

FreeDanse courtesy of
Larry Brahms, MTI Video.

Hip Hop for Kids courtesy of
Liz Milwe and graphic artist Josh Simons.

Phat Funk courtesy of Carol Scott, President
and CEO of ECA World Fitness,
www.ecaworldfitness.com.

Barroom Brawling courtesy of
Peyton Quinn, www.rmact.com.

Police Survival Shooting courtesy of
Lenny Magill.

Practical Self-Defense for Seniors courtesy of
Val DelVecchio.

Raising Canes courtesy of Ted Truscott.

American Bounty Hunter courtesy of
Bob Burton.

Metal Method courtesy of
Doug Marks, Metal Method Productions, Inc.

Parties of Sturgis courtesy of Big Sky Video &
Video Marines, Billings, Montana.

Fast Boats and Beautiful Women courtesy of
Bennett Marine Video, 2321 Abbot Kinney
Blvd., Venice, CA 90291.
www.bennettmarine.com,
Email: sale@bennettmarine.com,
Phone: 310-827-8064

War of the Monster Trucks courtesy of Tom Edinger, www.marshallpub.com. This program is now part of the DVD, *Monster Truck Classics*, available at www.monstertruckclassics.com.

A Woman's Guide to Firearms courtesy of Gary and John Lowe.

Yo-Yo Woman courtesy of Martha S. Cromleigh.

The Larger Woman's Workout courtesy of Idrea Lippman.

Women at Large courtesy of Sharlyne Powell.

Playgirl Morning Workout and *Playgirl SuperToner* courtesy of Playgirl, Inc.

How to Pick Up Men courtesy of Elliott Jaffa.

California Big Hunks courtesy of New & Unique Videos, www.newunique.com, with thanks to Mark Schulze and Patty Mooney.

F.A.R.T. The Movie courtesy of Ray and Migdalia Etheridge. The movie is available from Amazon.com.

Hawk Jones courtesy of Tor Lowry, www.torlowry.com.

Goldy III courtesy of Trevor Black.

Here We Are courtesy of Jamie Holt and the Pierce Arrow Theater.

Party with the Rovers courtesy of the Rovers, with thanks to John Orr and SL Feldman and Associates.

Shotgun Red courtesy of Steve Hall.

Carl Hurley courtesy of Carl Hurley: www.carlhurley.com, P.O. Box 5162, Louisville KY 40255. Phone: 502-583-8222.

Dirty Tennis courtesy of Jonathan Baker, www.jonathanbaker.com.

Incredible Cat Tricks courtesy of Karen Payne, www.princesskitty.com.

Cat Adventure Video, How to Spot Counterfeit Beanie Babies, and *How to Have Fun with Billy Bob Teeth* courtesy of Steve Cantin, www.stevecantin.com.

The Original Kitty Show: Video Toy for Cats courtesy of RJ Sorensen, CEO, Kitty Show.

Your Cat Wants a Massage! courtesy of MaryJean Ballner, www.catmassage.com.

Grooming and Bathing Your Cat courtesy of Bob Solomon. The video is now available in the DVD format at www.VideoCatnip.com.

Toilet Training the Feline courtesy of Jill Warnick, www.jillsnewenglandhedgehogs.com.

Jingle Cats courtesy of Mike Spalla, Jingle Cats Music, www.jinglecats.com.

Identifying Machine-Made Marbles courtesy of B. Alan Basinet, www.marblealan.com.

How to Build and Paint Military Figures courtesy of Kevin Campbell, KevinCampbellFilms.com.

Painting Wizard's Workshop courtesy of Scott Jenson. Cover design by Sarah Shockley.

Racewalking courtesy of Viisha Sedlak, www.viisha.com.

Finger Jazz courtesy of Tom Cutrofello. VHS copies of *Finger Jazz* are still available and they come with free string.

Lights . . . Cameras . . . Bubbles! courtesy of Louis Pearl.

Balloons for the Restaurant Worker courtesy of Dennis Regling.

Therapeutic Massage for Dogs courtesy of Mary Schreiber, www.equissage.com.

Face Aerobics courtesy of Judith Olivia, www.facelady.com.

Clown Ministry courtesy of Floyd Shaffer.

Y2K Family Survival Guide courtesy of Andy van Roon and Ken Goddard, www.film-com.com.

Almost Home: Living with Suffering and Dying courtesy of Liguori Publications, www.liguori.org.

Illuminazi 9-11 courtesy of Anthony J. Hilder, www.freeworldfilmworks.com.

Color Me a Rainbow courtesy of Linda King, www.themastersfineart.com.

Secrets of Pool Hustling courtesy of Key Media New York, with thanks to Elizabeth Key.

Sing Along with Frank Woehrle, *Babies of the Wild Ones*, and *Christy: Santa's First Female Reindeer* courtesy of Bill Porter, www.wildlifevideo.com.

Mark Rothstein's World of Rope Jumping courtesy of Mark Rothstein, www.worldofropejumping.com.

Refuse to Be a Victim courtesy of Bob Chaney, www.masterchaney.com.

Video Poker Strategies and *Winning Lotto Lottery Strategies* courtesy of Tiffany Designs, with thanks to David Wilhite.

Hank's Christmas Glitter 2004-2006, 2009 courtesy of Hank Brennan, www.hankschristmasglitter.com.

Nad's courtesy of Nad's, www.nads.com, 877-623-7435.

The Ultimate Pole Trick Instructional Video courtesy of Melody Obourn Moses.

Dare to Bare courtesy of the Sinclair Institute, www.bettersex.com.

Nude Law Enforcement courtesy of Woodhaven Entertainment, www.intermediavideo.com.

The Art of Aikido, The Laughing Dragon Exercises for Seniors, How to Spar Against Karate, How to Spar Against Tae-Kwon Do, Self Defense with Pressure Points, Chinese Moving Meditation, Balance and Coordination for Seniors, Chair Exercises for Seniors, Chinese Yoga, More Chair Exercises for Seniors, Practical Self Defense, Shaolin Sabre, Phantom Kung-Fu Vol. 1: Punching, Chinese Kickboxing Vol. 1, Zookinesis: Chair Exercises for Flexibility and Strength, Zookinesis: Chair Exercises for Weight Reduction courtesy of Bob Klein, Artistic Video, www.movementsofmagic.com.

Catfishin' with Willie P. Richardson courtesy of Willie P. Richardson, www.worldwidewillie.com.

Tony Little's Target Training Vol. 1: Stomach Reduction courtesy of Tony Little, www.tonylittle.com, with thanks to Tony Little and Janet Malure.

Less Stress in 5 Easy Steps (With Ed Asner) courtesy of Lois Winsen, www.editorontap.com.

Grupo Niche courtesy of Niche Business Enterprises, Inc., www.gruponiche.com, with thanks to Yanila Varela.

How to Avoid a Bozo courtesy of Destiny Image Publishers.

Laugh Out Loud courtesy of Tom Powell and the Addison Group, www.theaddisongroup.com.

Mighty Sanitation Machines courtesy of Nobuhito Noda.

Psalty's Funtastic Praise Party courtesy of Psalty's Kids Co., and Rettino/Kerner Publishing, www.psalty.com, 949-888-8811, with thanks to Debby Kerner Rettino.

10 Crunchy Carrots courtesy of Hug Bug Music Inc., under legal license from Charlotte Diamond Music / Charlotte Diamond Inc., www.charlottediamond.com, with thanks to Charlotte and Harry Diamond.

"Garbage Can Turkey" courtesy of Gerard Marquetty, 9740 1st Street North, Saint Petersburg, FL 33702, phone: 727-481-3983, with thanks to Chef Gerard, Live To Eat Inc.

Adventures in Customer Courtesy courtesy of Kantola Productions, LLC, www.kantola.com, thanks to Carla Fowler.

Meet a Real Giantess, Pushed Too Far, and *Jingle Bell Rockin' Christmas* courtesy of copyright holder John Kleiman, www.worldstallestwoman.com, www.hoosiermovies.com, www.bobbyhelms.com.

Jazz Dance Class courtesy of Wendell Moody and James F. Robinson, www.whitelionpictograph.com and www.jfrobinson.com.

Introduction to Muzzle Loading courtesy of Jay Warburton.

Win at Bridge with Eddie Kantar courtesy of Eddie Kantar, www.kantarbridge.com.

THE END

THE FOUND
FOOTAGE
FESTIVAL

RUNNING PRESS
PHILADELPHIA • LONDON

To find out more about the Found Footage Festival and see the show on tour, visit www.foundfootagefest.com

JIGS!

VHS
Approx. 30 min.

VIDEO COLLECTION SPORTS
PLAYGIRL Morning Workout
VHS hi-fi

Posh Impressions

Dee Gruenig

Magical Rainbow Sponge™

21276420
T-160
VHS

MORTEL COMBET ANIALATION

maxell
VIDEO CASSETTE

TREE STAND SAFETY

VHS

TOTAL BODY WORKOUT

PRISM
ENTERTAINMENT

NIGHT FRIEND

399
N-1

BREAKING INTO HOLLYWOOD

CAT. 29503

VHS

VHS HI-FI

KIDS' ROBICS

paige corbitt

8047

MAIER GROUP

DANCIN' GRANNIES™

Mature Fitness Beginners

VHS TMG 201

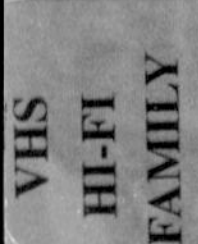

VHS
HI-FI
FAMILY

BABIES OF THE WILD ONES

$.49
4 66677 00049 9
Goodwill